When Truth
Is All
You Have

When Truth Is All You Have

A MEMOIR
OF FAITH, JUSTICE, AND FREEDOM
FOR THE WRONGLY CONVICTED

Jim McCloskey

with Philip Lerman

DOUBLEDAY
New York

Book design by Maria Carella
Jacket photograph © Psycho Shadow/500Px Plus/Getty Images
Jacket design by Michael J. Windsor

Library of Congress Cataloging-in-Publication Data
Names: McCloskey, Jim (Minister), author. | Lerman, Philip, author. |
Grisham, John, writer of foreword
Title: When truth is all you have : a memoir of faith, justice,
and freedom for the wrongly convicted / Jim McCloskey with Philip Lerman ;
foreword by John Grisham.
Identifiers: LCCN 2019054453 (print) | LCCN 2019054454 (ebook) |
ISBN 9780385545037 (hardcover) | ISBN 9780385545044 (ebook)
Subjects: LCSH: Judicial error—United States. | McCloskey, Jim (Minister) |
Centurion Ministries. | Church work with prisoners—United States.
Classification: LCC KF9756 .M33 2020 (print) |
LCC KF9756 (ebook) | DDC 365/.665092 [B]—dc23
LC record available at https://lccn.loc.gov/2019054453
LC ebook record available at https://lccn.loc.gov/2019054454

MANUFACTURED IN THE UNITED STATES OF AMERICA

1 3 5 7 9 10 8 6 4 2

First Edition

To my brother, Richard McCloskey,
and my sister, Lois McCloskey

In memory of our mom and dad,
Mary Fisher McCloskey and James C. McCloskey

Down here next to me in this lonely crowd
Is a man who swears he's not to blame
All day long I hear him cry so loud
Calling out that he's been framed
—Bob Dylan, "I Shall Be Released"

Certainly, this man was innocent.
—Luke 23:47

ι

FOREWORD

There are thousands of innocent people convicted and locked away in prison. Most Americans, or most white ones anyway, do not believe this. Those with darker skin know better because they have seen and lived this reality. But since the vast majority of Americans will never be affected by wrongful convictions they are not concerned with them. They see another sensational story of an exoneration and pause long enough to say, "What a shame." Which is usually followed by: "But he was probably guilty of something or he wouldn't have been convicted in the first place."

Few people care enough about wrongful convictions to volunteer with an innocence organization. Few even know how their elected officials vote on innocence issues. Wrongful convictions are on no one's list of our most important problems. Occasionally, when an exoneree retaliates with a big lawsuit and the taxpayers are forced to pay millions in damages, this gets attention and causes resentment but nothing changes. We hear the common refrain that "the system is broken" but there is little effort to fix it. So wrongful convictions continue, and the few lucky inmates are exonerated years later, while the majority serve long sentences for crimes committed by someone else. Life goes on for the rest of us.

With so little concern for the problem, why, then, do a handful of people dedicate their lives to freeing the innocent? I know some of these heroes: Peter Neufeld and Barry Scheck, who founded the Innocence Project in 1992 and have guided it to 367 DNA exonerations; Rob Warden of the Center on Wrongful Convictions at Northwestern, a group of advocates responsible for 30 exonerations to date; Emily Maw and the Innocence Project New Orleans, now with 36 exonerations; Shawn Armbrust of the Mid-Atlantic Innocence Project, with 36 clients walked to freedom. I could go on, but at the risk of neglecting someone or some organization, I'll stop here.

At any given time in the United States, there are about fifty innocence organizations at work. Most are attached to law schools and use students in their clinics and workshops. A few are freestanding and rely upon the generosity of others. And this does not include the tens of thousands of hours of pro bono work by big law firms and their attorneys who are committed to equal justice.

Each year one or two innocence organizations will fold because of a lack of funding, while one or two new ones will raise some money and open for business. There is never a lack of clients and every innocence group is deluged with letters from prison. Almost all receive help from private lawyers willing to work pro bono because they believe in justice. What the innocence organizations do not get is funding. Our flawed systems do not recognize the problem of wrongful convictions; thus, there are no public dollars to investigate bad convictions and litigate claims of relief. The funding is all private, from individuals and foundations, and this is unlikely to change.

Convicting an innocent person is relatively easy. Just put together a few of the usual causes—lying snitches, bogus forensic experts, cheating cops and prosecutors, a sleeping judge—and the jury can be convinced. On the other hand, exonerating that same defendant is virtually impossible. It takes years, some luck, and at least $200,000 squeezed from private donors.

And it also takes an advocate who is tireless, fearless, and dedicated to justice.

A man like Jim McCloskey, the dean of all innocence advocates—The Exonerator.

Forty years ago, when he was a seminary student at Princeton, Jim founded Centurion Ministries. He was neither a lawyer nor a reporter, but he was convinced that there were (and are) a lot of innocent people in prison. He gave up his plans to become a minister and instead dedicated his career to freeing the wrongfully convicted. As of today, sixty-three men and women are free because of his dogged efforts.

This book chronicles his unique journey. Jim started with nothing—no experience with the criminal justice system, no legal training, certainly no money—and he built Centurion Ministries into one of the most successful and important innocence organizations in the country.

In the pages that follow, Jim tells his remarkable story, and you will meet the amazing people who, though innocent, somehow survived in prison, most of them for decades. You will meet the New Jersey inmate who convinced Jim he was innocent and whose exoneration led Jim to follow a calling to spend his career freeing the wrongfully convicted. And the Texas inmate who spent ten years on death row for someone else's murder before Jim "walked him out." And two of Jim's clients, men whose executions he witnessed and only later came to question their innocence.

I've written one work of nonfiction, a story about two men who were wrongfully convicted in Oklahoma. The research was brutal and the writing took forever, but the story was so compelling I didn't want it to end. The same can be said for all the stories of wrongful convictions: They are so good because they are so tragic.

Jim could write a fascinating book about each of his cases, all sixty-three of them now, and the pages would turn. However, limited by time and space he has chosen his best. This book is far too thin and left me wanting more of Jim's "war stories."

Several years ago, Jim invited me to Princeton for the annual Centurion Ministries gala and fundraiser. It was a wonderful evening of celebration and made me feel that somewhere in the depths of the quagmire of our legal and judicial systems there are small victories to cheer about. The actor Brian Dennehy, a friend of Jim's, was there and served as the master of ceremonies.

The real stars that evening, though, were about two dozen exonerees, "his guys," as Jim likes to call them. These were men and women who had been banished to prison for the crimes of others and forgotten about. Men and women with no advocate, no lawyer, no voice, no hope. Men and women who had almost given up but somehow clung to the idea that one more letter, one last Hail Mary, to Centurion Ministries might bring a miracle.

Men and women lucky enough to meet Jim McCloskey.

JOHN GRISHAM
January 2020

AUTHOR'S NOTE

This is a work of nonfiction, and everything I've written is accurate to the best of my recollection. However, I've learned, in forty years of working to free innocent people and evaluating the testimony of countless supposedly credible witnesses, that memory can be more unreliable than we care to think.

In preparing this memoir, I have reviewed the historical record of Centurion Ministries and the relevant case files, comprising contemporaneous interview notes and detailed case memos, as well as trial transcripts, legal briefs, judicial opinions, and police reports. I have also consulted with a number of people associated with Centurion's work throughout the years, to help me recall conversations and events as accurately as possible. This is the truth as I know and remember it.

In writing about my personal life, I have referred to family letters, news clippings, and other archival material, as well as interviews with people who've occupied my life at different stages. I attest to the accuracy of these events as well.

I'd also like to note that due to the nature of the crimes our clients were convicted of, the book contains several graphic depictions of violence, as well as racially offensive language of the kind that, sadly, appeared in all too many of our cases.

My goal in writing this book is to provide readers with a glimpse into the world of the wrongly convicted. I hope to offer insight into our nation's criminal justice system: how it serves and doesn't serve those who are falsely accused of crimes. The views I express in this book are solely my own.

When Truth

Is All

You Have

One

░░░

NEW JERSEY, 1979

I guess if you saw him on the street, you might think he had just stepped off the floor of a disco, with his dusky good looks and his trimmed mustache and the tight shirts that were the style back in those days, although it was unlikely you'd see him on the street, and he was beginning to wonder if he'd ever see the streets again. Ever.

Jorge de los Santos paced back and forth in his jail cell in what was then known as Rahway State Prison. Maybe four steps to cover the entire length of it; if he reached his arms out, he could almost touch the walls on both sides at once. A toilet sat in the middle of the back wall; his bed covered most of the left side of the cell. And as he paced, he asked himself a question, over and over, a question for which there was no answer.

Soy un hombre inocente. ¿Cómo pueden encarcelarme por el resto de mi vida?

I am an innocent man. How can they put me in jail for the rest of my life?

Rahway was the place for housing the most violent, dangerous men in the state. It was an imposing structure—a huge copper dome over a large open central area, with long hallways radiating out like spokes of a wheel from a central hub. Those hallways were lined with cells stacked four levels tall. It was a fortress that told the outside world these prisoners were under control. But inside the opposite was true: The halls were so long, and the far reaches were so separated from that central area, and the prison was so overcrowded and understaffed, that chaos bubbled under the surface of every long, tedious day. Prisoners fashioned weapons out of whatever they could, and if someone crossed them, they could kill him in an instant. You had to watch your step around the guards as well, because they wouldn't think twice about getting physical with the inmates if they got out of line, or even if they didn't.

Jorge kept his head down when he was out among the other prisoners. He had good street sense. He'd been a heroin addict; he knew how to protect himself, who to watch out for and who to avoid. He never met the most famous of the prison's inmates, Rubin "Hurricane" Carter, but he knew all about him, as did everyone else: By the time Jorge arrived at Rahway, the fight to free the innocent Carter had gone nationwide. Bob Dylan immortalized him in song and lots of celebrities rallied to the cause. It seemed like just a matter of time before justice was done and Carter would be freed.

Some people, thought Jorge, had all the luck.

Jorge tried to keep himself sane, but all around him there was pain and despair. So much so that every guard was required to carry a "cut-down knife"—a curved heavy blade that folded into a metal handle—to cut down the men who tried to commit suicide.

Jorge was determined not to be one of them. He had reason to live. And he had reason to keep hope alive, hope that one day he would walk out of this prison a free man. His reason was named Elena.

Elena was a stunner, all flowing black hair and jet-black eyes, full-blooded Cherokee and as devoted to Jorge as he was to her. She came to see him at least twice a week, every Wednesday night and Saturday, sometimes Sunday as well. At first he told her not to; he said she should forget about him. But she knew he didn't mean it, and of course he didn't: He lived for her, he stayed alive for her, he thought about her all day.

And on this evening, he thought about the one bit of luck that had shined down on him in this awful hellhole: Prison officials had agreed to allow him and Elena to get married, in the prison chapel. The big day was just two weeks away.

There were, now and then, diversions that helped pass the oppressively long days: a boxing match, a concert, a movie. And as often as he was allowed to, he would spend time out in the yard with other inmates he knew from the Newark streets. But when Jorge sat in his cell at night, he would find himself lost in his own silent thoughts: wondering if, as someone had done for Hurricane Carter, anyone would ever take up his cause and help him find his way to freedom.

□

At that same moment, the noise level at my house was pretty high. I was living in a ranch-style home in the suburbs of Philadelphia, about twenty-five miles west of the city, in a town called Paoli, a nice, quiet, upscale place. I'd been at a management consulting firm called Hay Associates and making north of $50,000 a year, pretty good money for 1979, but had decided to give that up and make a big change in my life, and tonight was my going-away party. It was male only—twenty high school and college buddies—and it was getting about as raucous as you'd expect. But we'd saved a little surprise for them: One of the guys who helped me organize the party had said, "Hey, Matt"—the nickname came from my great-uncle Matthew McCloskey, who'd been JFK's ambassador to Ireland and was probably the most well-known guy in town—"Hey, Matt, I got a great idea. Why don't we bring in a stripper?"

So we worked out the details, and about nine o'clock that night, the same time that Jorge de los Santos was sitting quietly in his cell, listening to the subdued voices of the most dangerous men in the state echoing down the long hallways, I was drinking Maker's Mark with twenty good friends as Sandy the Stripper walked in the front door.

She was about thirty-five, brunette, couldn't have been more than five feet five, with a pretty, open face. She strode in the door with a boombox and a pink rug, and you should have seen the looks on the guys' faces. I took her in a back room and we negotiated the details—$150 for half an hour, one lap dance per customer.

So she came out and put on her music, and everyone was hooting and hollering, and she got naked except for her panties and sat on everyone's lap, and did a dance on the pink rug, and then went in the back room to get ready to leave.

Then one of the guests dragged me into the back room with her, and he said, "Sandy, do you know who this guy is? And what he's doing?" And she said, "No, I have no idea."

"This is his going-away party," he told her. "He's going away. To the seminary."

She stared at me, long and hard, trying to figure out if we were putting her on.

"You're going to be a *minister*?" she finally asked.

"Yes," I said sheepishly.

She looked over at my friend and then back at me.

"Get back in the other room," she said, pulling her shirt off. "I'll give you guys one more round."

□

How Jorge de los Santos would become the most important person in my life and how, I say humbly, I became the most important person in his still leave me with a sense of awe and wonder. All the odd occurrences that led us to each other, and put me on the path that I have followed to this day, leave me with no way to think about it other than that this is what God wanted me to do. You may think of it in any way you choose, and I'll be the first one to say that my faith has been shaken many, many times—shattered, even—but to this day I can only look back on the day Jorge came into my life, and I into his, as a matter of divine providence.

The party with Sandy the Stripper happened in late August 1979, and I did enter the seminary right after that. But by chance—or not—my seminary work would soon lead me to become a student chaplain behind prison bars, and sometime after that I would take a year's leave of absence from the seminary and dedicate myself to proving that Jorge de los Santos was an innocent man.

Out of my battle to liberate Jorge grew my life's work. I went on to found Centurion Ministries, dedicated to freeing the innocent. We have now freed sixty-three innocent men and women, all of whom were serving life sentences or were on death row, had collectively spent 1,330 years falsely imprisoned for the violent crimes of others, and were indigent and had no other path to freedom. They had only one other trait in common: I believed, in my heart, that they were innocent, and my colleagues at Centurion believed it as well; and we believed, truly and deeply, that we had no choice but to work to set them free. Despite our name, it mattered not a whit to us if those whom we served, or those who worked with us, had any religious affiliation or interest. All that mattered was the truth.

When I look back on all the simple twists of fate that brought me here, I can still put my hands on the first one that set in motion the chain of events that led me to my calling in life. It was in the mid-1970s; I was living the life of a successful American suburban businessman, commuting on the train from Paoli into Philadelphia to work. On the ride, I'd read the paper, and I used to cut out articles that I found inspiring. One morning, in September 1976, I read a story in *The Philadelphia Inquirer* about an investigator in a public defender's office named Fred Hogan who spent thousands of hours, all on his own time, reinvestigating the case of Rubin "Hurricane" Carter, the boxer wrongly convicted of a triple murder in Paterson, New Jersey (and who, I would realize later, was in prison with Jorge de los Santos).

I remember thinking, this Fred Hogan is amazing; the guy is exhausting himself, trying to free an innocent man. I thought, wouldn't it be great to live your life doing something so important, so purposeful. Just one of those passing thoughts you have on a train at eight in the morning. Nothing more than that, an idea that drifts by like one of the sailboats on the Schuylkill River that I'd cross on the way into the city. It would be years before I realized how deeply that article had affected me.

I got to know Rubin Carter over the years, along with his lesser-known co-defendant, John Artis (who is the unsung hero in that case, by the way, but that's another story). I first met Rubin in Toronto around 1995 when he and some associates started an innocence project called the Association in Defence of the Wrongly Convicted and they asked me to speak. Rubin used to razz me; he said that when I started freeing innocent people from prison, he had petitioned me to help in his case. I know I never heard from him, or I surely would have gotten involved. I would have jumped at the opportunity just to meet him. But he gave me a lot of grief about it nevertheless. In a good-hearted way, of course.

We stayed friends through the years. When Rubin was freed in 1985, he publicly vowed to never again set foot in New Jersey, and he never did—with the exception, in 2002, of coming to the twentieth anniversary celebration of Centurion at my home in Princeton. He asked if he could bring Fred Hogan with him.

"Are you kidding?" I said. "He's my hero!" I told him the story of reading the *Inquirer* article about Fred twenty-five years earlier. Rubin got a kick out of that and promised to bring Fred along. It was the first time I'd stood face to face with the man whose story, in a very real sense, was an inspiration for my own journey.

But when I enrolled in Princeton Theological Seminary's master of divinity degree program, I had no idea of the path that lay ahead of me.

Along the way, as I said, a lot would happen to shake my faith. I encountered police who lied on the witness stand, and prosecutors who knew it, and judges who turned a blind eye to the whole thing. I learned how terribly inaccurate eyewitness testimony could be, and how many people were sent to prison—or to their death—based on that flimsy, unreliable testimony. I learned that perjury on the stand was not only present; it was pervasive.

I learned how easy it was to get an innocent person to sign a confession just to end hour upon hour of unremitting interrogation, their decision hanging on the belief that recanting the confession the next day would set everything straight and put an end to these false accusations. And how incredibly hard it is—impossible, sometimes—to recant that testimony the next morning.

My work with Jorge de los Santos began ten years before DNA evidence came into use as a way to prove innocence and thirteen years before the founding of an extremely effective organization known as the Innocence Project, which has used DNA evidence to free hundreds of innocent inmates.

Like most people in the late 1970s, I still believed in the inherent justice of the criminal justice system—that cops had no reason to lie, that prosecutors would never want to put an innocent person behind bars, that judges were interested in the truth, the whole truth, and nothing but the truth.

I do not believe that now. What I have seen over the last forty years has shown me exactly the opposite. Many days, I wondered how it was possible the system had become so corrupt. And many nights, I looked up at the sky and wondered how, if there were a God, that God could possibly let these people suffer so. Some nights, I still do. So this is the story of how I learned what a cruel, mindless, mean machine the justice system can be. How, in trying to combat evil in the world, the system can become just as evil—more so, because it is evil done in the name of all of us.

But this is also the story of faith. How I learned to look that evil in the eye and still understand there is good in the world. And how, if you allow it, you can become a catalyst for that good.

I want to tell you the stories of some of the horrible injustices I've seen, and how we've managed to right some of those wrongs—including freeing two inmates from Texas's infamous death row. One of them was just eleven days away from execution. The other, just six. And I'll be honest and admit when we went wrong: I'll tell you about the inmates that Centurion fought for because I believed they were innocent, but later found out they weren't.

I also want to tell you of some of the terrible injustices we've seen that we could never unravel—that despite our best efforts we were unable to free innocent people from prison because of a justice system too cold to care. I want to confess to you how deeply that shook my faith. And how, in the end, that faith remains; beaten, certainly; battered, often; changed, irrevocably; but still, in the end, faith remains.

Because through it all I learned that there is hope. There is always hope.

There is always hope if you believe in God, or if you don't. One of my best investigators was an atheist—or at least someone who seemed to have had no interest in God or religion. And I have pondered, many a long night over many a good bourbon, who has it harder: those of us who see horrors and injustice in the world and wonder why God lets these things happen, or those who see those horrors and believe there's no God to turn to?

In the end, it doesn't matter if you believe in the existence of God or you don't. Because we worked together for a common cause, and when we did our work well, the prison doors opened, and those who had long ago lost any reason to keep hope alive—but kept it alive anyway—emerged, and walked back into the world, smiling and blinking in the brilliant sunlight of a new day.

I'm still trying to figure out how a regular guy like me wound up driving rental cars through the backwaters and seedy underbellies of towns across America in my minister's collar, knocking on all those doors and flying God knows how many miles from one end of the country to the other, hunting down witnesses and convincing them to admit they lied on the stand; or standing up to prosecutors who flat out screamed at me, their eyes wide and their faces red, that they didn't give a damn if my client was innocent or guilty because they were never going to reopen the case. Or how a regular guy like me, a businessman with no legal experience and no background in criminal justice, could find a way to get those clients free.

So in this book, I'd like to tell you my story, and how I came to the fateful night when I made the decision to give up my normal, everyday existence to join the seminary and dedicate my life to something greater than myself. But much more important, I want to tell you their stories. The stories of the brave men and women who suffered the greatest indignity the justice system can inflict upon a human being—to be convicted of a crime they did not commit, and sentenced to life, or death—and how, in keeping their own faith, in the end, they restored mine.

Two

NEW JERSEY, 1980

I'd given up a lot when I enrolled in the seminary, but one thing I couldn't bring myself to part with was my silver 1976 Lincoln Town Car. It was a boat of a car, and a beautiful boat at that: red leather plush seats and an enormous hood and that famous square-to-the-road grille. It might have gotten seven miles to the gallon if the wind was behind you, but I loved that car.

We had turned off the highway and were cruising down a two-lane tree-lined road, passing the New Jersey School for the Deaf, and inside the car things were tense and silent. It was a warm afternoon in September 1980, and seated beside me was another seminary student, Joseph Cejka. It had been about half an hour since we'd left the leafy peaceful campus of Princeton Theological Seminary, its stately buildings untouched by time, a place of serenity and isolation. Ahead of us, just down the road, was the Trenton Psychiatric Hospital, New Jersey's first mental institution, the site of unspeakable horrors in the early days of treating those who were considered criminally insane. Today it counted among other dark structures a building euphemistically named the Vroom Readjustment Unit, a forbidding fortress that housed 120 or so of the worst prisoners in the state—troublemakers, in the eyes of the law, so bad that they were sent there as punishment for their misbehavior at other state prisons, including Rahway.

To this day I'm not sure what possessed me to pick prison as the place to fulfill my field-education requirement. I could have chosen a church, or a hospital, or just about anything less intimidating than a prison. I'd heard a prison chaplain speak once, and I remember thinking, well, that's a world that's pretty alien to me. I bet that's fascinating.

There's the understatement of the century.

So when I started my second year of the three-year seminary program and had to choose a location, I said, well, I'll just go down to the state prison and serve as a student chaplain. I've never been in a prison before. I wonder what the people are like?

Now, as we approached Trenton Psychiatric, I knew I was about to find out, and I am not ashamed to tell you I was absolutely terrified. I thought, what the hell have I done? These are the worst of the worst, guys who are so bad they got tossed out of Rahway, for heaven's sake! You heard the stories—how the inmates would throw feces at you, how they were hostile and would mock you and curse at you and, even though you were separated by iron bars, could make you fear for your life. I hadn't slept at all the night before, imagining that an inmate would somehow take me hostage, maybe even slit my throat. And what would I say to the inmates who weren't trying to kill me, the ones who actually wanted to talk to me?

I looked over at Joseph. He was just twenty-eight, a good ten years my junior, and I could tell he was more scared than I was. He was a huge guy—six foot two and upwards of three hundred pounds, with glasses and thinning hair; the kind of guy who, because of his weight, could easily become the object of derision in a maximum-security prison filled with murderers, rapists, arsonists, armed robbers, and who knows what. I had gotten to know Joseph, and I liked him, which was good, because we were going to be spending a lot of time together, sharing this experience. He was an easygoing guy with a fine, self-deprecating sense of humor.

But on this afternoon, he was not joking at all. Normally, I'd have the radio playing. I liked to listen to the oldies station; I especially loved the Platters and Frankie Valli, and maybe stretching all the way up to the Fifth Dimension. But in this moment, I couldn't bring myself to turn the radio on. We just drove on, in dead silence, each lost in his own troubled thoughts.

We pulled into the parking lot of the grim four-story building topped by concertina wire. It was a few minutes before 1:00 p.m., the time we were due inside, so I broke the silence and suggested that we take a moment, sitting in the safety of the big, heavy Lincoln and the comfort of its soft leather seats, to pray, so that we might settle our nerves, and to ask for the spirit to be with us and guide us. Joseph looked as if the governor had handed him a reprieve. We bowed our heads and prayed.

"Dear Heavenly Father," I said, "please be with us as we enter this forbidding world. Please give us courage. Settle our nerves, and let us not show our fear." It was not the first time my prayers went unanswered, and sure as hell wouldn't be the last.

I looked down at my watch. It was time. As we got out of the car and walked toward the building, I tried to still the fear bubbling inside me. We were wearing our clerical garb, and I ran a finger under my white collar as I glanced back once over my shoulder. Everything behind me felt vague and unreal. I looked back up at the walls of Vroom.

This, I thought, is as real as it gets.

☐

Joe Ravenell, the Protestant chaplain at Trenton State Prison who had set up our program here, met us. Years later he told me he'd selected me for Vroom because I'd struck him as being a little too cocky at one of our orientation sessions, like I was Mister Tough Guy, and he decided to teach me a little humility.

At that orientation session, Reverend Ravenell had gone over the rules with us: Rule number one was, don't get involved, under any circumstances, in any way, shape, or form, with any of the inmates' cases or their personal lives. If we violated this cardinal rule, we would be immediately terminated from the program and forbidden to enter the prison ever again.

He sent Joseph down to the A and B blocks on the first floor, and came with me to my cell blocks upstairs. We walked down a long gray corridor where a corrections officer, his mouth set in a hard line, was stationed in a metal-and-glass booth. The booth was filthy with grease and smoke. The guard gave us a curt nod through the dim glass, then pressed a button, and a set of steel doors banged open loudly. I felt myself shiver as we walked through, the doors clanging shut behind us. Another set of closed doors sat in front of us, and then those doors slid open.

I was momentarily frozen, dreading the walk into the cell block. Twenty cells stretched away into the distance on my right, and a wall of ugly concrete sat on my left, with high barred windows along the top. In the very first cell, a guy was masturbating.

We decided to skip that one for now.

Reverend Ravenell and I started walking from one cell to the next, Joe introducing me to the inmates as their new seminarian and then stepping back so I could talk to them one-on-one. I first spoke with a friendly guy named Larry who smiled and reached out a hand for a surprisingly gentle handshake. I learned later that he was doing time for armed robbery of a jewelry store, but his relaxed stance and soft voice made him seem not at all like the violent type, so I felt at ease. A lot of the guys would wind up telling me right off what they had done to land in prison, and wouldn't pretend they were innocent for a second. I was a little surprised by that.

I worked my way down the line, and despite the ugly and forbidding surroundings I started to calm down. And then I got to the eighth or tenth cell, where an inmate was waiting for me. Before I could get two words out, he shouted, "Get the fuck out of here!"

I looked back at Joe Ravenell, but his face revealed nothing. I was on my own.

"I hate the fucking Catholic Church!" the inmate said, since

I guess my clerical garb made him think I was Catholic. "God is a fucking stool pigeon! I never want to see you on this cell block again!"

I looked down the row, and small mirrors were sticking out of every cell—the prisoners trying to get a glimpse of the action. I couldn't think. I couldn't react. I didn't know what the other inmates would think of me if I spoke back, or if I didn't. Which didn't matter because words failed me anyway. Finally, while the inmate was still screaming, Joe Ravenell intervened and suggested that maybe we'd had enough for the first day, and he took me back off the cell block. A while later, Joseph Cejka joined us, and I guess he'd had a rough first day too. We were comparing notes, and I turned to Joe Ravenell and asked, "By the way, who *was* that black guy screaming at me?"

Joe, who also happens to be African American, got a funny look on his face. "That was Butch Layton. He's white."

I am embarrassed to admit that in my moment of terror my inherent prejudice—prejudice of which I'd never been aware—had flooded my senses. I didn't just have the wrong face; I had the wrong race. This was my first experience with how unreliable eyewitness testimony can be. I had walked into that cell block filled with fear, and I had conjured up a face to go with the voice that had unleashed that fear—created that face, in my mind, out of my own prejudice.

Let me take a moment to say this: In the forty years of Centurion's work, we've had to unravel a lot of wrong eyewitness testimony. Some of it was just outright lying—people making up stories to curry favor with prosecutors, to cover up their own crimes or someone else's, to keep their own sorry selves out of prison. But some of it was just born of the strange kaleidoscope of images that we create in moments of fear and that we retain when those moments recede. This was the first time I experienced that firsthand.

Now, imagine if I had given a police statement at that moment. Imagine that Butch had committed a crime, but some innocent man—some innocent African American man—had been charged with the crime based on my identification. And now imagine six months later, putting me on the witness stand and telling me that I had to either stick with that statement or be charged with perjury, and by this time that image has crystallized into truth in my mind anyway, and I can either testify to the truth I have come to believe or face perjury charges and go to prison. So I get on the stand, and point a finger at that innocent man, and tell the jury, "That's the guy. I'll never forget his face." And I walk away. And he spends the rest of his life in prison.

That happens. That happens a lot.

So over the years, I would think back often to that first day at Vroom, and my misidentification of the man who told me to get the fuck off the cell block because God is a stool pigeon—whatever the hell that meant—and try to remember how easy it is for a witness to make a mistake.

□

Over the next couple of weeks I steeled myself each time I entered the awful, frightening hallways of Vroom for my three-hour shifts, 1:00 until 4:00 p.m., Tuesdays and Thursdays. I kept waiting for another outburst, another inmate to vent his fury at me. The block was a little quieter than I imagined it would be: Inmates weren't supposed to talk to each other, but the rule wasn't strictly enforced, so there was a constant murmur of voices, low and sinister, as though you were overhearing dangerous plots you weren't supposed to be privy to. I talked with the inmates and waited for the next explosion of anger.

But my fears started to abate as I realized that the inmates seemed to appreciate having someone who'd listen to them, and they treated me decently. Our mission wasn't to proselytize but just to be a friend, to talk to them about whatever they wanted to talk about. I was surprised at how many wanted to talk about why they were there.

Not only did some of the inmates easily confess their crimes, but some also seemed proud of them. One motorcycle gang leader bragged to me about killing a rival gang leader and burying him ass up on a New Jersey beach. Another seemed proud that he'd killed his attorney and kept his promise to his mother not to do it until after her death—his only regret being that he was so high on drugs at the time that he couldn't relive the killing clearly.

So, maybe I was getting a little more comfortable, but not *that* comfortable.

□

On my second day there, I had met an inmate who was a little different from the rest. He was friendly and gregarious, completely welcoming. He even seemed kind. The first thing he did was try to put me at ease over the Butch fiasco. I had tiptoed past Butch's cell, glad to see he was asleep this time; two cells farther down, I encountered Jorge.

"Don't worry about Butch Layton," he told me, that first time I met him. "I told him to lay off you for that. He's harmless anyway. He'll be fine."

He introduced himself to me as Jorge de los Santos but told me everyone called him Chiefie. He was about five seven, trim but muscular, with long dark hair, mustache, and goatee. He was dressed oddly—boxer shorts, flip-flops, bare-chested, with the name "Elena" tattooed over his heart. He held my gaze with an easy smile, and we started chatting. From the beginning, he was very truthful with me. He was honest about his past as a heroin addict, committing petty crimes on the streets of Newark. He never went to high school and couldn't read or write that well, and he and his brother Ruben had lived the junkie life. He'd been picked up in early 1975 on a narcotics charge about a month after a murder went down at a used-car lot, and a few months after that, while he was still in Newark's Essex County Jail, he found himself charged with that murder. He was later convicted and, at the age of twenty-eight, given a life sentence. He told me he'd been sent to Vroom, along with another inmate, for encouraging a work-stoppage movement at Rahway in an attempt to improve their living conditions.

Then he said the words that would set everything else in motion. In contrast to all those prisoners who were admitting to their crimes, Jorge insisted he was innocent.

"I don't belong here," he said, his smile fading. "They got the wrong man."

I had no reason to believe him. And besides, we had been told at orientation that we would be immediately terminated from the program and forbidden to enter the prison ever again if we got involved with any of the inmates' cases or their personal lives. So I gently turned the conversation elsewhere.

Jorge began to tell me about his wife, Elena, the love of his life, whom he'd married behind bars about a year before. As he did, his face brightened like someone had punched a hole in the prison wall and let the light shine in on him.

"I would be dead without her," he told me. "If something ever happens to Elena, I'm taking myself out. I couldn't live without her. She always stood by me, even in my drug addict days, man. She brought me out of my stupors. I was terrible, man. She was a saint."

He paused a moment, letting that sink in, as though mentioning a saint to a man of the cloth would have some special meaning. And maybe it did. But then the words kept flowing out of him: "I love her to death. I just miss her so much. I just want to be home with her. I didn't do this thing, Jim. I didn't do it. And no one believed me except Elena, even as bad as I treated her with my life on the street, she stood by me. She was the only one who was there for me during my trial, no friends, no family, only Elena. She comes to visit me every week, and then I go back to my cell and cry."

He fell silent then. His chin dropped to his chest, and I thought for a second he might start crying right then and there. It was the most personal and emotional moment I'd experienced so far, and I had to admit I was touched by his plight, even though I still didn't believe he was innocent, but I did sense, for the first time, how deeply difficult it must feel to be locked away, far from someone who loves you and whom you love more than life itself.

I had experienced a love that deep, once, and a separation that painful. I thought of her, just for a moment, and then turned my attention back to Chiefie.

"How did you get the name Chiefie?" I asked, trying to lighten the moment.

He smiled up at me, smart enough to understand what I was doing, good-hearted enough to appreciate the kind intent behind the gesture.

"My boys on the street," he said. "I was, like, leader of the pack."

"Your boys? You had a gang?"

"No. Nothing that organized. Just, you know, street junkies, and my boys from the McCarter projects. But I was their chief. They all called me Chiefie. Still do. You can call me Chiefie, too."

"Well, Chiefie, it's nice to meet you," I told him. "I'll pray for you, and for Elena too."

He thanked me, like I was a guest who had visited his home but now had to leave. I turned toward the next cell and realized, with a little bit of amazement, how much I was looking forward to talking to Chiefie again.

Over the next few weeks, the work became a little easier. Even Butch, once he found out I was neither a Catholic nor a priest, started to come around, and we had some interesting discussions. He was really puzzled by the question of why God, if God truly exists, allowed so much evil and unjust suffering in the world. I think he appreciated my honest response: "Damned if I know."

But my favorite was Chiefie. He and I hit it off immediately; he had an engaging and friendly personality, a good sense of humor, and an articulate way of expressing his feelings, and he wore his heart on his sleeve.

And he held Elena as indelibly in his heart as the ink on the tattoo of her name above it: She wrote him passionate, loving letters, and though his reading and writing weren't the best, he sent heartfelt letters in return. He told me she was a beautician with four children, ages ten to eighteen, from a prior relationship. He related to me the story of how he'd tried to tell her to forget him, to move on with her life, that she was wasting her time waiting for him. She got angry and told him she'd never give up on him. He was so happy he lost that argument.

One Thursday afternoon he showed me some of Elena's letters, and one that he was about to send to her. I didn't ask, but I assumed he dictated it and had another inmate write it down for him.

"I know I done a lot of bad things in life," it read, "but I never killed anyone in my life but what hurts me the most is that no one cares about what happens to me except you and some of my family. That is why I so fuck up about my family they turn their backs on me, and what hurts the most is they know I'm innocent. I want to cry but I can't, all I can feel is the hurt that is in my heart. Smile cause I truly love and need you!"

I looked up from the letter. I don't know what possessed me, but I went where I wasn't supposed to go.

"You keep telling me you're innocent, Chiefie. Tell me the truth. You really didn't commit this murder?"

He got quiet and looked down, and his hands gripped the bars in front of me. I could see his knuckles turning white. His whole body tensed up. He looked up at me. "I am a lot of things. I am a junkie, I robbed people, I beat people up. I'm not saying I'm a saint. But I swear to God, I did not kill anybody. I never kill anybody."

I was a little scared, but I pressed forward. I asked him how he wound up in prison for murder. He proceeded to tell me a tale I found unbelievable: He said there were two witnesses against him. Both of them lied to make a deal with the prosecutors. The prosecutors knew they were lying, Chiefie said. And they didn't care. They just wanted a conviction.

At that, I stopped believing him. With a crime as serious as murder, I couldn't imagine a prosecutor not wanting to put the real killer behind bars, let alone accept that an innocent man had been framed for the crime. It felt like some old Warner Bros. movie, where Chiefie was Jimmy Cagney and I was Pat O'Brien. I imagined saying a prayer for him and leaving it at that. But something made me press on.

"Let me get this straight," I said, my palms in front of me to make sure he didn't interrupt me. "The witnesses for the prosecution are lying, and the DA knows it, and doesn't care, because he wants to put you in prison? Is that what you're saying?"

"That is exactly what I am saying," Chiefie told me. He started to run down the details for me, but again I put up my palms to stop him.

"I'm sorry, Chiefie, but you were just one of a hundred Newark junkies walking in and out of the police station. Why did they have it in for you? You were nobody to them."

"That's exactly the point!" Chiefie cried. "They needed a conviction. They needed to clear the case. If they leave it open, it makes them look bad. So why not pin it on some junkie who keeps getting hauled into jail? What do they care? You said it yourself, Jim. I'm nothing to them."

"Did your lawyers appeal? What's happening with your case?"

Now, for the first time, he looked at me with something like exasperation. "You don't get it. My lawyers don't believe me. Nobody believes me. Only Elena believes me. And I thought maybe you. But maybe not."

A silence fell between us. I was about to break it when Chiefie beat me to it. He had the sober, stern look of a judge as he spoke.

"Do you know what it is like when I tell people I'm innocent and they laugh at me?" he said. "Those words hurt more than any beating the guards have given me. They make me sink into a deep and dark depression. I feel as if I'm at the bottom of a pit and I can't climb out because the sides are so slimy. I yell for someone to help me, but no one answers."

I was stunned. I didn't know what to say. Chiefie sure seemed to be telling the truth, and the passion of his words felt true and sincere. On the one hand I believed he wouldn't lie to me because of the relationship we'd built up, but on the other hand I couldn't imagine that what he was saying was true. It just seemed so outlandish.

In the course of the next few months, as we talked more about the case, I started to wonder. Maybe the witnesses did lie to save their own skin, and the prosecutors didn't know about it. Or maybe they'd made an honest mistake, and Chiefie had built it up into a big conspiracy in his mind, sitting and stewing over it in his cell, day after day, month after month, year after year.

I was driving to Vroom one gloomy Thursday, a few weeks before Thanksgiving, turning all this around in my mind. I had a lot of inmates who had come to trust me, and my days at Vroom were pretty busy, but all I could think of was Chiefie's outrageous claim—that the prosecutors had, knowingly and intentionally, framed him. I hadn't seen him in more than a week and was burning to talk to him about it, to really question him, to find out how he knew what he says he knew.

But when I got to his cell, it was empty. I asked the shift officer where he was. He told me that inmate de los Santos had been sent to "the hole." The words sent a jolt through me. They seemed to echo off the cold, hard cell-block walls.

The hole.

I'd heard about the hole. It was a dark, dank, stinking place in the Vroom basement where they sent inmates for punishment. Apparently, Chiefie had mouthed off to a guard or something and had been sent down there. I had been hoping to make it through my time at Vroom without ever having to experience the hole, but now, as I walked down the cement staircase to find Chiefie, I really felt like I was descending to hell.

When I got there, I found out I was right. There was one row of cells, maybe eight or nine of them, and a guard stationed outside a set of metal doors. He let me through, and the doors slammed behind me. It was so dark I could barely see; one bare lightbulb lit the entire cell block, and the smell of feces and urine was so power-ful I thought I'd get sick. An inmate in the first cell had thrown his feces around and smeared it on the walls. I looked in and it was so dark I couldn't make out the figure inside.

The inmate screamed at me, incoherently, and I backed away and stepped down the cell block. "Chiefie!" I called out. "Are you here?"

From deep in the darkness, I heard his voice. He sounded frail, defeated, lost. "Down here, Jim," he said.

I made my way to the sound of his voice, in a cell in the middle of the block. I couldn't see him in his windowless cell; it was that dark. "I think I am going crazy in here, man," he said, his voice as thin as tissue paper. I crouched down, and we talked for a while. He told me he'd been there for a week, and this was the first time he'd spoken to anyone. It was driving him nuts.

I couldn't imagine his utter loneliness and desperation, and if he was indeed innocent, as he claimed, he must have held more anger in his heart than I could possibly fathom. To my surprise, he said that wasn't the case. "I don't hate anybody. I don't want to be a man with hate in his heart. I used to be a bitter man, when they put me in prison. But I can't be bitter. That destroys you. I don't hate nobody. I just wanna go home." He begged me to believe him, to help him. "I believe there is a God," he said. "But if there is a God, He's gotta work through you."

I promised to come back and see him as soon as I could, and walked out of the building to breathe some fresh air. I stood there in the failing light of a late fall day and looked up at a blank sky that offered no answers. I was free in this moment to do whatever I wanted—to come, to go, to help Chiefie, to not help Chiefie. I thought about how much freedom I had in life, that I had always had in life. And I thought about Chiefie in the hole. His words came back to me then, as they come back to me now, as they have come back to me so many times since.

If there is a God, He's gotta work through you.

Three

||||

Neither of my parents came from a perfect home.

Far from it. When my mom, Mary, was about three years old, her dad—a successful buyer of fine linens for Gimbels department store in Philadelphia—left the house one morning in 1919 to go to work and never came back. Later, it turned out that in his travels he'd met a woman in Sioux City, Iowa, and had gone to live with her. My mother was just a toddler when her mom, devastated at being abandoned, had a nervous breakdown; my mom's last memory of their lives together was sitting under the kitchen table, watching men in white coats come and grab her and take her away to the State Lunatic Hospital at Norristown, outside Philadelphia.

My father, whose name I share, didn't have it any easier. His father left the family when Dad was in high school, to go live with his secretary. My dad's mom was just as disturbed by it as my mom's mom had been: She eventually descended into the sad, untethered life of the homeless, living in hovels and shelters in Philadelphia. I remember when I was a kid, she would come to our house at Christmas, smelling worse than anyone I'd ever met. She would give us Christmas gifts, but I knew my dad would take them the next day and return them to the department store from which she'd stolen them.

So, for better or for worse, these were my grandparents: men who abandoned their families, women driven crazy by the betrayal. Neither my mom nor my dad came from a home that engendered feelings of faith, or loyalty, or devotion, or fealty, or any of the higher qualities I'd later come to associate with the scriptures.

And yet. From the beginning, Dad was determined that his life would turn out differently.

It happened just after he graduated from the University of Pennsylvania, the summer of 1937. They met on a blind date on the Fourth of July weekend, on the boardwalk in Ocean City, New Jersey. For Dad, it was love at first sight. They immediately started dating. But soon after, he gave her an ultimatum that must have come from the depths of the pain of abandonment he experienced as a teenager but never spoke of as an adult: You date me and me only, he said, or you don't date me at all.

She said goodbye, and he was heartbroken. He pined for her but didn't pursue her, out of pride or fear or whatever motivates a man who grew up the way he did, in the times he did. He didn't see her again until the Mummers Parade in Philadelphia on the first day of 1939. If you've never seen a Mummers march, imagine the goofiest parade you've ever seen, and double it. Thousands upon thousands of people line the streets; in those days women with parasols and men in bowlers watched brass bands and floats made up to look like army tanks or prop airplanes or royal thrones or God-knows-what, and guys with tinfoil hats with giant feathers, and clowns in cars and clowns on bicycles and clowns on other clowns' backs, and in the middle of it all my dad looks over, and standing right there, on that same street corner, Chestnut and Broad Streets, is my mom. The woman who left him heartbroken. And somehow, in the middle of that ridiculous chaos, they had a moment of crystal clarity, and their true feelings overcame whatever pain had crossed between them. They patched things up and started dating again, and got married a year later. He moved her into a nice little house in the suburbs west of Philadelphia.

It was a good marriage, though maybe not a great one. Dad could be very difficult: He was a strict disciplinarian, and if you ever questioned his authority, there would be hell to pay. But he was a solid citizen with a good job; right out of college he went to work for McCloskey and Co., the construction firm owned and operated by his uncle Matthew. My father, Jim McCloskey, became something of a Renaissance man: He was a civil engineer, and yet he spoke Spanish fluently and played piano marvelously. He loved the classical composers: Bach, Beethoven, Tchaikovsky, all of that. He was an accomplished bridge player who could hold his own with the best of them. He was an artist, too; he would sketch our portraits, in pencil, and they were amazingly good. And when he wanted to, he could be the life of the party.

But most important, he was someone who took care of his family. He knew the importance of devotion and loyalty. I was very little when I learned just how much.

When I was five, my mother, just thirty years old, was stricken with polio. It hit like lightning in the night, as it did to ten thousand others that summer of '47. She went to bed one Friday night feeling tired and feverish, like she had the flu. By Sunday morning, she was paralyzed from the waist down.

The next week, my dad went up to our neighbors' house and got blistering drunk. He was never a big drinker before, as far as I know, and my neighbors told me later that it was the only time they or anyone else had ever seen him smashed. But he came back, sobered up, and from that moment on was absolutely devoted to my mother. For ten years, every Tuesday and Thursday, he would pile us all into the car to drive to a physical therapist in North Philadelphia.

Mom didn't want anyone feeling sorry for her: Even through this tough time, she always kept a beautiful smile on her face, was always the one that everybody wanted to be around. She was determined not to allow paralysis to stop her from living a normal and productive life as a loving mother and wife. For example, she knew my dad's deepest desire was to have a daughter, and so despite her condition, and the enormous difficulties she'd face, she agreed to try. And miracle of miracles, in 1954 Mom had a baby girl, my sister, Lois.

And as for Dad, he never strayed, as far as I know; he never complained; he never got drunk again, or anything close to it; he just did whatever he could to help his wife, my mother, the love of his life.

So if in my life I developed a sense of giving yourself up to someone else, of devoting yourself to those who have suffered terrible wrongs, hoping to right that wrong in the face of overwhelming odds—and the feeling of having faith when reason fails—it begins, in part, with my dad.

It begins, as well, with a kid named Tommy Boyd and his family. Tommy and I were born within a month of each other and were raised on the same block. After my mom was stricken with polio, I lived with Tommy's family for six months, and my brother, Rich, lived with another family until Dad could get the right full-time help to assist him in tending to Mom's everyday needs.

Because the polio virus was so contagious, people would cross the street and walk on the other side when they got near our house. But the Boyds, and the family who took Rich in, didn't think twice about it, even though they must have thought they were risking the danger of polio attacking the members of their own family. They just ignored that and did the right thing, because it was the right thing to do.

So when I search for the roots of it all, what would later lead me to the seminary and the kind of work I found myself devoting my life to, I'd have to say that in spite of all that had happened—or maybe because of it—I had some pretty decent role models to show me the kinds of values that can see you through.

And from the early days, I was no stranger to the church, either. When I was in fourth grade, and my brother was in third, we moved from one part of my hometown, Haverford Township, to another, a part of town that was fairly well-to-do. And right around the corner from our new house was The Bethany Presbyterian Church, a trim and unimposing two-story building that looks like the bishop from a chess set, its modest spire topped with a simple white cross.

Everything about it said *this is simple, this is easy, just come in and have a seat.* Which is what our parents decided we should do; they were virtually unchurched, but they thought it was a good idea for their kids to go to Sunday school. Pretty soon I asked Mom and Dad why we had to go to Sunday school when they didn't go to church themselves, and my father—a man of great integrity and conviction, I would realize later, when I was old enough to understand the concepts—said, "Well, you've got me there." And they began attending Sunday services and soon became important leaders in the church.

The church became important to me, too. I turned into a very Christian young boy, very religious, a Sunday-school kind of kid. I stayed out of trouble. I didn't hang around with the cool kids, the bad boys. It planted a seed in my soul, and I nourished it, and it grew.

Until junior high school, anyway. Then all hell broke loose.

I'm not sure why my life took that turn; maybe I was rebelling against my disciplinarian father, the way he became the mirror opposite of his own dad. Or maybe it's just what teenagers do. But I went from choirboy to hell-raiser pretty darn quick.

I was an athlete, and I quickly fell in with the sports clique. Some kids resented us because they imagined we thought we were better than everyone else. To be fair, they were right. We did. We just couldn't get over how *cool* we were. The same gang carried through to high school, and when my parents bought me a shiny new 1957 black Ford Fairlane 500—with the fender skirts and the low tail fins, possibly the coolest car ever invented, or so I thought at the time—we were unstoppable. I drove that car as far and as fast in the opposite direction of the church as the law would allow, and usually a lot faster than that.

I was a popular guy in the clique and the captain of the baseball team. But the undisputed leader of the gang was Tommy Boyd, the kid whose family had taken me in all those years ago, the kid who was now my best friend. Tall, good-looking, brown curly hair, perfect white teeth, captain of the football team, charming with the girls, and the center of attention with the guys. He called himself "All World," and he lived up to the title. All I wanted in life—or so I thought at the time—was to be that guy. I yearned to have half the attention he got without trying; I would do anything to get it.

One of the things I did was drive that Ford Fairlane like a madman, just to get laughs. I would load the car up with seven or eight guys and yell, "Roll 'em!" which was my cue to drive off the road into the woods, going through bushes and sideswiping trees, laughing and screaming like lunatics. In that moment, I was giving everybody a good time, and I was the center of attention, and I loved it.

The next morning, my dad would see the branches and scratches all over the car and he would ground me. But as soon as I got the car back, I'd do the same thing again. I didn't care about my dad. I didn't care about anything, really, other than having a good time with my good friends.

That same spirit carried me through to college. Tommy and I both went to Bucknell. He became my roommate and fraternity brother, and I became the class clown. I'd do anything for a laugh. In college I had moved on to a brand-new red 1960 Volvo Sport car (again given to me by Mom and Dad—I guess parents never learn). One night, drunk and behind the wheel, I drove it right into a metal pole, got out, and saw that it put a V in the front bumper. I proudly announced to the boys that it was a V for Volvo and continued driving like nothing happened.

Our fraternity, Phi Gamma Delta, could have been Delta Tau Chi from *Animal House* for all the partying that went on, and I was always at the center of it. How we didn't wind up on double secret probation—and how I managed to graduate in 1964 (albeit with a GPA that barely peeked above a 2.0)—I'll never know.

So when I tell you that my father's example helped plant the seeds of my later life, I'd have to just as quickly admit that they lay dormant for a long time. The path back to the place where I'd started, and the values that my father tried to instill in me, was a long and winding road. And when I tell you a few of the twists and turns, you're probably going to think I'm making some of it up, but I promise you, it all happened. This much I know: If you're going to spend your life uncovering the horrible lies that put innocent people in prison, you've got to be honest as hell.

Four

NEW JERSEY, 1980

Bill Martindale, a good friend of mine from high school, had invited me to spend Thanksgiving with him and his family. It didn't turn out the way we planned.

In the weeks since that first fateful visit to Chiefie in the hole, I'd listened more carefully to his story. He got out of the hole, finally, and the very next time I visited his cell, I promised I'd look into his claim of innocence. This was, of course, breaking the first rule they'd taught us when I volunteered to be a student chaplain, but I put that aside for now. I told him I wanted to read the trial transcripts, because there are two sides to every story and if I'm going to believe him I have to hear all the facts. Chiefie brightened up at this; he told me he was going to suggest just that. He did have a copy, he said, but he'd lent it to a student whom he'd met on some prison study project a year earlier. The student never gave it back, and he'd never heard from the guy again.

I tracked the student down, who was very apologetic about putting the transcript aside and ignoring Chiefie's pleas for its return— just another tiny heartless injustice in what was appearing, more and more, to be a river of them. I sat down, over Thanksgiving, to pore over the twenty-one hundred pages of documents.

Some people think reading trial transcripts is the most boring thing you can do in life. But I was transfixed. I begged off Thanksgiving dinner with Bill, and while he sat down to turkey and wine and the warmth of family at his parents' home, I sat at a desk in Bill's apartment a few miles away with a pile of papers and my Thanksgiving dinner of a McDonald's cheeseburger and fries, and fell deeply into the case of Jorge de los Santos.

The murder took place on January 10, 1975, in a seedy part of Newark, New Jersey. That evening, the owner and operator of a used-car lot, Robert Thomas, was working in his office. At about 7:30, someone rushed in to rob the place, and Thomas took four shots from a .38-caliber pistol, including one to the face and one to the chest. Thomas staggered to the front door of a business called Mack Floor Covering, about a hundred feet away, and banged on the front door. Someone inside let him in and, terrified, called the cops.

Thomas didn't die that night. He was rushed to the hospital, where he lingered for nearly a month. Something went wrong in the hospital, and he died of blood poisoning. He was interviewed twice by police during those twenty-eight days in the hospital, but because his tongue was severed by the shot to his face, it was difficult to understand what he was saying, and the officers later offered contradicting accounts of what information they were able to glean from the victim before he passed away.

There was no physical evidence placing Chiefie at the scene of the murder in that Newark car lot on the night of the crime. As Chiefie had told me many times, the case against him, I could see in the transcripts, rested squarely on the testimony of two neighborhood junkies. One of them, Pat Pucillo, worked at another nearby car lot, called Mike's Auto Sales, owned by his father-in-law. He said he was driving his tow truck back to Mike's when he heard shots, looked in his rearview mirror, and saw two men running from the scene—one of whom he identified as a short black man from the neighborhood who went by the name of Grasshopper, and the other as a guy he knew by the name of Chiefie. As I pored over the transcripts, I found that Grasshopper—real name Lamont Harvey—was in California at the time of the murder, so the case against him was dropped right before it went to trial. It puzzled me, though: If

Pucillo's testimony was already discredited because he got one guy wrong, how could his identification of Chiefie be trusted? But I put that aside and read on.

The other real damning evidence came from another neighborhood addict named Richard Delli Santi. He said that Jorge had confessed to him behind bars at the Essex County Jail. What seemed odd to me here, as I read through his testimony, was the amount of detail he knew about the crime and how squarely his testimony synced up with Pucillo's already suspicious account. It was almost too perfect. According to the testimony, Pucillo and Delli Santi didn't know each other, and Delli Santi had never been an informant or testified in a case before. So there was no real reason for the jury to have doubts about their testimony.

I was sure having mixed feelings about their testimony, though. I wondered if these two guys really didn't know each other as they'd claimed; it seemed unlikely to me somehow, given that they traveled in the same sordid circles. And I could dismiss Pucillo's identification as wrong, but was it a lie, or did he just mistake Chiefie for someone else? I also wondered, even if Chiefie had confessed—and I sincerely doubted that he did—how could Delli Santi's recounting of that confession contain so much detail? And yet, if Delli Santi concocted the confession, what would his motivation be to lie? These and a thousand other questions swirled in my mind. I was perplexed.

When I appeared at Chiefie's cell the following Tuesday, I could see that he was nervous as a cat. He knew I had read the transcripts and was anxious about what I thought. So when I ran my questions past him—starting with the idea that the two state witnesses didn't know each other—he nearly jumped out of his flip-flops.

"I saw them together all the time!" Jorge said. "Knew each other? We all bought drugs from the same guys! They're lying! I told you they're both lying!"

Why? I asked him. Why would they lie?

He got a sheepish look on his face. He told me that he and Grasshopper had once robbed Pucillo, at knifepoint, of $88 at a drug house.

"I told you I wasn't no saint," he said. "I did a lot of things. But I never murdered anyone. I swear."

I didn't like hearing that, but it did explain a lot. About one of the witnesses, anyway. I suppose Pucillo might have testified against Chiefie out of revenge. But what about Delli Santi's testimony? How did he know so much about the crime scene, the details of the murder, all that?

At that, Jorge slumped. "I feel stupid," he said. "I didn't want to tell you, because I feel so stupid."

I pressed him, and he elaborated: It was about six months after he was imprisoned and getting ready for his trial. His lawyers had given him copies of the police reports. Chiefie couldn't read well enough to understand these complex documents. He knew he shouldn't trust anyone around him, but he was desperate to know what was in those papers, to find out who was saying what about him. So he asked another inmate, one he knew from the streets, to read them to him and help him understand what they said.

That inmate was Richard Delli Santi.

"Chiefie," I said, "you can't blame yourself. You were doing what you thought was best." I tried to console him, but I could tell his soul was weighing heavy on him.

"Jim," he said, staring straight at me—through me—"you can't imagine what it was like. My trial. I am sitting next to my no-good lawyer and the prosecutor is showing photos of the victim to the jury, and I'm praying, in my mind, for him to get up, I'm saying, please, get up, Mr. Thomas, get up and tell these good people that they got the wrong man. But then Pucillo gets up and tells them that he saw me flee the scene of the crime and Delli Santi gets up and tells them I confessed killing Mr. Thomas to him. I—"

He stopped short. There was nothing more to say.

I drove home that night feeling sick. It was like I was being pulled into some dark hole. Could all this be true? Could these two men have conspired to put Chiefie behind bars? And if so, it seemed impossible that the police and the prosecutors wouldn't have known about it. It would have been so obvious.

But what if it were all true? What could I do about it? I didn't know anything about law, about police procedure, about criminal investigations, about filing appeals, anything. Hell, I had never been in a courtroom in my entire life. I was a former businessman and a seminary student. How could my training possibly help me now?

The next time I saw Chiefie, I confronted him with all of my doubts about whether I could help him. What he said tore me apart.

"Jim, you've read the transcripts and I've answered all your questions. Now I have a question for you: Do you believe I'm innocent?"

"Yes, I do," I said. And for the first time, I realized, I truly did.

Then he said, "Well, what are you going to do about it? Are you just going to go back to your nice little safe seminary and pray for me? That's not enough. That's not going to free me. I've been on my knees for the last six years praying for God to send me an angel, like he sent Bob Dylan for Rubin Carter. I need someone to free me from this hell on earth. Whether you like it or not, you are that man. You are the answer to my prayers."

I promised him I'd think about it, long and hard. And as I drove away that night, a funny thought occurred to me. It dawned on me for the first time, though I can't imagine why it didn't dawn on me earlier, that in their own languages, Spanish and Italian, "de los Santos" and "Delli Santi" both mean the same thing.

Of the saints.

The accused and the accuser.

After eighteen months of sitting in my room in the seminary, studying scripture, church history, and theology, I'll have to admit I was probably suggestible to things like that. But in that moment, as I drove the lonely roads back from the depressing cell blocks of Vroom to the bright, warm environs of the seminary in Princeton, it certainly felt like a sign. Almost like a passage out of the Gospel According to Chiefie, in a chapter and verse about the saints:

If there is a God, then God's gonna have to work through me.

□

The road ahead of me was becoming clearer and clearer. I was getting closer and closer to a decision. One cold December evening at the seminary I was in my dorm room in Brown Hall studying—my studies aided by a bottle of Maker's Mark, I'll admit—when I came across a passage from Isaiah 59. I put down my drink and stared at the lines on the page, and I can close my eyes right now and see them as clearly as I saw them then: "Justice is turned back. For truth has fallen in the public squares and uprightness cannot enter. Truth is lacking. The Lord saw it, and it displeased him that there was no justice. He saw that there was no man and wondered that there was no one to intervene."

Well, yes, I thought. There is. There is one to intervene.

When I told my fellow students at the seminary what I had decided to do, they told me I was an idiot. A junkie from the streets of Newark is conning you, they said.

"You don't know Chiefie," I told them. "I do. And I believe him."

They just shook their heads. It would not be the last time someone questioned why I was putting my own life on the line for someone who lived a less than stellar existence.

Because if I learned anything in the seminary, it was to show compassion to the lost sheep among us. I remembered the story that Jesus told his followers about the shepherd who had a hundred sheep. One of them wandered away, and he left the other ninety-nine to find that one and bring it back. The others were in a safe place, he reasoned; the lost sheep is the one who needs me most.

Was Chiefie my lost sheep? It sure felt that way. He'd wandered far from the fold, I could see that. And if he was, then I could only see how it was incumbent upon me to bring him back.

Maybe I had a little extra sympathy for the lost sheep among us as someone who had once been something of a lost sheep myself. I hadn't been living that exemplary a life before I got into this work (I'll confess that part of my story later). So I wasn't one to judge.

Still, I was worried about what my parents were going to say. It had been only a little more than a year since I'd dropped the bomb on them that I was leaving a high-paying job in the business world to enter the seminary. Now to hear that I was taking a leave from the seminary to help some heroin addict in prison for murder? And that I was naive and foolish enough to believe he was innocent, just because he said so?

My dad was quiet when I broke the news. My mom did most of the talking and said all the right mom things. She didn't come right out and say she thought I was maybe a little crazy, although I could tell that was probably what she and my dad were thinking. She talked about how she was worried about my safety. In those days, a young white man telling his parents he was going to prowl the streets of Newark, New Jersey, looking for clues to a murder had to have been a pretty scary notion for them. It was almost as though she was reading my mind, because tears began to well up in her eyes. She said, "Jimmy, I won't be able to sleep. I'll be up all night, worrying about you, just like I did when you were in Vietnam."

That stopped me cold. I hadn't considered, at all, how difficult this would be for her. But I knew it now. We went silent for a while. Finally, my father spoke.

"We're both worried about you," he said. "But we'll support you."

I couldn't find any way to reassure them. And there wasn't much more to say. But when I looked in the mirror, I had no doubts. I had made my decision. I felt alert, and alive, and aware of what I was about to do. I was about to leave the seminary—for a year, at least—and devote my time to freeing Jorge de los Santos from prison.

□

I drove to Vroom that Thursday, a week before Christmas 1980, filled with wonder. I thought about all the forks in the road, all the twists and turns, I had to take to come to this moment: What if I hadn't decided to quit my job and give up my business career? Or what if I had decided to go to a seminary closer to my home? Or if Reverend Ravenell hadn't set up that student chaplaincy program? Or I hadn't gotten mouthy with him so that he would decide to take me down a notch by placing me in Vroom? What if the random chance, like the flip of a coin, had gone the other way, and the reverend had sent me downstairs to cell blocks A and B, and sent Joseph Cejka upstairs? Or if Chiefie hadn't started a ruckus at Rahway and gotten himself sent to Vroom to begin with? So many intricate little movements, a complex ballet, all designed to bring me to this place, this moment, this decision.

You can take that any way you want. My dear friends who are not religious call it coincidence. I call it providence.

I also call it the luckiest moment of my life. Because for the first time in my life, I knew my purpose, my mission, and it was an important one. It was to take the most horrible injustice there is— putting an innocent man in prison—and make it right. I believed this was more than a decision. I believed this was destiny, that this was why God put me on earth. That everything that came before, all the ups and downs of my life, was in preparation for this work.

I couldn't wait to tell Chiefie. I had that Lincoln going eighty miles an hour down Route 95 on the way to Vroom. For the first time, I couldn't wait to get there.

When I broke the news to him that I was taking a leave from the seminary and devoting a year of my life to setting him free, Chiefie stood in shocked silence. I told him that if I ever, ever caught him lying to me, even once, I was done with the case. I told him this was helping me as much as it was helping him. I told him a lot of things.

He said nothing. He stood, staring at me, silent, tears streaming down his face. And then he began thanking me, over and over, and I told him no, I thank you, for showing me my purpose in life. This is my Christmas gift to you and Elena, and this is my Christmas gift to myself. And now I was crying as well, and we reached our arms through the bars and hugged each other, an awkward but loving embrace. And then it was time for me to go.

I walked out of Vroom that afternoon just as the sun was sinking low in the sky. It was freezing cold, but I didn't feel it at all: I felt warmed by the glow of—well, I don't know what, but a song filled my head, and I'm not the kind of guy who just bursts into song, but I began to think of the words of my favorite hymn as I headed to my car:

> Amazing grace. How sweet the sound,
> that saved a wretch like me.
> I once was lost; but now I'm found. Was blind—but now I see.

I started my car and pulled out of the parking lot, trying not to think of the one dark cloud that hovered on my sunny horizon: I had committed myself to working to free Chiefie, but I didn't have the slightest idea how to do it.

□

One of the first things I did was go to the crime scene, at the same time of night that the crime happened, and stand in the street at the same spot where Pucillo claimed his truck was when he looked in his rearview mirror and saw the two men running away. It was immediately clear to me: This far away, this time of night, this dark? You couldn't identify two men running if you had a pair of binoculars, let alone if you saw them in your rearview mirror. It was ridiculous. I had no doubts about Chiefie's story now: I knew that he was an innocent man, and I knew it was up to me to prove it. So it was time to go to work.

I had to move out of the seminary, of course, after I let the higher-ups there know that I was taking a year's leave. The president and the dean were both speechless when I told them. When they regained their composure, they asked me if what I was doing was legal, then seemed to want to usher me off campus as fast as possible. Lucky for me I had met a guy named Charlie Gregory a few months earlier in the seminary library; his grandmother Elizabeth Yeatman, a delightful and intelligent eighty-three-year-old with a wicked sense of humor, lived in a beautiful house nearby, a two-story affair that Woodrow Wilson lived in when he was a professor at the university in the 1890s. It was a stately Victorian home on Princeton's most prestigious street, Library Place, but by the time I got there, it was in need of some pretty extensive repairs. She was looking for someone to live in her house rent-free in exchange for doing errands and helping around the house.

I didn't mention that I was incapable of fixing anything more complicated than changing a lightbulb. Since I was going to have exactly zero income for the next year, the rent sounded about right. And this would give me a base of operations. I moved in right away.

I was relieved of my chaplaincy and barred from Vroom. I knew that was coming but wondered how I could possibly proceed without being able to meet with Chiefie. As luck would have it, though, he was transferred back to Rahway, where the visiting privileges were more negotiable, so our meetings could continue.

I decided I had to part with my beloved Lincoln, and as much as it pained me, I traded it in on a 1975 Ford Pinto with great gas mileage and zero sex appeal. But I had bigger fish to fry. And right now, Richard Delli Santi was my great white whale.

I soon found out that fingering Jorge de los Santos was not the only phony jailhouse confession that Richard Delli Santi had concocted. He'd actually been instrumental in getting his own cousin Danny convicted for murder, by making up another bogus confession. I was thinking, Richard Delli Santi must have missed his calling; he should have gone into the ministry instead of me, given the fact that everyone seems to confess to him.

Now Danny Delli Santi was not exactly "of the saints" either, but it seemed pretty clear that his conviction was built on flimsy ground. So I had a hunch that he wasn't exactly delighted with his cousin Richard for testifying against him. I guessed that if I could show that Richard was lying in Chiefie's case, that would only help Danny's own case, and maybe if Danny knew I was trying to do that, he would help me out.

It turns out that's just what happened. Sure enough, cousin Danny was eager to help. When I met him in Trenton State Prison, we hit it off right away. For a convicted murderer, he was pretty charming, and he immediately gave me two things I needed: one, authorization to get his complete files from his lawyers so I could see whether there was anything on Richard in there that I could use; and two, an introduction to his mom, Dottie.

Dottie was living in a little row house in Newark with her nephew Richard's wife, Wendy, and their two kids. Dottie was a short, plump woman with short brown hair and a fierce dedication to getting her son Danny sprung from jail. The house was neat as a pin, and not to play into the stereotype of an Italian Jersey family, but the first time I walked in the door there was a pot of spaghetti sauce simmering on the stove. They fed me the biggest bowl of pasta I'd ever seen before we got down to business.

Over dinner, she laid it out for me: She was disgusted by Richard Delli Santi and what he'd done to her son, but she maintained the facade of family kinship with him, hoping that he'd do the right thing one day and admit his fabrication. Or at least that at some point their relationship would come in handy.

"You showing up here tells me maybe now is the time," she said.

I decided to trust her, I guess because she'd decided she could trust me too. And besides, she was agreeing to help me out, and I was feeling kind of lost and alone as I started out on this venture. So I told her I'd share everything I learned with her if she'd do the same.

"Done," she said, with the solemnity of having made a sacred pact. I was nervous, but I was excited to hear what she had to say.

In the course of the next hour, I learned a lot. She told me

Richard Delli Santi—Chiefie's alleged confessor, my great white whale—was sitting in the Bronx House of Detention on some minor burglary charge. Wendy, Richard's wife and Dottie's housemate, had been talking to her husband in prison. And—more miraculous than I could have dreamed of—Dottie had already been *taping their phone calls.* (I wondered at first why Richard's wife would be so cooperative with Dottie's scheme, but I soon realized that without Dottie, Wendy would be homeless. Dottie had only agreed to take her in if she would help get Danny freed.)

They brought out the little mini-cassette tape recorder they were using, and played me a conversation from the fall of 1980. It made clear what Richard's motivation was for lying about Danny: He made no bones about having been an informer for the police, and he knew what happens to informers in prison. They wind up dead pretty quick.

His voice was tinny and there was a lot of noise on the recording, but I could make it out okay, and what I heard sent a chill through me, how cold and calculating he was in justifying his lying.

"I'll do whatever I have to do to make sure I don't go to prison and that's the bottom line," he said. "My life is more important than somebody doing a life sentence."

During the next few months, Dottie and Wendy and I kept meeting, and they played me more of the tapes. In the meantime, I had gotten ahold of Danny's complete legal files, and they puzzled me. In the transcript of his post-conviction hearing there was clear evidence that Richard Delli Santi had a long history as an informer. But I remembered that at Chiefie's trial, Richard had denied it under oath:

THE COURT: Were you concerned about your being an informant in any matter other than this?

DELLI SANTI: No, I wasn't an informer.

THE COURT: You were not in fact an informant?

DELLI SANTI: No.

There were other times in Chiefie's trial that Delli Santi denied it under oath. But in Danny's papers, it was clear that Richard was an informant; even an Essex County prosecutor admitted it.

So I felt that I'd established a decent step one: If Richard Delli Santi lied at Chiefie's trial about being an informant, wouldn't that damage his credibility as one of the main witnesses against him? I couldn't square in my mind why the prosecutors would even put Delli Santi on the stand; they obviously knew he was lying. I made a mental note to follow up on that.

The more Dottie and Wendy played me Richard's taped conversations, the more I was convinced that he was a little weasel who'd lie about anything if it would get him out of jail, or keep him from being transferred to a state prison.

The next bit of insight came from a guy named Joe Leonardos, a detective from the Newark burglary squad. "It's common knowledge that Richard Delli Santi is an informer," he told me when we met. "They gave him a license to steal. Look at his rap sheet. He's always out on the streets. He is a wheeler-dealer." He told me that one time he arrested Delli Santi and immediately got a call from an Essex County detective named Ronnie Donahue, asking him to go easy on Richard. "Go to bat for us," was the term he'd used. He said Donahue wanted help lowering Delli Santi's bail so the cops could get him out of jail. Leonardos refused.

Ronnie Donahue. It's the kind of name that sticks with you. I knew I'd heard it before. It took me a moment to place it, but then I remembered. Dottie had mentioned the name. He and another guy, she said, were Richard's "handlers" at the Essex County Prosecutor's Office.

I went back to Danny's files, and sure enough there was the proof: Ronnie Donahue *was* one of Richard's handlers. A prosecutor testified at one of Richard's sentencing hearings that "Donahue is more familiar with Richard Delli Santi than any prosecutor." And I found other evidence that Richard had been in the Essex County prosecutor's office for one reason or another at least thirty times.

Thirty times. Holy cow.

And there was more, too: The files showed that Richard had eleven convictions and thirty-six arrests from 1968 through 1975 for everything from assault and battery to arson to drugs to you name it. But he testified at Chiefie's trial that he had only two convictions.

I felt like I had cracked the case! Richard had lied at Chiefie's trial about being an informant, and about his own record. That had to be cause for a new trial! Didn't it? And now I had the names of his handlers; certainly they'd back me up on this.

I made an appointment in April 1981 to go see Kevin Kelly, Chiefie's trial prosecutor. I was thinking, on the way there, that once Kelly realized that through no fault of his own he had convicted an innocent man, he'd join me in working to get Chiefie a new trial.

Yep. I was really that naive.

I sat in a chair across the desk from Kelly, and he was friendly enough when we started talking, but seemed to become more and more agitated as I laid out my suspicions about Richard Delli Santi. Impulsively, he picked up the phone and called Donahue—the guy I already knew was Richard's handler.

"Ronnie," he said after some chitchat, "I have a minister here who thinks Jorge de los Santos is innocent. Do you think Richard Delli Santi's testimony was a bunch of shit?"

He listened for a while, then ended the conversation and hung up. "He said there's nothing," Kelly told me. "The jury convicted the guy, didn't they? Look, don't lose any sleep over it. The guy's guilty."

I left his office feeling like I was playing a chess game with people who'd been at it all their lives and I was just learning how to move the pieces. But I was catching on quick. I knew what my next move had to be. And it wasn't going to come from that pile of papers stacking up in my room at Mrs. Yeatman's. It was going to come from old-fashioned detective work, which I'd never done before but which I was obsessed with now.

Here's what happened. One of the linchpins of Chiefie's conviction, which Kelly had driven home to the jury, was that the two so-called witnesses were strangers to each other. "Patrick Pucillo and Richard Delli Santi will tell you they don't know one another," prosecutor Kelly said at the start of Chiefie's trial. "They never met one another until last week in preparation for this trial." So how could their stories, immortalized in statements recorded long before that, be so consistent with each other, if they'd never discussed them? Must be true, right?

Wrong. Chiefie had told me that the two of them knew each other pretty well, and the more I pounded the pavement, the more what he said proved to be true, and the more prosecutor Kelly's story began to unravel right before my eyes.

My travels led me to McKinley Elementary School. Turns out Pucillo and Richard Delli Santi went to school there together. They'd known each other since they were kids! I spoke to the principal and he showed me the records. They were in the fifth grade together.

I also stopped by Mike's car lot, where Pat Pucillo worked. I met a guy named Johnny Bellini there. He was nervous about talking to me, but somehow I got him to open up. And when I did, what flowed out was amazing. First of all, he told me that Richard and Pat were good friends; Richard used to come hang with Pat all the time, he said. They used to cop drugs together.

I decided to ask the $64,000 question.

"Do you have any idea why Pucillo would finger Chiefie for the murder? And that guy Lamont—Grasshopper? Why would he pick them out of thin air?"

Johnny didn't answer right away. He looked like he was turning things over in his mind. And then he looked back at me, stared me straight in the eye, and said, point-blank, "Pat told me before the trial he was gonna take care of Chiefie for robbing him of $88, at that place on Mount Pleasant."

Eighty-eight dollars! The exact same thing that Chiefie had told me! And Mount Pleasant—that had to be the joint at 77 Mount

Pleasant Avenue where Chiefie had told me these guys all bought and shot up their heroin. Man, I thought. These guys are pretty desperate. And pretty vindictive. You cross them for eighty-eight bucks and they'll send you up for murder. Not the sort of thing my seminary courses had prepared me for.

I already knew the answer, but I had to ask anyway: I wanted to know if Johnny would testify to any of this. Of course, he said he wouldn't. Which meant I had to stop with the preliminaries and get on to the main event. Meaning I was going to have to get the truth out of Richard Delli Santi.

□

I have to admit I was feeling more alive than I ever had before. I was living a film noir life. I was Humphrey Bogart, tracking down the Maltese Falcon; I was Philip Marlowe and Sam Spade all wrapped up in one.

But if I wasn't an actual detective, I *really* wasn't an attorney, and so I went in search of one. A Presbyterian Church executive recommended I contact Morton Stavis, a renowned constitutional and defense lawyer based in Hoboken, New Jersey, about fifty miles from my home in Princeton. Mr. Stavis agreed to take the case and passed it along to his associate Paul Casteleiro, a thirty-four-year-old former public defender. He had an interesting history; back when he was still a clerk for Stavis, they worked together on the famed Chicago Seven case, helping to defend Abbie Hoffman and Jerry Rubin and other hippie icons of the 1960s. He had retained that passion for fighting for justice in civil rights cases.

I can't say I warmed up to the guy right away. He was kind of stoical and hard to read; I was a little thrown by the way his shock of red hair seemed out of sync with his laconic manner. He didn't show any enthusiasm for the case and seemed way too laid back for my taste. I didn't think he cared much about me, or Jorge, for that matter. I couldn't have been more wrong. I learned pretty quickly what a dedicated lawyer Paul was. He dove deeply into the case and immediately started working on the writ of habeas corpus that we'd need to get this all back before a judge.

I suppose I should confess at this point that I didn't have a clue what a writ of habeas corpus is. But I was all Paul had, and he was all I had. So there we were, a Hoboken lawyer and a Princeton seminary dropout. Not exactly the dynamic duo from the outside, but from the inside we were working like a house on fire.

Paul, in addition to trying to get the case back into a courtroom, was educating me in the ways of the criminal justice system. He was my mentor and my guru. I'll never forget one of our first conversations. I told him that I thought I was well on the way to establishing a great case for Chiefie's innocence, and he looked me straight in the eye and told me, "Doesn't matter."

Doesn't matter? That a convicted man is innocent?

"Doesn't matter," he repeated matter-of-factly.

"What are you *talking* about?" I said, incredulous.

He laid it out for me. The federal courts, he said, won't accept claims based on evidence of innocence alone. You have to demonstrate that the petitioner's trial was constitutionally flawed and as a result he did not get a fair trial—regardless of whether he's innocent or not. Flawed, meaning that the convicted person's rights were violated; that evidence was suppressed which could have pointed to the innocence of the defendant; that the trial was unfair; that the prosecutor made prejudicial comments during summation; that the court-appointed defense attorney was inept.

Or that the prosecutor knew he was asking a witness to lie.

I thought about what he was telling me and let out a deep breath.

Well, if that's what I had to do, I thought, then that's what I was going to do.

□

My year's leave from the seminary was up. It wasn't much of a decision to go back to my studies; that had been my plan all along, to graduate with a master of divinity degree in order to become an ordained Presbyterian church minister. That was my goal when I started, and that was still my goal.

But it wasn't much of a decision to continue my fight to free Chiefie, either.

I didn't attract all that much attention from the administration or from the students, who were too caught up in their studies to show much interest in my work for Chiefie, and I didn't offer them much to attract their interest anyway. I was taking a full load of courses, but I kept living at Mrs. Yeatman's instead of moving back into Brown Hall on the seminary grounds, so no one saw me coming and going.

I found myself—not for the first time—living in two worlds. I was rooted in, and drew my sustenance from, the bucolic, leafy, peaceful, kind environs of the Princeton seminary. But some of my days and many of my early evenings were spent wearing out the fifty-mile stretch of Route 1 between that world and the rough part of Newark I was working in now.

I was still visiting Chiefie every Wednesday night at Rahway and keeping him up-to-date on my activities. He was thrilled at the progress I was making, how much of what he'd told me I had corroborated. When I told Chiefie I was getting ready to talk to Richard Delli Santi, he nearly jumped out of his skin. He told me he was praying that I could get Richard to tell the truth. He didn't need to. I was doing a heck of a lot of praying myself.

The first time I had seen Richard Delli Santi was at the Bronx County Courthouse. Dottie was keeping careful tabs on him, and she alerted me to the fact that he had a court hearing coming up. So I went, just to have a look at him. I'd been circling this guy for about six months, and now I was going to do a little incognito reconnaissance. I think if I had a fedora and a raincoat, I would have put them on; that's how much I was feeling the part that I was playing in this drama.

But when he walked in, the film noir fantasy I was living out fell apart. He was no movie villain. This, I thought, is Richard Delli Santi? He had greasy, slicked-back hair and a wispy mustache; he was missing a few front teeth and had yellow skin and a long pointy nose. He was about thirty-five but looked a good ten years older.

Now, at least, I had a real face to put to all the facts I collected. We didn't even make eye contact that day, but when I got home, I wrote him a letter, to which he never responded. I persisted and wrote him a few more letters, and Dottie kept vouching for me and pushing for Richard to talk to me. *I don't want to talk to him*, Richard would reply. *Why should I help Chiefie? Chiefie's an asshole. Fuck Chiefie.* They tried to convince him that if he helped me help Chiefie, it would wind up helping Danny. It's all about the family, they kept telling him. *La famiglia.*

And then, one day in February 1982—around the time I returned to the seminary—I got an unexpected call.

The voice was deep and mellifluous. It took me a moment to put that resonant voice with that disheveled, scrawny man I'd seen in the courtroom. "This is Richard Delli Santi," he crooned in my ear. "I got your letters."

It was nine at night, and I was knee-deep in papers on my bed, but when I heard who it was, I bolted straight up.

He got right to the point—no banter, no bullshit: "I know who you are, I know what you're doing, I know what you're up to. I know what you want from me." I was listening intently. "Dottie's been after me to talk to you, I've gotten your letters, and so if you want to come up, I'll meet with you. No guarantees or nothing, but I'll meet with you."

□

I was full of anticipation as I walked into the Hudson County jail-house in Jersey City, where he'd been moved on a separate breaking-and-entering charge. They'd given us a small room to talk privately in, where we sat face to face. Suddenly I was as excited as I'd ever been. Here I was, about to talk to the guy who had lied on the stand and sent Chiefie to jail. And what on earth made me think he was going to tell me anything? What on earth made me believe I could accomplish anything here?

Well, maybe it wasn't anything on earth. I believe it was something in heaven. You can believe that or you can not. But for whatever reason, Richard Delli Santi decided, then and there, to tell me everything.

Everything.

I'm no priest—I'm not even an ordained minister, to this day—but I will tell you, in that moment, it was like taking confession. We met for two consecutive days. First, he confirmed to me that he and Pat Pucillo, the other witness, went way back, all the way to McKinley Elementary School. He said all that business at Chiefie's trial about them never having met until a week before the trial was absolute bullshit. Ronnie Donahue, his main handler in Essex County, and Kevin Kelly, the prosecutor, had come up with that idea, he said. Donahue I could understand, but Kelly? The prosecutor? He knew that was a lie? My heart was leaping in my throat, but I kept quiet, because Richard had more to tell me.

He went on to say that Pat told him before the trial that he didn't see a thing the night of the murder—that he was motivated by the pure pleasure of framing Chiefie and Grasshopper for ripping him off for $88.

Then he laid out for me his history as an informant and told me that he was told to lie on the stand about it. So he did.

And finally—and most explosively—he told me that he had framed Chiefie and Grasshopper because Donahue had put him up to it.

I could barely breathe as I asked him, "Why are you telling me this?"

"I've been thinking about this for a while," he said. "I didn't have the guts to go forward with this before. I'm not going to say there is no fear. There is. But I want to get all of this out of the way and start life all over again."

He said he'd decided to talk to me because Dottie had vouched for me. And he said he believed that the statute of limitations for perjury had run out. But he said the main reason was a simple one: "I'm just fucking tired of these guys using me." He told me that Donahue in particular would constantly put the squeeze on him for everything he was worth: Do what I tell you or you're going back to prison. Do what I tell you and you're back on the street. It was always, Do what I tell you.

Fucking unbelievable.

I felt like my feet were barely touching the ground as I walked back to my car; that's how elated I was. I drove home thinking, this isn't Humphrey Bogart anymore. This is Serpico. This is a world of criminals and junkies and thieves and murderers and police corruption, and I'm in the middle of it all. And in my fantasies, I was going to bring it all down.

I couldn't wait to get ahold of Kelly, the prosecutor. He was the one who'd told the jury that Pucillo and Delli Santi didn't know each other. I still didn't believe that Kelly was in on the scam. I was sure that once I showed him the evidence that he was wrong, and all the evidence about Delli Santi's history as an informant, and told him about Pucillo confessing to Richard that he'd lied—I was sure that Kelly would rush to correct the injustice that resulted from it. Surely a prosecutor wouldn't want an innocent man to sit in jail because of his own mistake—an unwitting mistake, I assumed, based on the lies he was fed by the cops—but either way it was a mistake I was sure he would want to set right.

Yep. I was still that naive.

I managed, after a few tries, to get Kelly on the phone. I told him what I had, and waited eagerly for his response. It wasn't exactly what I was expecting.

"I don't give a fuck if ten people come forward and confess to this crime!" Kelly screamed over the phone. "I will still believe that your boy Chiefie is good for this!"

With that, he hung up. I sat on my bed and stared at the receiver.

He knows, I thought. He knows Chiefie is innocent. Either that or he doesn't care. But one way or the other, he's not going to help me out. Paul and I are going to have to do this ourselves. Paul already knew that, I guess; I was just coming to that realization.

I had no illusions at this point about how hard this would be: Kelly and Donahue would fight fiercely to protect their reputations. I was sure of it. This was going to be a war.

I called Paul to tell him what happened. He could not have been less surprised.

"Well, what did you expect?" he said. "You thought a prosecutor is gonna just admit that he's wrong? That doesn't happen. That's not how this works."

It was like a veil was lifted from my eyes. I could feel the naivete falling away from me. This son of a gun is holding on to this conviction because of his own reputation. He'd rather let an innocent man rot in hell than have a blot on his own record!

Now I understood the nature of the job in front of me. And I was more determined than ever to do it.

□

Over the course of the next few months, I kept talking with Delli Santi over the phone. One of the things I needed to know was his motivation for lying to set up a guy he barely knew. He wasn't shy about telling me: He knew the prosecutors would send him to prison if he didn't play ball.

"Look, Jim," he said to me at one point. "It's a matter of survival. Either I go away or he goes away. And I ain't going away."

I don't know why, but I was the first person he had confessed to. Somehow I'd gained his trust, and it was like blowing up a dam. The truth flowed out of him. As weird as it is to call this criminal my mentor, I have to admit that as the conversations went on, it became clear that he was schooling me in the true relationship of cops and prosecutors and informants. I was getting a first-class education. "I was their ace in the hole," he said. "When they had something that wasn't the way they wanted it, that's when they brought me in. To bolster something weak. When they needed a missing link, I was their missing link."

And that filled in the missing link for me as well: I got Richard's motivation all right, but now I was understanding what motivated Donahue and Kelly. They knew their case was really weak, relying only on Pucillo, so they went to their bullpen and brought in their old reliable closer, Richard Delli Santi.

According to Richard, here's how it went down. When Chiefie was on the twelfth floor of the Essex County Jail awaiting trial and Richard Delli Santi was housed in the same cell block, Donahue brought Richard over to the prosecutor's office and threatened him. "I have proof positive that you are a member of an arson ring," he said. "We have an eyewitness who puts you at the scene of the arson.

"You're on the tier with Chiefie," Donahue continued. "And we want to burn him."

"But the jailhouse confession was my idea, not Donahue's," Richard admitted to me. "At that time I believed he did it, so the ends justified the means."

After my meetings with Delli Santi, I took stock of the situation. I certainly couldn't prove this was a conspiracy—yet—but I did have hard evidence that Delli Santi lied on the stand. And now I had come to believe that Kelly was complicit in the web of lies that led to Chiefie's conviction. I was sure of that, too.

But remember, I was brand-new at this. Convincing myself and convincing a judge were two different things. And I knew that at best Paul and I were going to get one shot at this.

□

I did manage, at one point, to wrangle a meeting with Ronnie Dona-hue, Richard Delli Santi's main handler. I can't tell you how excited I was; in my mind, this guy was as corrupt as a cop can get. And I knew a lot more than he knew I knew. I was in pretty deep, and I was loving it.

We met in a parking lot outside an office building. He didn't fit my image of a homicide detective; I expected someone sharply dressed, not this rumpled figure standing before me. And he was charming in a way I didn't expect, either. Disarmingly so, really: Here I am, some guy trying to overturn one of his convictions, and he couldn't be friendlier.

"Look, Jim," he said to me, "the last thing in the world we want is to have an innocent man in prison. If there's any way I can be of any help, please let me know." Now, I'd already been far enough down this rabbit hole to know that was a big pile of bullcrap, but I didn't let on. I played it as friendly as he was playing it.

"I happen to believe Chiefie's innocent," I said. "But I could be wrong. We're just trying to get to the truth."

Just two charming Irish guys, passing the time of day in a park-ing lot. Couldn't have been more pleasant.

"So, how are you guys making out? You going back to court, or what?" he asked, like he was wondering if I had the chicken or the fish on my last airplane flight.

"Well, you know, to be honest with you, Ronnie, it's tough," I said to him, trying to play it cool. "I got some lawyers working on it, but we're a long way from getting back into court." I stubbed out a cigarette. "That's why I wanted to talk to you. Since you were the one who was so involved in the case."

"Whoa, whoa," he said, holding his hands up. "I don't know where you're getting that from."

"Well," I said, "it was my understanding you were Richard Delli Santi's handler."

"What do you mean, 'handler'?" he asked, as though I was inventing the idea of police using informants out of thin air.

"That he was a regular informant, and you used him on other cases."

"No, no, no," he insisted, in a tone that implied I was the dumbest person he'd met all day and he'd already met a lot of them. "Other guys might have used him, but I didn't. Where did you get the idea that I was working Delli Santi?"

I was ready to drop the bombshell. This will shake him, I thought. I lit another Marlboro and said, in as matter-of-fact a tone as I could manage, "Bob Cerefice." Cerefice was one of the assistant prosecutors I'd tripped across in my travels. "I met with him twice," I told Donahue. "He said that any case that came up, anytime Richard Delli Santi's name surfaced in an investigation, the prosecutors knew to contact you, that you were his main guy."

If I thought that would rattle Donahue, I was mistaken.

"Well, I don't know where he's getting that," he said.

And it just went on that way: me dropping little tidbits of what I'd learned, and Donahue lying through his teeth.

"Well, we'll keep working at it and see what we can come up with. Listen, thanks for meeting with me. It's been a big help," I lied.

"Like I said, anything I can do to help," he lied.

And that was that.

As I walked away, I thought about how far I'd come in just a year. I had started out as a naive greenhorn, someone who believed that cops and prosecutors and judges were out to find the truth, to protect the innocent and prosecute the guilty. And now I was meeting with a cop who was clearly lying and a prosecutor who didn't care whether a guy he'd put in prison was innocent or guilty. None of this surprised me anymore.

□

It was now a year since I'd returned to the seminary, and more than two years since I'd started investigating Chiefie's case. Paul had actually managed to secure us a court date, and it was fast approaching. I was still carrying a full course load and visiting Chiefie every Wednesday night. Every once in a while I'd check in on Elena at the housing project where she lived in Newark, just to see how she was doing and keep her updated on Chiefie's case. She drank in the details: She believed I was going to set Chiefie free. I only prayed that she was right.

Once, when I was visiting her, her sister walked in, and right away I knew I was in trouble. Elena introduced her as Gladys, but said she went by the name Crystal Star. As pretty as Elena was, that's how alluring her sister was, with her long black hair, copper skin, and penetrating black eyes. We chatted for a while, and I know that for a schlubby guy like me it's going to sound like boasting, but I swear Crystal was looking me up and down. We all made small talk, but I was nervous, so I thought I'd address, ever so slightly, what I thought we were all thinking. I said, as politely as I could, "Well, Crystal, I see good looks run in the family. You and your sister both have beautiful black eyes and beautiful black hair."

I know. Not the smoothest guy in the world, but, hey, for a seminary student it was the best I could come up with.

What she said in return nearly knocked me off my feet: "I've got something else that's black too." And her eyes drifted slowly down, her gaze moving from my eyes to her own ample hips, and then back up to meet my eyes, with a devilish grin on her face.

Oh, jeez.

My embarrassment, I hope, was covered by the two women's cackling laughter. "Gladys!" Elena said. "Don't talk that way in front of Jim! He's a minister!"

"That's okay, Elena, I don't mind," I said, kind of sheepishly. Because yes, I was a minister. But that didn't make me immune to the allure of an attractive woman. After all, I was trying to walk the straight and narrow after a long path of debauchery, which I'll tell you about a little later.

But talking with Crystal, I felt the old feelings rise in me again and thought, I'm back in the seminary now; I can't begin living a double life again.

I'd like to tell you that nothing happened between Crystal Star and Minister Jim.

I'd like to tell you that. But of course, it's a sin to tell a lie.

When I got home that night, I got a phone call from Crystal. She said she just wanted to make sure I got home okay. We started chatting, and the next thing I know she's inviting me up to her place. A few days later I went.

I fell into her like a man dying of thirst falls into water, and the next week as well, and the next. She started calling me "the Night Rider" because I'd drive down to her place, about an hour outside Princeton, around midnight, after I'd finished my seminary work and my work on Chiefie's case, and I'd stay the night and get up and drive home at dawn.

It was the first time the words "sexual addiction" crossed my mind, because I had to admit I was sexually addicted to that woman. After sex we would talk, and she told me her story: She had left her Cherokee family in North Carolina and hit Newark when she was nineteen. She started working at one of those hamburger joints where the waitresses work on roller skates. One night, an older man, around forty-five, drives in, and she waits on him, and they get to talking. She winds up his common-law wife, has three kids, and then they finally break up after twenty years, about a year before I met her.

I was three years younger than Crystal, but I have to admit, as I lay there in the dark next to her and lit up a cigarette, I felt like that older guy, taking advantage of this beautiful woman, knowing that I'd eventually leave her. It made me feel terribly guilty. Not guilty enough to stop, of course. But guilty nevertheless.

It also troubled me to admit to myself that the way I'd lived before the seminary, the life I promised myself I was leaving behind, was now right back with me, here, in the dark, surrounding me like a halo of cigarette smoke.

It was the only halo I deserved, for sure. I was certainly not of the saints.

I promised myself, then and there, that I would stop seeing Crystal, stop living this double life.

It was not the first promise to myself that I broke in this regard. And it wouldn't be the last.

□

Paul Casteleiro was also making great headway in proving that Delli Santi had been an informant many times before, despite what had come out in Chiefie's trial. One Saturday morning, he drove down to Trenton on a fishing expedition. Digging through old musty card catalogs in the state library in Trenton, he came across a card for Delli Santi, which led him to the microfiche room. He loaded a reel onto one of those old machines and turned the knob to focus in on the page he was looking for. It was a transcript of some minor case that Delli Santi was involved in.

But for us, it was the biggest find of the year. Paul had, just on a hunch, managed to dig up a 1973 Delli Santi sentencing transcript showing that the judge was so worried about Delli Santi's informant history he couldn't figure out where to send him. "I can't send him to state prison," the judge wrote. "Word gets around. His life won't be worth a plug nickel. He is going to have Dutch Cleanser or Bab-O in his coffee."

Paul called me up, more excited than I'd ever heard him. In fact, he was such a low-key guy I don't think I'd ever heard him excited at all. But he sure was now. Even though we had other evidence pointing to Delli Santi's informant history, having a judge spell it out so clearly and powerfully felt like finding the Holy Grail.

"Jim, this is it!" he was saying. "This is it! This is the whole thing! I mean they're saying the guy is not a snitch for the prosecutor's office, and here it is, before Chiefie's trial, saying that's exactly what he is! I mean, eureka!"

But that wasn't even the best of it. When we were about a month ahead of our court date, Paul decided to play an ace he'd been hiding up his sleeve. "Jim," he said to me, "I think it's time to see what the other side's got."

What he meant, he told me, was that he was going to ask the judge in the case for a subpoena to go through the prosecutor's files. The judge granted the subpoena, and the next day Paul was in the prosecutor's office. That afternoon, my phone rang. Paul sounded like he was ready to jump through the receiver.

"Jim! You're not going to believe this! We have Kelly dead to rights! Dead! To! Rights!"

What he'd found, he told me when he settled down, was the mother lode of all mother lodes: documents in Kelly's own handwriting saying that Delli Santi was in the habit of giving testimony and acting as an informant. I knew right away how crucial and damning that was, because Kelly asked him at Chiefie's trial whether he'd ever informed on anyone in his life and Richard said no, he hadn't. So if that's not suborning perjury—persuading someone to lie under oath—I don't know what is. Paul called it our "smoking gun."

A few weeks later, on March 23, 1983, as we headed for the U.S. Courthouse in Newark, I ran over all the evidence in my mind again and again. I was confident that we had the goods on Kelly, the prosecutor in Chiefie's case, a whole treasure trove of documents proving that Richard Delli Santi had been an informant in other cases before Chiefie's trial and that he was in the habit of giving testimony. We had proof that Kelly was aware of it, and we had Kelly, at Chiefie's trial, asking Richard if he'd ever informed on anyone else in his life and Richard saying no.

We had a ton of proof that the two witnesses—Richard and Pat Pucillo—went way back, went to school together, shot heroin together. And yet there in the transcript was Kelly, at Chiefie's trial, saying that the two men had never met until a week before the trial.

In 1982, I got to visit Chiefie in Rahway State Prison with his wife, Elena. There was no doubt that she was the thing that kept him going. *Courtesy of the author*

So we got out of the car, the three of us—me, Paul, and Neil Mullin, another lawyer at Paul's firm—and walked into the courthouse. I sat down on a bench outside the courtroom and tried to take a few deep breaths to calm myself. But I looked up, and there, looking down at me, was Kelly himself.

It jarred me to see him standing right there. We had subpoenaed this guy, and now we were about to bury him. He had to know it. He took his hand out of his pocket, and part of me thought he was going to sock me, but he just shook my hand and said, as friendly as the guy behind the counter at your favorite coffee shop, "Jim! Good to see you. How have you been?"

We exchanged some pleasantries, and at one point I looked up, and walking past us, in chains and handcuffs, escorted by two corrections officers, was Chiefie de los Santos.

I turned away from Kelly, suppressing the urge to run over and hug Chiefie. This was the first time I had ever seen him outside the walls of a prison. Chiefie was dressed sharply in civilian clothes. Elena had ironed a crease into his jeans so sharp you could have cut your hand on it.

"Holy jeez," Kelly said as Chiefie walked by. "He looks a lot better than he did eight years ago."

"Clean living," I said, and left it at that.

Paul and Neil and I headed toward the courtroom door. Kelly was sequestered, meaning he had to stay out in the hallway until it was his turn to testify. Just as we were walking in, Paul turned to me and said, "Jim, I want you to stay out here. Keep an eye on Kelly and make sure no one comes up to talk to him."

Are you out of your mind? Two years and change I've been waiting for this moment, and you want me to stay outside? No fucking way, I said.

I stood my ground, and Paul stood his, and we started to argue way too loudly for the courtroom hallway until Neil stepped in and separated us.

"Let's take a breath," Neil said. "We're all a little anxious."

After a few minutes, Paul relented and we went in, and what for me was the Trial of the Century (or at least the Evidentiary Hearing of the Century) began.

Paul started laying out our case for the judge, Frederick B. Lacey. Lacey had a police background—his father was Newark's chief of police in the 1950s—and a conservative reputation. But I was sure Paul could prevail. And even though I knew every ounce of our case, every document that showed Richard Delli Santi was a longtime informant, every document that showed Kelly knew it and suborned perjury around it—even though I knew all that, hearing it here, in open court, made me think how an actor must feel when he steps out onstage on opening night on Broadway. No more rehearsals: It's showtime.

And Paul was putting on a hell of a show. He had decided, before we came to court, not to put Richard Delli Santi on the witness stand. We all knew the judge would hate him, and we felt we had enough evidence without him. I didn't like that decision, but I knew that was not for me to say. I was sorry I wouldn't get to hear Richard confess before the judge, but I was eager to see Paul take Kelly apart in court. And now, I knew, that time had come. Paul had already presented most of his evidence; Kelly was called into the courtroom and sat down not ten feet from me. Paul and Neil were at the defense table with Chiefie; I was back in the audience area.

After Kelly was sworn in, Paul started leading him through the documentary evidence of Delli Santi's informant history, asking him if he'd been aware of any of the many instances of Richard's informant activities. Of course Kelly denied any knowledge.

Paul then handed him our smoking gun. It was the document Paul obtained through the subpoena of the prosecutor's case files: Kelly's own notes in preparation for Chiefie's trial.

And there, in Kelly's own handwriting, plain as day, it read, "DELLI SANTI IS IN HABIT OF GIVING TESTIMONY."

And, "Get in Richard Delli Santi—TESTIFIED AGAINST JOE DEMARE."

The smile was gone from Kelly's lips. He seemed to shrink in the witness chair. I knew we had him.

Look, I know what you're probably thinking. This is not exactly the thrilling moment of exoneration you'd see in the movie version of a story like this. I was hoping for one of those, too. I would have loved to get Richard Delli Santi up there on the stand and have him break down, screaming, "He's innocent! He's innocent! I made it all up! Kelly and Donahue made me do it!"

That would have been so satisfying. But I'd learned a lot in the couple of years I'd worked on Chiefie's case, a lot about how this game is played. Paul had taught me well: Getting some lying convict who'd testified and recanted his testimony, and recanted that recantation in another case, back in front of the judge, to recant one more time—that was not going to get Chiefie free.

This, what Paul was doing—this was going to get Chiefie free.

It's not about those great movie moments, most of the time.

Getting the innocent out of jail is about diligence and pounding the pavement and poring over musty documents in a dimly lit room in the middle of the night with a glass of bourbon in one hand and a yellow highlighter in the other. But you do what it takes, and if you work hard, and you're lucky, and you have a good lawyer on your side, sometimes you can do what you set out to do.

Paul continued, relentlessly, presenting Kelly with documents proving that he'd flat-out lied, again and again, and with each one Kelly seemed to be shriveling before my eyes. It was like watching a prizefighter finishing off some big galoot against the ropes. I almost felt sorry for Kelly.

Almost.

When it was over, they led Chiefie from the courtroom, and he looked our way with a huge grin on his face and gave me a big thumbs-up, and I gave one back. He went back to Rahway; Paul and Neil and I went to a bar. We knew the day could not have gone better, and we knew there was nothing left for now but to wait.

□

Judge Lacey's decision came on July 5, 1983, two months shy of three years since the day I first walked into the Vroom correctional facility.

In it, he said it was clear that Delli Santi had committed perjury.

In it, he said that Kelly must have known it.

In it, he said, "Even a casual reading of his testimony demonstrates that it reeks of perjury ... that [Delli Santi] is a person of reprehensible character ... and that he committed numerous crimes is undisputed."

In it, he said, "Delli Santi fabricated the petitioner's alleged jailhouse confession in order to avoid death or violence in state prison at the hands of inmates who knew of his informant status. . . . Delli Santi had for years told the prosecutor what he wanted to hear in exchange for his life and a license to commit crime . . . and that the facts established regarding Delli Santi's informant activities and the State's knowing use of his perjured testimony mandate the conclusion that ... the suppressed evidence could have affected the judgment of the jury."

In it, I read, with tears in my eyes, that he was ordering a new trial for Jorge de los Santos, which meant that in the interest of justice Jorge would be set free.

□

Three weeks later, on July 26, 1983, Paul and I stood outside a gate at what was then called Trenton State Prison, where Chiefie had been transferred. The early afternoon sun blazed down, the heat making the street behind us shimmer. The prison, a block long on all sides, sits in the middle of a downtown neighborhood. You might mistake it at first for a giant monastery if it weren't for the barbed wire atop the walls, and the imposing watchtower—a modern glass-and-white-metal guardroom atop an old, fading brick tower. The tower made a nice metaphor for the day, I thought: a gleaming future rising above a sad, hard past.

We stood sweating and pacing outside a heavy brown steel garage door next to one of the towers, which had a smaller exit door within it. The minutes passed like hours, and part of me didn't believe the door would ever open, but finally it did, and there, clutching a paper bag with all of his possessions, looking tiny inside the frame of that huge garage door, a little hunched over and squinting in the bright sunlight, was Chiefie. He shaded his eyes with his free hand to find us, then walked toward us, slowly at first, then breaking almost into a run. He and I threw our arms around each other, without a word, and held on tight for the longest time. Paul stood back and let us have this moment, and finally I leaned back and looked at Chiefie, and we just started laughing and crying at the same time. It felt like the greatest moment of my life, up to this point.

I truly believed Christ had led me here and that this was the work he had led me to do. And I had done it. With a huge smile on his face, Paul gave Chiefie a big bear hug, then turned to me and in his typical understatement said, "I think it's time we get the hell out of here."

Truer words were never spoken.

Our first stop was the Princetonian Diner: For eight years, Chiefie had told me, he had dreamed of having a banana split, and before we headed home, we decided to stop and have one. As I sat and watched him devour it, I couldn't help thinking how much he looked like a child, completely lost in the pleasure of whipped cream and walnuts and chocolate syrup, as though they were the only things in the world. And at that moment it struck me. I have never had a child, and I'll never know what it's like to bring a child into the world, but in this moment I felt as though I'd delivered one. Chiefie was, in that moment, an innocent that I, through the grace of God, helped bring out into the world, through great struggle, to a place of great joy.

As soon as he finished, Chiefie stood up. He was aching to get to Elena. We stopped off at my room at Mrs. Yeatman's so he could call her, and I could hear her shrieking on the phone. Chiefie called his mother in Puerto Rico too, and I don't speak much Spanish, but I did hear one phrase, over and over, that I understood as deeply as I understand anything.

Soy libre, mama. Soy libre.

I am free.

It was about 6:00 p.m. when we pulled into the parking lot of the McKinney housing projects in Newark. I couldn't believe my eyes: There must have been a hundred people there, children and grown-ups and music blaring from a boombox the size of a small Volkswagen, and "Welcome Home Chiefie" signs, and a reporter from the Newark *Star-Ledger.* A huge cheer went up as Chiefie got out of the car. I was stunned by the sight, but I don't think Chiefie saw or heard any of it. His eyes were like lasers, scanning the crowd.

And then he saw her.

The beautiful Elena: she was dressed, as usual, in Bermuda shorts and a halter top, but for my money she could just as well have been wearing the robes of an angel. As Chiefie walked toward her, she let out a shriek that pierced the sky. They held each other for what seemed like an hour, his face buried in her thick mane of jet-black hair, the crowd cheering and hollering around them, and finally he stepped back, his hands on the sides of her face, and he looked into her eyes. I couldn't hear what he said to her, but the looks on their faces, looks of pure joy, said everything I'd needed to hear since I started this strange and difficult and messy and marvelous journey.

I finally left them and got back to my room, alone, about nine that night. Mrs. Yeatman was already asleep. I poured myself a bourbon and tried to savor the glow of the day—the glorious, mind-boggling victory we'd achieved, the astounding feeling of freeing an innocent man from prison. And yet, I felt . . . empty.

It was hard to admit it, but I was envious of Chiefie. He was celebrating in the glow of love and home, and here I was, a forty-one-year-old man, almost broke, living rent-free in the home of an eighty-five-year-old woman. There was no one in my life: I still saw Crystal from time to time, but it wasn't anywhere near the consolation I needed in this moment.

I flipped on Johnny Carson, and he was talking to Linda Evans, the beautiful star of the hit TV show at the time, *Dynasty,* but I couldn't really focus on it. There's Johnny with Linda, and Chiefie with Elena, and Paul home with his wife, Darcy, and here's me, with my second bourbon of the night, getting ready to pour my third.

I flicked off the TV, went to the window, and peered into the night. Out of the corner of my eye, I noticed some papers on my desk, a little pile I'd put aside for months as Chiefie's hearing date approached, papers I'd almost forgotten about. I picked them up, and smiled, and realized, no, I'm not alone. Not at all.

I realized, God's here with me.

And has more work for me to do.

Five

||||

In college, I could still feel the weight of my father's disciplinarian demeanor pressing down on me, and I needed to get out from under it. Maybe I just needed to strike out on my own, to figure out how to be myself. Or maybe it was just the moment in time when college kids did this sort of thing. But for whatever reason, at the end of my freshman year, I decided to pick up and bum around the country for the summer. I had all of a hundred bucks in my pocket.

My buddy Bill Martindale and I hitched a ride to L.A. with a friend; four days and three thousand miles later, he dropped us off at the Phi Gamma Delta fraternity house on the USC campus. Billy was a Phi Gam at Gettysburg and I was one at Bucknell, so they let us stay for free for as long as we liked.

Then I got a job as a doorman at the classic Tower Theatre in downtown Los Angeles, famous as the first theater in L.A. to be wired for sound back in the 1920s and the place where *The Jazz Singer* premiered on the West Coast. It was a beautiful, majestic theater, grand and elegant, modeled after the Paris Opera House inside, all chandeliers and golden archways and long carpeted stairways. They outfitted me in a red uniform with shoulder braids and a fancy hat, and I got to see all the movies for free. I probably watched *The Guns of Navarone* five times that summer, and had a little crush on Maureen O'Hara in *The Parent Trap*. It was all pretty cool and cushy.

One weekend, we decided to drive down to Tijuana, Mexico, where, sometime south of 3:00 a.m. and under the influence of the local tequila, we apparently made some remarks to three prostitutes on a street corner. Unfortunately, they weren't the only ones at that corner; a local cop was there as well, overheard the remarks, and immediately arrested us.

They were hauling us away to the Tijuana jail, which we all knew from a pop song by the Kingston Trio a couple years back. "So here we are in the Tijuana Jail/Ain't got no friend to go our bail," we crooned drunkenly. We thought it was the coolest thing in the world to be headed to the jail from that song.

That is, until we got there. There were ten of us, squeezed into a twelve-foot-by-seven-foot cell, with a toilet overflowing with human waste. The place reeked of vomit and urine and shit. The mattresses were pitch-black and filled with fleas, a guy was masturbating on the top bunk, and I was afraid to drink the water or eat the piece of bread they gave us.

The next morning, we were hauled in front of a judge, who told us we were charged with "sexually assaulting women." He sentenced us to twelve days or $16. We had only ten bucks between us, so we went back to the hellhole of a cell, where the guy in the top bunk was masturbating again and four drag queens in the next cell were shouting at us. I sank to the floor, and sat there, and wondered how in the hell I'd ever get out.

What seemed like a thousand hours later, a guy showed up at the cell and said he was the American consul. He told us these false accusations were a pretty common occurrence and asked if we had anyone to pay the fine for us. By happenstance I'd stopped to visit a friend of the family in Coronado when I first got to California. I gave her name to the consul, and a few hours later she'd driven down and bailed us out. I don't know which was worse: her look of horror when she got to the cell, or her attempt not to act disgusted when these three smelly teenagers piled into her car. I've thanked her many, many times over the years, but probably never enough.

She drove us back to our car, which by the grace of God—although I don't think God was very pleased with the whole sordid affair—we found, miraculously, in the same condition we left it. We piled in and headed back to USC.

I took two things away from that experience: how easy it is to find yourself behind bars, and how easy it can be for nice white college kids with connections to get out of that scrape. I wasn't aware enough in that moment to imagine what life might be like for innocent men and women to find themselves behind bars, not for just a few uncomfortable hours or days, but for the rest of their lives, with no one to come to their rescue. But later, when I started to meet some of them, I think that experience in Tijuana—and more important, the understanding of how easily some people can get out of a situation like that and how unfair it is that others have no recourse—I think all that helped motivate me to become someone who could help.

A week or so later, I said goodbye to the Tower Theatre and was on the road again. I hit Vegas and Yellowstone and ran out of money in Laramie, Wyoming, where just by chance I had one of the most formative experiences of my life.

I checked in at the local unemployment office, because I'd heard that some of the ranchers would stop in there, looking for ranch hands to stack hay. Just after I got there, a rancher named Roy Githens stopped in looking for help. He could have been the Marlboro Man—dungarees, boots, cowboy hat, stubble of a beard on a weathered face. He rolled a cigarette as he looked at me with piercing blue eyes, sized up my skinny 135-pound frame, thought it over for a minute, and—probably against his better instincts—muttered, "You'll do. Come with me. Get in the pickup."

An hour later he showed me to a bunkhouse, which I shared with two itinerant workers. The next morning, I found out what I'd gotten myself into.

We got up at 6:15 a.m., threw some water on our faces, had a decent breakfast—Mrs. Githens, the rancher's wife, was a terrific cook—and headed out to the fields. From 7:00 a.m. until 6:00 p.m., we stacked huge, heavy, lumbering hay bales, pulling them first off a mechanical lift onto a long flat wagon, then off the wagon onto big stacks of bales.

The bales weighed upwards of eighty pounds each, and there was an endless supply of them. And every day, in the hot, grueling sun, we lifted and tossed and lifted and tossed. For eight dollars a day, plus room and board.

The food at least was a godsend. Every night, Mrs. Githens made us steaks and stews and potatoes and vegetables and hot rolls and cakes and pies, and we'd eat and wash up in a basin—you'd have to go to town to find a shower—and smoke a few Pall Malls and collapse, exhausted.

After a week I announced that I was quitting. Roy Githens looked me up and down, spit on the ground, and said, "Well, shit." He stared at me cold and hard, and I think I was literally trembling in my shoes. He proceeded to dress me down like I'd never been dressed down before.

"You're nothing but a soft, spoiled kid from the East," he said. "You should be ashamed of yourself—turning tail and going home to Mommy when the going gets tough. That how you're gonna live your life, you little piss?"

I felt ashamed. "No, sir," I said. "It's not." I asked him if I could stay on and, from that day forward, kept my mouth shut and did the work. For six weeks, I hauled those damned hay bales, and at the end of the summer he dropped me off on Highway 80 to hitchhike back home. As I got out of the car, he told me to be sure to let him know I got home safely. He told me his wife wanted to talk to my mom about my hard work—all of which was, I like to think, a small way of letting me know that I'd earned his respect.

I put my thumb out in the early morning sun, standing on the side of the highway, about fifteen pounds of muscle heavier than when I showed up, probably twice as strong, and, most important, with a lesson in my back pocket that stayed with me for a long time.

The lesson being: You don't quit. Ever. No matter how tough things get.

Six

NEW JERSEY, 1983

In the days after we freed Chiefie, I felt a sense of peace and accomplishment, but also a sense that something was missing. I found myself at a fork in the road. I had, by then, graduated from the seminary with a master of divinity degree. Now it was time to continue down that path, as I had planned from the start and promised my parents: to become an ordained church pastor.

Or was it?

At heart, when I dig down, I'm not a settle-into-a-routine kind of guy. I love adventure and the entrepreneurial spirit, and whether it was God telling me which way to go or just my own love of the feeling of freedom, the idea of setting out on my own, to do good in my own way, started to sound better and better. I was still living in my sparsely furnished room at Mrs. Yeatman's. It contained a three-by-four-foot wooden table that served as my desk, a threadbare green easy chair, my bed, and an unused fireplace that piled up with the leaves that blew down the chimney that early fall.

It also, in the form of that pile of papers on the desk, contained my future.

I returned again and again to those pages—letters and legal documents from other inmates I'd met through Chiefie, professing their innocence and asking for my help—in the early evenings, when the sun had already set outside my window and I huddled under the desk lamp, wondering whether I was going to continue this crazy notion of spending my life trying to free innocent people from prison.

It was right around that time that I first had The Dream. The dream took me back to Vietnam, where I had served what felt like a million years before. The dream was this: I'm standing on a river-bank in Vietnam's Mekong Delta. A boat chugs by, filled to over-flowing with people. And all of a sudden the boat starts to sink. I'm standing next to another man and I turn to him and say, it's so sad, there's nothing we can do, they're all going to drown. And then, all of a sudden, a helicopter flies in, and Navy SEALs jump out and dive into the water and bring up the people, one by one, and save them all.

I bolted awake and thought about what the dream meant. And listen, I'm not a new age kind of guy, and I don't put a lot of stock in dreams, but I have to tell you, in that moment, I felt that it was a sign. We can talk all day about whether it's a sign from God, as I believed it was, or a message from my subconscious, but it doesn't matter.

What matters was, I believed the dream was revealing my path to me: The prisons were full of innocent men and women. They were drowning. And they were all going to die unless someone jumped in and tried to save them.

And so, I began to realize, I was coming to a decision; or rather, as I now believe, that decision was coming to me.

Something else occurred in that moment that made me feel that way. It just so happened that I was, to put it mildly, dead broke. Mrs. Yeatman had long ago decided I could stay in that house rent-free for as long as I liked, and God bless her for that, but there was no way I could afford to keep pursuing this quixotic quest. And then, out of nowhere, my dad got an unexpected return on a long-forgotten busi-ness investment and decided to give each of his kids $10,000.

It was like manna from heaven to me, and if you believe in this sort of thing, which I certainly did then (and probably still do now), it was a sign from heaven, too. I had prayed very hard for a sign, something to help me understand what I should do. I truly believed that this was the omen I was waiting for.

And so I put aside the idea of becoming an ordained minister, because it was clear that God had another path in store for me. With this funding, I could start my new venture. A nonprofit corporation dedicated to freeing the innocent. I was certain now that this was why Christ had led me to Chiefie's cell block. That everything I had done in my life until this point was in preparation for this purpose. At last, at the age of forty-one, I had finally discovered—or been led to—my destiny, and found my rightful place in the world.

I struggled with what to call this new venture of mine, but one day, driving up the New Jersey Turnpike to visit Chiefie and Elena in Newark, it hit me: Luke 23. A Roman centurion at the foot of the cross looks up at the crucified Christ and exclaims, "Certainly, this man was innocent!"

And in that moment, Centurion Ministries was born.

And I knew just what the first case would be.

□

I had met Rene Santana back when I was visiting Chiefie at Rahway on Wednesday nights, figuring out how to get him freed. Chiefie and I were so excited and full of energy that we couldn't sit still, so we'd spend the hour walking around: the visitors' yard, on warm days; and, on colder days, a big room where all the prisoners and their visitors could congregate. We'd circle the room, talking and plotting and planning. And wherever Chiefie and I would walk, there was this inmate, Rene Santana, who would follow us around. Santana was a plumber from Newark who sometimes worked undercover for the Bureau of Alcohol, Tobacco, and Firearms. He would set up illegal gun deals; then the agents would swoop in. In 1976, Santana had been convicted of murder in a case of robbery-gone-bad that left two people dead. He swore he was innocent, and he knew what I was doing for Chiefie. He wanted me to do the same for him.

The prisoners were allowed to wear civilian clothes, and Rene, a short guy from the Dominican Republic with thinning hair and glasses, was a sharp dresser: always a nice shirt, polished shoes, well-pressed pants. He spoke good English and was very polite.

But very assertive, too. As Chiefie and I would walk the yard or the visitors' room, he was like a little terrier, nipping at my heels. He kept asking, Chiefie, can I join you guys for five minutes? I just want to talk to Jim for five minutes. And five would become ten, and ten, fifteen, and Chiefie would get irritated and chase him away. But over time, he wore me down. Maybe just to get him out of our hair or maybe because I was starting to believe him, I said, okay, when I'm done with Chiefie's case, I'll look at yours. No promises, but I'll get the transcripts and I'll take a look.

By the time Chiefie was freed, I'd obtained those transcripts and begun to dig into them. They were voluminous and, from the beginning, very confusing and filled with contradictions.

The crime had taken place in December 1974. A gambler by the name of Remigio Sanchez had been running a numbers game out of his Newark apartment building; some local thugs got wind of it and heard rumors he had upwards of $20,000 in the apartment. So on the morning of Monday, December 16, they decided to rob the place.

The testimony remains unclear, to this day, whether it was two or three men in ski masks who knocked on the door. When Sanchez made the mistake of cracking it open, they tried to force their way through. For a moment there was a tense stalemate, with the robbers pushing on the door and Sanchez and one of his sons desperately trying to hold them back. Eventually, they burst in. Sanchez grabbed a baseball bat and bashed in the head of one of the robbers before taking a fatal gunshot to the gut.

By the time the county prosecutors got around to sorting out their case, they said there were two men who'd burst in and one who remained outside as a getaway driver. The identity of one of the robbers was pretty clear: When they peeled the ski mask off the dead robber, they were able to identify him as a tough Newark Puerto Rican guy who went by the nickname Columbia. They identified the getaway driver as a man named Jose Rodriguez. And they said the third member of the team was a Dominican plumber from Newark named Rene Santana.

□

As I pored over the case file in my room at Mrs. Yeatman's, it all started to look suspicious to me, right from the get-go. For one, the case had seemed pretty flimsy, up until the start of the trial. A bunch of the dead robber's associates said they'd all been at a christening the night before the robbery. They said Rene was there and that he and Columbia had planned the robbery that night. They said Rene supplied the guns and ski masks the next morning and told Jose that he was supposed to be the lookout driver.

I didn't see how any of this, even if it were true (which I doubted), put Rene at the scene of the crime. The prosecutors must have felt their case was shaky, too, because just as jury selection for Rene's case concluded—out of nowhere, eighteen months after the crime— the state came up with a new, surprise witness.

His name was Roberto Gutierrez, a thirty-year-old longshore-man who lived in the same building as Sanchez, the victim who had been running the numbers game. I read on, incredulous, as Gutier-rez took the stand. The defense raised objection after objection as he testified that he heard the shots that morning, looked out of his first-floor apartment window, and saw a man walking quickly, pulling off his ski mask, and fleeing on foot up the street to the north. He identified that man as Rene Santana.

"I never forget the face in the front over here," he said on the stand. "I never forget that day."

The jury never got to hear from Santana's handlers at the Bureau of Alcohol, Tobacco, and Firearms, who wanted to vouch for his character, because the prosecutors objected to their testifying and the judge sided with them. And apparently the jury didn't take much stock in the testimony of Columbia's partners in crime—the ones who testified that Jose Rodriguez was the designated getaway driver—because they acquitted Jose.

So based, it seems, primarily on the testimony of the surprise "eyewitness," they convicted Rene Santana of two counts of murder.

I looked up from the giant case file and out the window: It had turned dark while I was reading. I hadn't even stopped for dinner. I was tired and bleary-eyed and ready to go get something to eat. But I did know I had come to a decision. Rene Santana was an innocent man. And just as in Chiefie's case, I felt compelled to try to prove it.

□

When I told Rene I was taking his case, he was almost in tears. "It is amazing, Jim, it is amazing," he kept saying. "I write to so many people, crying to help me. I cry about my innocence. Nobody help me. Sometimes I showed them a little bit of money and they help me a little bit. But nobody really help me. Now you will help me. It is amazing."

I didn't know how amazing it was. I was just doing what I felt God had called me to do. But I guess when you've been in prison for nine years for a crime you didn't commit, and nobody seems to care, simply finding someone who believes you can feel like a miracle.

I began by trying to find Roberto Gutierrez. I knew, in my bones, that he was the key. I found his magical appearance eighteen months after the crime to be problematic. How can you recognize someone eighteen months later when you got only a quick look at him supposedly fleeing a shooting? Heck, I can't recognize somebody's face two days after I meet the person.

Somebody had put him up to this, I was sure of it. I was still pretty new at this, but I decided to trust my instincts. That hasn't always served me well in my life, but it's what I had. And it's what I went with.

I had three things on Gutierrez: I knew his date of birth, I knew he was from the Dominican Republic, and I knew that he was a New

York City longshoreman. After months of getting exactly nowhere, I hit on the idea of trying the Immigration and Naturalization Service. It's located in a big federal building in downtown Manhattan, so on the morning of June 6, 1984, I drove up to the city to try my luck.

It was a ridiculously hot day for early June, and I was sweating under my clerical collar as I climbed the steps of the federal building, the blinding sun already glinting off the Twin Towers.

I walked into the first floor, and it was like walking into the Tower of Babel: There was a long, long line of immigrants, all talking at once in every language imaginable, all waiting to be served by three clerks. I was looking around and couldn't see any indication of how to find the INS, somewhere within this towering government building, and realized at the same time that I'd walked in with absolutely no plan—can you even walk into the INS and ask for information on an immigrant?—when one of the three clerks called out to me.

"Father," he said, "you look lost. Can I help you out?"

I looked down at his name tag and saw that he was a Mr. P. McConnell, probably a good Irish Catholic, and here's me, big red Irish face and the white collar. I guess he figures I'm a Catholic priest. I didn't do anything to dissuade him of that notion.

"I'm trying to get some background information on a Dominican fellow by the name of Roberto Gutierrez," I told him. "I need to talk to somebody from the INS." I was about to launch into my explanation of why, but he didn't even wait for that. He picked up the phone, and after a few seconds I heard him saying, "Yeah, I got a priest down here who wants to talk to somebody up in INS. Will you let him come up?" He puts the phone to his chest and asks me my name. "Jim McCloskey," I told him, careful not to say "Father Jim." "Yeah, the priest is Jim McCloskey. Can I send him up?"

My heart was pounding as I waited for the response, but he put down the phone and said, "Yeah, go on up to nine. Go see a fella named Ed Grecsek. He's waitin' for ya. Have a nice day, Father."

I resisted the urge to say, "Bless you, my son." With a big smile on my face, I thanked him for his trouble and headed to the elevators.

Ed Grecsek took me to his little cubicle, and I told him what I was doing. I told him about this Dominican man, Rene Santana, who was a good guy, who used to work for the ATF, and who got convicted because another man lied about a murder. I needed to find the other man, and I was wondering if he could help me out.

He listened, and after what seemed like an hour, he called in his secretary and said to me, "What's the guy's name?" After a little back-and-forth about where he might live, and did I have a date of birth, and all that, he gave all the information to his secretary and told her to get the file. She brought it in, and he started going through it and, without looking up, said, "Oh, this is a bad guy. What do you want to know about him?"

Before I knew it, he was running down Gutierrez's criminal history. Weapons possession, menacing, drunk driving, unlawful possession of gambling records, and one I was particularly interested in: 1972, Newark, charges of attempted bribery, possession of a dangerous weapon, and eluding a police officer. Maybe not Public Enemy No. 1 stuff. But fascinating to me, because I remembered, when I read the trial transcript, that the prosecutor said he had no criminal record at all!

Meaning somebody was lying. And I had the proof, sitting on the desk in front of me, in a cramped cubicle in the possession of an INS agent named Grecsek. I figured I most likely had no right to get this information without a court order. But I decided to press my luck.

"Um," I said, my voice as dry as chalk, "do you think I could get a copy of that file?" He said I couldn't, but he did let me write down all the details—the case numbers, charges, courts, dispositions, the whole shebang. Ten minutes later, I was walking out onto the scorching streets of Lower Manhattan with the goods tucked under my arm. There was an address in the file, too—unfortunately, an address that turned out to be long out of date—but I had something better. I was sure of it. I had the proof that Roberto had lied. And that the prosecutor, more than likely, had suborned perjury.

Not bad for a day's work.

□

I shared the information with David Ruhnke, the lawyer who was handling Rene Santana's appeals. He was a good guy, pretty strait-laced but very friendly. He wasn't much one for praise, but I could tell he was pretty impressed that I had ferreted out this information, and told me he'd get to work on it.

I had my work cut out for me too: I still needed to find Roberto Gutierrez. My next stop was the waterfront. I figured, the guy's a longshoreman; there must be some union card or work record or something that has his current address. So a few days later I put my collar back on, drove up to the city, and started working the docks. I felt like Karl Malden in *On the Waterfront*, trying to root out corruption in the shadows of the pier buildings in Lower Manhattan. On a hunch I stopped at the hiring hall at Pier 42, right on the East River, and sure enough, they had given Roberto work that very day. I left a message and hoped for the best.

A few days after my visit, I got a call from a woman who said her name was Ida and that she was Roberto's sister. She agreed to let me come visit her and gave me her address, on Ocean Avenue in Brooklyn. I didn't know that was Gutierrez's address, too. The very address I was looking for. But sometimes, when you're mining for gold, you can't tell right away what's going to pan out.

I went there the next day, a nice little six-story brick building across from a park. I rang the bell for her apartment, and she buzzed me up and was waiting in the hall as I climbed the stairs. She was probably about forty years old, with short brown hair and a round, kind face, which lit up when she saw me in my clerical collar. "Father!" she said. "Come in! Come in! Are you from the local parish?"

I went inside; the place was small but tidy and well maintained. There were two men sitting on the couch, glumly drinking wine and staring into space. They didn't acknowledge my presence, and I decided to just ignore them.

Ida and I sat at the kitchen table and sorted out who was who: I wasn't from the local parish, I told her. I was from New Jersey. I slowly got around to the point: Roberto had testified in a murder trial, and I didn't think he was telling the truth. An innocent man—a Dominican man, I made a point of mentioning—was sitting in prison as a result.

"Roberto . . . testified in a murder trial?" she said, emphasizing each word, slowly, as though she was trying to find the truth in the statement. "I did not . . ."

I waited for her to finish. A look of realization, or acceptance, or perhaps anger, flashed across her face.

". . . know."

But I knew, at that moment, that she would be an ally. I explained everything about Centurion Ministries, and pulled out a picture of Chiefie and Elena, and told her that whole tale. I will admit, a white male has an advantage in a situation like this, especially a white male in a clerical collar: Immigrants tend to see you as an authority figure and offer you perhaps more respect than you're entitled to— perhaps more than you deserve. But I felt good about my cause, and so, I'll admit, I used it to my advantage.

"Do you think maybe you and me and Roberto could sit down and talk this over? I'd be more than happy to come back and maybe the three of us could sort this out."

"Oh, he'll talk to you all right," she said, her voice rising in fury. I don't know if she was more angry that he had lied on the stand or that he'd withheld the story from her. Either way, the anger was flashing in her eyes. "I guaran-*tee* he will talk with you."

I left, feeling flushed with victory. I was sure she was telling the truth. She would get Gutierrez to talk to me.

It turned out she was sort of right. She did, eventually, get him to agree to see me.

It only took a year.

□

"Shut up and stay out of my business!" is what Roberto said to Ida when she confronted him about his role in the trial. She stayed in touch with me as the weeks turned into months, and remained very friendly; she said she was trying to get Roberto to change his mind and talk to me, but so far, no luck.

She did tell me that the victim's two sons, Guido and Felipe, had warned Roberto not to talk to me. They were the two men in the apartment when I met her, and when I left, Felipe told her, "I don't care what he says, that motherfucker Santana, he's trying to get out of this. I know he killed my father because Roberto saw him."

After months of silence, I started to think that maybe we'd have to move forward without him. After all, I still had the info on Roberto's criminal history, evidence of his perjury. Before the trial, the judge had grown increasingly angry at the prosecutor, Ralph Fusco, for withholding evidence—behavior, the judge said, that "borders on the shameful." When the trial did finally begin, Rene Santana's lawyer—a great public defender named Robert Graves—growing more and more frustrated, kept asking to see Roberto Gutierrez's rap sheet. Fusco kept saying that there were no pending charges in Essex County. The file I was holding, listing all the charges against Gutierrez, showed that Fusco was lying, pure and simple.

Or so I thought. Actually, as I dug a little deeper, I found out that he was, technically, telling the truth. There were no "pending charges." Because one day before Gutierrez's testimony, Fusco or one of his detectives had a judge dismiss all the charges against him. I found that evidence at the municipal court in Newark. The Essex

County prosecutors, the ones who'd pulled the dirty tricks in Chiefie's case, were at it again! There it was, in black and white: Gutierrez's record was whitewashed the day before he took the stand.

So I thought there was plenty of reason to call shenanigans on the prosecutor; Dave Ruhnke, Rene's attorney, agreed. We started the process of asking for a new trial.

And then, one Sunday in September of 1985, just as I was getting ready to watch my beloved Philadelphia Eagles' opening game against the New York Giants, I got a call from Ida. She wanted me to come to her apartment right away. Roberto had decided to talk. I guessed that seeing how well Ron Jaworski had recovered from his broken leg would have to wait. I grabbed my collar and my car keys and headed up to New York.

Roberto was sitting at the same table I'd sat at with Ida several times before. Even seated, he obviously wasn't a big guy, maybe five nine, and not muscular at all—certainly not my image of a bulky longshoreman. He apologized for ducking me for so long, but I brushed it off. We made small talk for a few minutes, but when I got to the point—telling him, flat out, that I thought he hadn't told the truth on the stand—he got sullen and silent and wouldn't look me in the eye.

Ida broke the silence. "Tell him what you told me," she said, her voice a glacier of ice. "Tell him."

It was very clear who was the boss here, and after a moment's hesitation he did just that. "They made me do it," he said. "I didn't want to do it. They made me."

My heart was in my mouth, but I tried to sound as matter-of-fact as I could, as though I was asking where he got that nice khaki shirt he was wearing.

"Who made you?" I asked, knowing the answer and hoping I'd hear it from him.

Roberto, sounding sheepish and ashamed, told me the whole story: how a detective named Robert Flaminio from the Essex County Prosecutor's Office had come to him and told him that if he didn't testify against Santana, they'd get him deported back to the Dominican Republic. He was terrified: This is a man who grew up under the iron fist of Rafael Trujillo, one of the most fearful dictators of our lifetime. The oppressive and violent rule left Roberto, and everyone of his generation, forever terrified of authority, knowing the horrors that awaited anyone who dared defy them. He was physically trembling as he told me this, his eyes pleading for me to understand.

He said the pressure had come from the victim's family as well: He was good friends with them, he told me, and Sanchez had helped him out many times; the cops had convinced Sanchez's sons that Santana was the killer, and they prevailed upon Gutierrez to testify as such.

"They said, 'Listen, this is my dad, you know,'" Roberto told me. "'Think of everything he's done for our family. Everything he's done for you.'"

He paused and considered me for a long moment.

"Thank you, Mr. McCloskey," he said to me, much to my amazement. "This is the first time I get to tell the truth. Please don't judge me."

I saw now how important that was to him. He had hit on a basic truth for me—one I hadn't realized until that moment. I told him then what I've told many more since.

"I'm not going to judge you, Roberto," I said. "God knows, if I were in your shoes, I probably would have done the same thing. I don't have that kind of courage to stand up to those kinds of people—and especially being told they were going to deport you or throw you in jail or whatever they were going to do. I understand. I don't blame you. I'm just happy you could tell me the truth. And Rene—Rene will be so happy. You can't imagine what this means. Roberto, you have just saved a man's life."

There wasn't much to say after that. He hugged me, his arms pressing into my back. I asked him if he'd sign an affidavit stating what he just told me. He glanced at Ida, saw her nod her head slowly, then looked back at me and said he would.

I walked out into the late afternoon daylight, trying to make sense of what had just happened. I was amazed at how relieved Roberto had seemed. Lying on the stand, putting an innocent man in prison, was a burden he had carried for nine long years.

This is what I was there for. To help him lay that burden down.

As incredible as that moment was, I wasn't prepared for what came next. About two weeks later I got a call. "Hello, Jaime?" said the voice on the other end. I knew right away it was Ida; she liked to call me Jaime. "So, Roberto and I have been doing some thinking," she said. I was worried, although the tone in her voice told me not to be. What she said next was the last thing I could have possibly expected. "He wants to go down to Rahway to tell Mr. Santana how sorry he is and ask for his forgiveness."

□

Rene was sitting at a table in the outside visitors' area when I showed up with Roberto and Ida in tow. We walked slowly toward him, and I was trying, from a distance, to read Rene's face. When I had asked him, the week before, if he would agree to this meeting, and told him why Roberto wanted to see him, his reaction had surprised me. "I hated that man," he told me, seething. "Hated him. If it wasn't for him, I wouldn't be here. But now, now that you tell me why he did it—I wouldn't have caved," he said, a hint of bravado in his voice. "But I understand why somebody would cave under that pressure. Those bastards," he said, and let that hang. I knew who he meant.

"It takes a lot for him to come here and face me," he said. "It takes a lot to apologize. You can bring him here. It will be fine."

Now, a week later—as he came face to face with the man who put him behind bars—I didn't know what his reaction would be. Would seeing this man dig up all those years of buried hostility? Would he react in anger and fury?

Roberto and I reached the table. Rene stood up, and without a word he moved toward Roberto and put his arms around him.

"I think I'll leave the two of you to this," I said. Ida and I excused ourselves. As I looked back, I could see them talking. Rene was gesticulating a lot, and then Roberto seemed to be talking, and then the two of them stood up and started hugging again. That's when Ida and I went back.

"Thank you, Mr. McCloskey," Roberto said to me. "Rene has forgiven me. I told him how terrible I feel about this, how guilty I felt all these years. I've been carrying this in me, for all these years. And then for me to be able to come and tell him how sorry I am. That I did this, I allowed myself to be coerced by these people. I cannot accept that in myself. But he is accepting of me." He turned to Rene. "Thank you," he said simply.

I looked at Rene, and he was just nodding. He told me again how much anger he had held in his heart for so many years and how that anger had dissolved when he saw this man, in person, apologizing and promising to set things right.

The anger, I realized, had weighed on Rene, just as the guilt had weighed on Roberto. Both men had found, on their own, a way to lift those heavy loads from off their shoulders.

Ida, her voice quivering, asked Rene if he would retaliate against Roberto when he was freed, and Rene assured her he would do no such thing. Instinctively, she reached out to hug him, and then so did I. I left that day feeling proud and humbled. Things were really going my way.

Until they weren't. Sometimes, cases move in a straight line. And sometimes, I was about to learn, just when the train seems to be pulling into the station, it goes right off the rails.

The case was moving along briskly, and based on the evidence I'd collected proving that the prosecutor's office had lied about Gutierrez's record, the lawyer, David Ruhnke, had gotten us an evidentiary hearing. But I was getting nervous: I hadn't heard from Roberto or Ida for several weeks. I soon figured out why. When the prosecution and defense exchanged documents—standard procedure before a trial—I discovered two things. One surprising, the other devastating.

I learned that Ida wasn't Roberto's sister; she was his longtime live-in girlfriend. But that was nothing. I also learned that Roberto had recanted his recantation; he took it all back. As soon as I learned that from the documents, I called Ida.

She was ashamed and sad. "Please, Jaime," she said. "Don't call us again. Roberto is scared of the prosecutor. He is scared of Felipe Sanchez." I tried to protest, but she interrupted. "We are just so tired," she said. "And we don't want any more trouble." With that, she hung up.

I soon discovered what had happened: As we geared up for our hearing, and the prosecutors saw that Roberto had given us an affidavit recanting his trial testimony, they began to play hardball with him. They had the New York City waterfront police pick him up and deliver him to Essex County detectives, who interrogated him something fierce.

Roberto caved. He gave a statement declaring that I had manipulated him into saying Santana was innocent. At the conclusion of this new statement, the detective asked him, "One final question, Roberto. Who did you see running from the scene of the murder?" His answer: "Rene Santana."

At first, I was heartbroken. All that work was for nothing! I couldn't believe it. I wanted to go back and try to change his mind. But I knew, in my bones, it wouldn't do any good. So I was just bereft.

But quickly, my sadness turned to rage: Incredibly, once again, the prosecutors had subverted justice—with blind disregard for the truth—just to preserve their phony conviction. It was outrageous! If there were ever a moment that I realized what a mean machine I was dealing with, this was it.

I tried to keep my wits about me. We still had Gutierrez's record, which the prosecutors had lied about at trial. I prayed it would be enough.

□

The day of the hearing came. Dave Ruhnke put me on the stand first, and I laid out everything I had found—the conflict with Gutierrez's record and the fact that the prosecutors had whitewashed it. I left out all that had happened with Gutierrez, of course, because he'd recanted his recantation. In fact, both sides decided not to call him.

I kept looking over at the prosecutors, to see if they were rattled at all. If they were, I couldn't tell. It was like playing poker with a statue of a poker player. They were utterly impassive.

But clearly, what I said had an effect. A big one. Shortly after I testified, the prosecutors—caught red-handed—offered a plea deal. They were going to let Santana plea down to supplying the weapon the night before the crime (another thing I'm sure he didn't do, by the way).

I was taken aback when I learned that Dave had convinced Rene to accept the deal. He'd kept me in the dark about it the whole time. I guess he was afraid I'd throw a monkey wrench into the conversations. And I would have, too. We hadn't fought for the truth all this time just to settle for a lie, even if it was a smaller one.

I insisted that the three of us—Rene, Dave, and myself—meet in Rene's cell in the courthouse the next day. I wanted to make sure that Rene hadn't been coerced by Dave to accept the plea deal, that this was what he really wanted to do.

Rene stood up when he saw me and gave me the biggest hug in the world, thanking me once more for getting him free. I tried to stay as positive as he was, but I had to ask the question.

"Rene," I said, "why did you do it? Why did you accept the plea deal? I know you didn't give those guys the gun. Why did you admit to a crime you didn't do?"

He looked down for a long time before he looked back up at me.

"I'm tired, Jim," he said. "It's been ten and a half years. I didn't want to do it, but this was my way out of prison and just to get out of there, be a free man."

"Oh, Rene," I said. "Man, but this was going so good."

He put a hand on my shoulder. "This is good, Jim. This is good. You gave me my life back. I'm okay."

So, in open court on Tuesday, February 18, 1986, Rene pleaded guilty to aiding and abetting the robbery. The judge vacated the murder conviction, issued a motion for a new trial, and gave Rene a sentence of time served. Meaning, he was free to go.

Free to go.

I know I should have been elated at that moment, but something seemed wrong to me. I mean, yes, it was my goal to free this man from prison. But it was also my goal to exonerate an innocent man. Now he would still have this stain on his record. I didn't know what consequence that would have.

I found out seconds later. Because who was sitting in the back of the courtroom but some agents from the Immigration and Naturalization Service. Rene's freedom lasted all of about ten seconds. Before I could even talk to him, they grabbed him, took him into custody, and threw him in jail. His green card had run out while he was in prison. They were going to immediately deport him back to Santo Domingo.

Once again, I was seeing just what a mean machine the justice system is. I couldn't believe how cold, how heartless this was. The prosecutor's office flat-out lied to put a man in prison for ten years, and now that they were caught doing it, they made sure he got thrown out of the country—just for spite? I gave Dave Ruhnke a lot of credit for doing this case pro bono and had to give him credit for getting Rene free. But I was furious at him, too, partly for keeping me in the dark, but mostly for caving in to this deal when we were so close—*so* close—to getting Rene fully exonerated.

Dave had a different objective than I did. Freedom was good enough for him. As it turned out, neither of us got what we wanted.

Rene was being sent away. Now he could never come back to the United States, where his mother lived, where his brother lived, where his wife and daughter lived.

I know I should have been thinking, well, at least I got the guy out of prison. But that's not what I was thinking. I was thinking, "You make a deal with the devil and this is what happens."

If only I had known their plan was in the works, I thought. I could have done something. I could have at least fought with the INS. I could have gotten an immigration hearing. I could have leaned on the ATF agents he'd collaborated with, who'd testified before about how Santana "was constantly endangering his life" to help them set up stings on gun smugglers. I could have brought in Paul Casteleiro, the guy who helped me in the Chiefie case. I could have—

Paul.

Thinking about him, I suddenly felt the urge to call him, to unburden myself. I got him on the phone and started telling him the story. I poured my heart out. He was very sympathetic. He really got it. But he kept telling me to focus on the positive—that I'd done a great job, that I'd gotten another innocent man out of prison, and that sometimes you get what you get.

I felt better after talking to Paul, but I promised myself, whenever possible, total exoneration would be the goal. Of course we would accept freedom if that wasn't possible, but I would always keep my eye on the prize.

I thought about the similarities between Rene's case and Chiefie's. In both, the star witness agreed to meet with me after refusing to do so; in both, telling the truth had lifted a weight off them in a way I could never have expected. In both cases, we wound up not putting them on the stand, because we had enough evidence without them (and obviously in Rene's case, because the witness recanted his recantation).

So I was starting to learn how this works: Gather all the cards you can, and when you get to the table, figure out which ones to play. We'd played them well in each instance. Both times, the Essex

County prosecutors suppressed evidence, and we proved it, and they were upbraided by the judges. That was something. It wasn't going to keep Rene in the country, but it was something.

At 4:00 in the morning, six days after he was grabbed by INS, Rene was informed that he was being put on a 7:00 a.m. flight to Miami, and then on to Santo Domingo. He called me right away, and I realized that in all the confusion I'd never gotten to say good-bye to Rene and once he was on that plane, I'd never see him again.

I got up and drove frantically to Newark Airport, ran to the ticket area, and sure enough I spotted Rene just before he headed for the gate. He stood up and embraced me, thanking me once more for freeing him from prison. I tried to stay as positive as he was. I didn't let him know how angry I'd been, or how sad. We just talked about how amazing it was that he was out of prison. I promised to keep in contact with his family members here in the States, and he promised to keep in touch with me.

There was nothing more to say. I watched him walk through the gate in the company of two INS agents, then turned and headed home.

I knew Rene was landing in the Dominican Republic dead broke, so I managed to scrape together some funds, sending him $1,200 to get him started. He called me as soon as he arrived, sounding despondent.

"I am so lonely, Jim," he said. "I don't know what I am going to do."

It was rough going for him those first few months. Some friends took him in for a few weeks, and a little while later one of his sisters came back from the States and got an apartment for the two of them. He bounced around doing real estate and some other jobs until he landed a position with the government; his English had gotten pretty good in prison, and he was able to teach practical English to intelligence agents who worked with the president.

Things started looking up: He remarried, had children, and kept working, building a new life for himself as year folded upon year, decade upon decade. It had its ups and downs; that marriage broke apart after his son, then an adult, was murdered. It was a crime that remained unsolved, probably because the killers were powerful drug dealers, Rene believes.

But then he got married again, and he and his wife are still together. He has been working for the government for twenty-two years and has a seven-year-old son who loves baseball and, like any red-blooded Dominican, wants to grow up to be a shortstop.

Rene still calls me every couple of months. We've stayed close to this day.

"You saved my life," Rene told me recently. "If it was not for you, I would be in prison the rest of my life. But Jesus Christ! That prosecutor nailed me. They know I was innocent. I cannot believe it."

Clearly, his anger, the anger I had seen him lay down the day Gutierrez appeared to make amends, has returned. It remains to this day. So does his sadness.

"Right now, if the judge told me, 'Do you want to come back to the United States?' I would say no. I don't feel like I can go back. What they did to me is too much. I miss my family, but it was too much. I tried to meditate about this, I tried to analyze how politics works, but I can't understand why they keep me in prison and the real killer is on the streets. I never understand this. I never understand."

It's hard for me to hear how that pain endures. But it helps me, too. It helps me to know I'm on the right path. To know what I'm doing matters. And especially, to know it matters to people like Rene.

"I have a nice life now, Jim," Rene told me a little while ago. "People love me here. I am around good people. I have respect and I have a life."

And sometimes, maybe, that's all you can ask.

Seven

▥

NEW JERSEY, 1985

As much as the work I was doing was starting to feel like the best way I could possibly spend my life, I was having to face a hard fact: I had no idea how I was going to keep it up.

It was a pretty lonely road I was walking. At that time there was no one else anywhere in the United States, or elsewhere in the world for that matter, committed to freeing the imprisoned innocent. I was up against the strong headwinds of a prevailing belief that the criminal justice system was about as foolproof as it gets. Today I think people are more willing to accept the idea that many in prison have been wrongly convicted, but back then talking about the notion that the greatest country on earth was systematically imprisoning innocent people fell on deaf ears in many corners.

For that reason—and because I had exactly zero expertise in trying to raise money for a nonprofit—it was a struggle to get Centurion Ministries up and running, to say the least. I was raising less than $20,000 a year for both my living expenses and my work, and I was spending every penny of it. Paul and Dave offered me outstanding legal support, of course. But otherwise I was alone as I worked the Chiefie and Santana cases, and I was quickly running out of money to pour into the 1974 VW Rabbit that had replaced my Pinto.

But the thought of giving up never crossed my mind. Not once. I knew this was what God wanted me to do. I just wished God had given me a hint or two about how to pay for it.

Around Christmas 1985, at the end of my rope (and down to my last five hundred bucks), I decided to apply for a dinnertime waiter's job at the Annex, a local Princeton restaurant I used to hang out at when I could afford to.

But then a greater force—in the form of my old high school buddies—intervened. Out of the blue, I got a check for $1,200 from a high school friend, Lin Haly, who had taken up a collection among the rest of my high school gang. That, and a Christmas present from my parents, kept me from putting on the apron at the Annex. It wasn't much, but it was enough to keep Centurion afloat.

I said three prayers of thanks—one to God, one to my parents, and one to my dear friends at Haverford High—and got back to work on my next case.

□

I met Nate Walker through Chiefie, the same way I'd met Rene Santana. Walker and Santana were convicted in the same month, May 1976, and both had professed their innocence from the start; just as Rene, at his sentencing, had interrupted the judge to say "they found the wrong man guilty," so did Nate Walker interrupt the judge in the middle of his sentencing, saying, "It wasn't me, Your Honor. The man you want is probably still in the street. You got the wrong man." What they got the wrong man for was a brutal rape and kidnapping of a young white woman by a black man in Elizabeth, New Jersey, in October 1974, for which Nate was serving life plus a fifty-year consecutive sentence.

I had decided to take a look at Rene Santana's case because of his dogged determination. In Nate's case it was the quiet dignity of his mother that persuaded me.

They barely had to say anything to me, really, when I walked into the visitors' room at Trenton State Prison to talk with them in the fall of 1984. Nate and his mom were sitting quietly, their faces filled with hope and patience: Nate with the large, thick glasses he'd worn since he was a teenager; and his mother, Irene, composed and polite, immaculate in appearance and demeanor alike. I asked her about herself and learned that she was a faithful member of Grace Episcopal Church in Elizabeth, where she was trying to raise money for Nate's defense by organizing rummage sales. She was the only black person on the board of the local Salvation Army.

We started talking about Nate's case, and I could tell from the start how much pain she was in. Nate remained expressionless throughout our conversation, but the emotion showed on his mother's face as she pleaded her son's innocence to me and told me that no one had been assigned to work on his appeals.

"We are at a crossroads," she said. "We can't afford to hire a lawyer. We don't know where else to go. I really feel that God has sent you to us, Mr. McCloskey. I have to walk past that courthouse every day on my way to work. You cannot imagine how hard that is. To look at that every day. And know that my son is innocent. He did not do this. I swear to you. He did not do this. Please, please help us."

She stared at me, and the words that followed tolled, each one, like a church bell calling me to prayer: "Do. Not. Let. My. Son. Die. In. Prison."

I was shaken by her words. I promised I'd study the record of the case when I could. I was still buried in the Santana case at the time, but I knew, sooner or later, that I would take up their plight. What I didn't know was how profoundly this case would change my life.

The facts of the case itself are fairly clear, though there are some critically important gray areas. On the night of October 19, 1974, a woman I'll call Jean (to protect her identity) was visiting a friend in Elizabeth, New Jersey. Just before midnight, or maybe just after midnight—one of those critically important gray areas—she says she left and walked toward her car; the next thing she knew, a man forced her into the car at knifepoint, got in the passenger's seat, and ordered her to drive to Newark. But a few miles down the road he ordered her to stop, and for the next two or three hours he raped her repeatedly. In her initial statements she said she let him out in

Newark and then drove back to Elizabeth. Where she actually let him out is another one of those gray areas.

She was taken to the hospital; a rape test was performed, and the vaginal swabs indicated the presence of semen. And the hunt was on for the rapist.

As I read the transcripts, I understood why the case drew so much attention—black assailant, white victim, community outrage. It was unclear to me, however, how Nate Walker became a suspect. Nevertheless, about four months later, in February 1975, he was yanked off the street and put in a lineup, and the victim identified him as her assailant. He was shocked as hell and insisted he didn't do it. She insisted he did.

And so the trial began.

Nate's alibi was rock solid: He worked at a large copper plant, and he clocked out at 11:31 p.m. His time card was put into evidence at the trial. The guy who gave him a lift to and from work testified, too, saying he and Nate went to wash up after they clocked out, then walked to the parking lot, which was a ways away, and then he dropped Nate off at home at 12:15 a.m. Nate's wife, Tina, was home with their child.

In her testimony, Jean said she was positive that her assailant did not wear glasses, but Nate Walker, due to a condition called structural myopia, was virtually blind without his glasses. Couldn't see anything more than ten inches from his face in fact. It's inconceivable that Nate could have done the things she said—especially directing her where to go on the drive—and not have his glasses on.

If all that wasn't enough, Jean also testified that the assailant forced her to perform oral sex, and as a result she knew that he was circumcised and had one testicle. Nate Walker matches neither of those descriptions.

Armed with all that information, the jury deliberated for three days and came back with a verdict.

Guilty.

□

I decided not to start the investigation with the victim, although it seemed like a logical place to begin. It was clear that she'd been through a terrible trauma, and I didn't want to bother her if I didn't have to. But I did need to know if she was just wrong about her identification of Nate or if something more sinister was going on. The jury never heard about it, but Jean had a record of her own. She was under indictment in Middlesex County, the next county over, on drug charges and possession of nine illegal weapons. Just the kind of person the cops could squeeze, if they wanted to. But why would they want to?

When I started poking around, I was shocked to learn that nobody—nobody!—had ever talked to the young woman Jean was visiting on the night of the rape. So I went to see her. Sure enough, she told me that she remembered that night really well. And she remembered that Jean left her house at about eleven o'clock at night.

Eleven o'clock. I got a little dizzy when she said that. That was about an hour earlier than the victim had said she had left. Which is crucial, because Nate was still working at eleven o'clock.

The thought was still buzzing around in my head when I made my next stop, at the office of Union County sheriff Ralph Froehlich. Ralph was a highly regarded law enforcement officer who spent twenty years as an Elizabeth cop before being elected sheriff. This wasn't his case—it was a police case, not sheriff's department—but Irene suggested I see him, because he had been kind and sympathetic to her over the years. Besides, he was an Elizabeth police officer at the time of the crime, so maybe he knew something about what went down. I got right to the point with him and told him why I thought Nate was innocent.

At first, he rebuffed my assertion. But I was persistent: I kept finding excuses to go back and see him, and after a while I guess he finally came around to trusting me. And to admitting that maybe, just maybe, they had the wrong guy.

"Nate's just not the kind of guy to do this," the sheriff conceded one afternoon. "He just doesn't do this kind of thing." Apparently, they all knew Nate as a small-time car thief. Not a violent rapist. "Listen, Jim. You're a good guy," he said. "I've always had doubts about Nate's guilt. The woman's testimony is full of inconsistencies. I hope you can get this thing straight." He suggested I talk to Joseph Brennan, director of the Elizabeth Police Department—the office that actually arrested Nate.

Joseph Brennan was friendly to me, though not as forthcoming as the sheriff had been. But persistence pays off, and over time he opened up to me as well. In fact, Brennan was so forthcoming I decided to double down. I put together a memo for him, outlining everything I knew. The next time he saw me, it was like the floodgates had opened.

"I've reviewed our files on this case and they confirm what you've told me," he said. "This case should be reopened. It is the right thing to do, and I think it should be done. You write the prosecutor and ask him to do that, and tell him we'll be glad to cooperate from our end."

"Well, I appreciate that," I said as calmly as I could, though inside I was about to burst.

The case is as good as solved, I thought. The police are saying my guy is innocent. What more could I need?

You guessed it. I was *still* that naive.

□

The next time I saw Nate, I told him what I'd heard. As always, he remained composed, peering at me through those big thick glasses. He smiled at the news, but I was primed by now not to expect him to jump out of his seat with excitement. I think he didn't want to get his hopes up. His mom, when she joined us, was emotional enough for the two of them, always thanking me, always crossing her fingers and asking God to guide my hand. But this time, it was just me and

Nate. I asked him something I'd never thought to ask him before, and to my surprise he took no time to answer.

"Nate," I said, "do you know why they did this to you? Why did they set you up like this?"

"You don't know?" he said to me, tilting his head to one side. "It's because of that dead police officer."

Nate began to tell me a story I could barely believe, but over the next month, as I pressed my Union County police sources for more information, they all confirmed the incredible story Nate was telling me. Here's what I pieced together.

Back in 1971, in the town of Clark, a few towns over from Elizabeth, a well-respected police officer was killed—career guy, father's a senior officer in the same police department. They found a stolen car at the scene of the murder, and they surmised that the killer was a car thief.

They decided to lean on the car thieves they knew in the area. Why they decided to lean on Nate as the guy they were going to squeeze, I have no idea. But they did. They hauled him in and grilled him. "We know whoever did this was a car thief," they told him. "You're a car thief. You've got to know who did this. You're out in the street. You hear things. What do you know about this?"

Nate insisted he didn't know anything. But the department grew obsessed with finding the killer of one of their own—as police departments do, understandably. That obsession kept bringing them back to Nate. They gave him a polygraph. They hounded him.

And then, when the opportunity presented itself, in the form of the kidnapping and rape of a young woman, they charged him, figuring it was the pressure that would finally cause him to crack. That would make him give up the cop killer in his midst.

Only Nate couldn't give up the killer, because he didn't know who the killer was. In fact, here's something else that made me swear allegiance to Nate Walker, if I hadn't already. I was able to confirm a story that he told me about the murder of the police officer, because in July 1977 another man was put on trial for that crime.

The prosecutors' case was weak—the defendant was acquitted in the end—but just before the trial they hauled Nate out of his Rahway cell, brought him downtown, and said, if you'll testify against this guy, we'll let you go. You'll be a free man and can go home to live with your wife and son. And if you don't testify, you'll never see the light of day again.

Now, I'd been at this long enough to know how easy it is to get people to cave in and commit perjury to save their own hides and stay out of prison. I'd seen it with Delli Santi in Chiefie's case; I'd seen it with Roberto Gutierrez in Rene Santana's case. I've seen it in plenty of other cases I've worked on, too. I knew how little the cops cared if Nate was telling the truth. They only cared to have him testify. If that meant suborning perjury, so be it. They were desperate for a conviction. So there was Nate's out. Tell one lie, like so many others have done, and you walk away, free and clear.

Nate peered at them through those Coke-bottle lenses and said, "I don't know anything about that policeman's murder."

And for that, they put an innocent man in prison. They all knew it. And no one said, maybe we should stop this.

The more I heard about it, the angrier I became. The next time I saw Brennan, I asked him about the dead cop theory. He didn't confirm it, of course, but he didn't deny it either. He just sat there, with the bearing of an ex-marine and the starched, pressed uniform of a career no-nonsense cop, and told me, again, that he believed me, and added, "As I said, I believe this case should be reopened. You write the prosecutor and ask him to do that, and tell him we'll be glad to cooperate from our end."

I was glad to hear it again, but at the same time I wanted to explode. Well, if you know the guy is innocent, why don't you do something? Why are you asking me to talk to the prosecutor? Why don't *you* push to reopen the damn case?

But I held my tongue. I knew that's not how this works. Here's how this works: If there's a God, then God's gotta work through me.

□

My next step took me back to the Union County Courthouse in Elizabeth, trying to unearth any files I could on the Walker case. I was focused on trying to find out if any other rapes had gone down around that time, maybe done by someone who fit the description the victim had given. I was cooling my heels, waiting for a clerk to come back with some files, when whom did I run into but Paul Casteleiro, the attorney who'd helped me free Chiefie. We greeted each other like old friends. Or old battle buddies, anyway. Which, in a sense, we were.

"So, Jim," he asked me, "what are you doing down here? What are you up to now? Still fighting the good fight?"

"As a matter of fact," I told him, "I'm looking for a one-balled rapist. You know any?"

When he stopped laughing, I filled him in on the case—how the victim had testified that her assailant had one testicle, and if I could find someone who fit that description, it would help the case enormously.

"Aw, man, that sounds like a great case," Paul said, a curious look on his face. "Hey, why don't I join you? Be your lawyer? I mean, you know, be Nate's lawyer? You got one?"

No, I didn't have one. No, I didn't know where I was gonna find one. And no, I wasn't gonna let this moment go by. What to some people might seem like a living nightmare, to someone in Paul's line of work sounded like an exciting opportunity, and that's just what I needed.

"Paul, that's great," I said. "Offer accepted."

I didn't know it at the time, but that chance encounter started Paul and me on a lifelong journey. He stayed with Centurion from that day to this one, more than thirty years later. It began with our hunt for Jean's rapist.

And it didn't take us long to find our prime suspect. In the wake of Jean's rape, it began to seem very clear that a serial rapist was on the loose: Jean's was the first of ten rapes, all from mid-October to mid-December 1974. A perp named James Jackson Johnson—who came to be known as JJ—was arrested and charged with eight of those ten assaults. The ninth case was thrown out for lack of evidence because the victim never got a good look at her assailant. Of the eight cases he was charged with, Johnson pleaded guilty to two and was found guilty at trial for three others. He got a hundred years, total.

"Why the hell wasn't JJ Johnson charged with our case?" Paul asked me once we'd uncovered this mountain of evidence.

I explained to him the whole theory about the killing of the police officer. Which is why, I believed, they'd saved that last rape case for Nate. Now, I should point out that to this day JJ has never been charged in Jean's case, and given that he's already rotting away in prison, the chances are mighty unlikely he ever will be. Still, if we could find evidence that he was a likely suspect in her case, that sure would help Nate.

"If only there was a way to find out if JJ has one ball," Paul said, jokingly.

"Well," I said, "as a matter of fact—you're not gonna believe this—but I know how we can find out."

□

I was still working the Rene Santana case and still visiting him at Rahway every Wednesday night. And guess who else was spending the rest of his life at Rahway? None other than our possibly single-testicled suspect, JJ Johnson.

"Hey, Rene," I said one cool Wednesday evening on the visitation yard, "do you see that inmate over there by the fence? The guy in the blue workshirt with his hands in his pockets?"

Rene scanned the yard. "Yeah, I see him. What about him?"

"Rene," I said, not sure I even wanted to go through with this, "I have about the strangest favor I could possibly ask you."

"You are doing so much for me, my friend," he said. "I will do anything you ask me to."

"Well, that's good," I said. "But I don't know if you're going to want to do this."

I told him my plan. When visitation hours are over, all the inmates are lined up and strip-searched to make sure their visitors didn't leave them any souvenirs—drugs, a file, whatever. What if Rene just happened to be in line right after JJ when they strip-searched him and happened to get close enough to do some testicle surveillance?

Rene's face lit up like I'd just told him the funniest joke in the world. "Yes! I'll do it! I find out for you!" he said. I don't know if it was the chance to help the guy who was helping him, or just the sheer delight of doing something ridiculous, or putting one over on a no-good serial rapist. But when our time was up, I saw them get in line, and there, right behind JJ, was Rene; he looked back at me, nodded ever so slightly, and put his head down, like it was just another rotten moment in a rotten day in the rotten place they call Rahway.

The next morning, Rene couldn't wait to call me. He was bursting at the seams to tell me what he'd found out.

"I did it!" he said. "I saw! You were right, Jim! He only has one ball! *¡Uno cojone!* How did you know?"

"How did I know?" I asked, incredulous. "How do *you* know?"

He told me a whole lot more detail than I ever cared to know about the testicles of JJ Johnson, how they'd made him bend over and spread his legs during the strip search, and how he was a tall man so Rene could tell from behind that he had only one testicle, and—

"Rene, I get it," I said, not needing to hear any more of the sordid details. "So you're not just telling me this because you know it's what I want to hear, right? I mean, you're sure you're sure?"

"I'm sure I'm sure, Jim. The son of a bitch has one testicle. As sure as I have two."

I was pretty pleased with myself for pulling off that little stunt, with Rene's help (and extremely happy that I was never going to have to try to verify the fact myself!). But on its own, I knew it wasn't going to get Nate off. The jury convicted him despite the difference between his physical attributes and the witness's testimony; this wasn't going to get him a new trial. It was time to dispense with the preliminaries and get on to the main event.

I had to track down Jean.

☐

I contacted her family's rabbi, who told me he had an appreciation of my mission (he called me a "mensch," in fact—the first time I'd ever heard the word), and he gave me her address in Gainesville, Florida. I wrote her a letter; I didn't expect a response, really, and sure enough I didn't get one. So I decided to fly down there.

She wasn't home, but her neighbors told me where she worked. I showed up there the next day; she was a secretary, working at a row of desks, and the minute I showed up in my clerical collar, she knew exactly who I was and why I was there.

"Jean, I'm sorry to pop in on you like this," I said, as friendly as can be, "but I didn't know any other way. I wrote you a letter, did you get my letter?"

She just stared at me.

"Hey, could I maybe take you out for a sandwich or for lunch so we can talk about this situation?"

"Get out of here," she snarled back. "I don't want to talk to you. I never want— How dare you!" At that, her voice started to rise, and some of the other secretaries looked over. She lowered her voice, but I could still hear the fury in it. "How dare you come down here and intrude on me and bring up this terrible, traumatic"—she searched for a word—"*situation* that I had to endure all those years ago! Get the hell out of here. Right now."

And that was that. I turned and left, and flew home.

I was thinking we were at a dead end, but while I was away, the amazing Paul Casteleiro, the man with an eye for detail like no one I'd ever known, had found something in the file that no one seemed to have noticed before. Namely, that the semen taken on the vaginal swab from the victim on the night of the crime had never been tested for blood type. Remember, this was before DNA had been used to exonerate anyone; that was still four years in the future. But if the blood type didn't match Nate's, it would be proof positive of his innocence.

Now all we had to do was see if the man who originally prosecuted the case would help us find that evidence. How hard could that be?

Richard Rodbart, the trial prosecutor who put Nate Walker away, was the trial supervisor of the Union County Prosecutor's Office when Paul and I approached him about the possible wrongful conviction of Nate Walker. The way I figured it, maybe he was just a rookie trying to make his bones back when he earned that conviction against Nate. Maybe he didn't test the swab, because he felt he had a decent case, and why roll the dice on getting a bad result that would prevent a conviction? And I could guess why the defense attorney didn't ask for the swab: He already had what he felt was a rock-solid alibi—Nate was at work that night—and so maybe he figured there was no reason to take a chance on the test results.

I just couldn't fathom why everyone was so afraid of the truth— why truth had no place in this equation. Everyone was just trying to prevail; truth was sacrificed at that altar of winning.

I didn't confront him with any of that, of course. I was hoping we could get on his good side.

I have to give Rodbart all the credit in the world. We all agreed that if the blood type in the swab didn't match Nate's, he was innocent. And if it did match—well, that didn't prove him guilty, but it certainly meant we didn't have a leg to stand on. Talk about rolling the dice.

By another incredible twist of fate—or something bigger than that—it turns out that we were just in time. That vaginal swab was sitting in a plastic bottle with a cork top, collecting dust on a shelf in the Elizabeth Police Department's evidence locker room—a building that was scheduled to be torn down in less than a month, and all the old unneeded evidence in it was scheduled to be destroyed with it. And this was now evidence in an eleven-year-old, settled case; no one, aside from Paul and me, thought there would ever be any use for it.

But there was. Rodbart rescued that swab and sent it to the FBI. We held our breath until the results came back.

On October 22, 1986, I was at Newark Airport. I'd asked Paul to meet me there. I'll never forget the moment: He was coming up the escalator, and I was at the top, and he had a sheaf of papers in his hand and a huge smile on his face.

He couldn't wait until he reached the top.

"Jim, we won!" he said, shaking the sheaf of papers above his head. "Nate's been exonerated!"

When he got off the escalator, he showed me that what he was holding was the FBI report. Rodbart had just given it to him. It showed conclusively:

Nate's blood type was A. The victim's blood type was A.

The blood type found in the semen was B.

Nate Walker was an innocent man.

☐

Two weeks later we were all in a courtroom in Elizabeth, judge Alfred Wolin presiding. Rodbart, bless him, had actually joined Paul in drawing up a motion stipulating Nate's innocence.

After Rodbart told the judge that the crucial evidence in the case had been "overlooked" at trial—a dubious way of putting it, to say it mildly, but let's let that go—Nate's conviction was vacated. At the same time, he was sentenced to time served on a guilty plea for a 1974 car theft because, Rodbart told the judge, Nate had already "overpaid his debt to society."

I sat in the front row of the public gallery, next to his mother, Irene, and right behind Nate and Paul, and I thought to myself, well, that's the understatement of the year.

The judge took a moment to say that he considered the evidence for dismissal "unequivocal" and said this moment demonstrates "the strength and perhaps the virtue of the criminal justice system," in recognizing that justice must be accomplished and making sure that's done when the system is "confronted with its own fallibility."

I'm not sure how much I agreed with that sentiment. It felt more like every facet of the justice system had conspired, knowingly and wittingly and with evil intent, to convict an innocent man. From the police who squeezed him, to the jury who ignored the fact that the defendant didn't remotely match the description of the perpetrator, to the prosecutor who didn't bother to test the obvious evidence. And only when forced, by sheer dint of will, to look at what it was refusing to see, was justice done.

But at least, in this moment, justice *was* done. Nate had been fully and completely exonerated. I looked to my left; Irene was still as composed and dignified as the day I met her. She sat straight up, her back away from the bench behind her, and I could tell she was tense until the moment the judge vacated Nate's sentence, and then I could see her physically relax, as though a pain she had held in her heart for twelve years had finally released its grip.

When the proceedings were over, Nate came out, and he and his mother held each other for the longest time. Finally, they turned to me. Nate could barely speak; he was just beaming, holding his mother's hand, and shaking his head side to side. His mother said what I think he was thinking, too.

"I can't believe it," Irene said to me. "I can't believe it," she said again. "Every morning since he was sent away. Every morning. I would wake up asking myself, 'Is it real? Is it real?' And then I realize, yes, it really happened to me. And no one cared. No one cared."

She stared at me a long time.

"But you cared."

I didn't know what to say. "I'm just glad it's over, Irene. It's over."

"Today it's finally over," she proclaimed, as though she had to hear herself say the words. "Thank God. Thank God."

I thought, thank God, indeed.

□

I hadn't realized that a reporter from *The New York Times* was at the courtroom. The article appeared the next day, and from there things began to snowball. In those days, getting an innocent person out of prison the way we did was still a rarity. Even so, the press was treating this like it was the most unusual story to come out of New Jersey since the Lindbergh kidnapping.

I only wish Nate's story was unusual. I was already starting to learn how very, very common this would be. Nowadays, DNA evidence frees innocent people every day, but back then Nate's story was one that still had the power to grip the public's imagination. And so things exploded. Quickly.

By the next day, I was getting calls from reporters and producers all over the country. *The Today Show* wanted us on, and the next thing I knew, there was a stretch limo in front of Mrs. Yeatman's house. She stared wide-eyed as I got in and drove off; we picked up Nate and headed to Manhattan.

"I've never been in a limo before, Nate," I said.

"Me neither, Jim. This is amazing. To think that last week I was sitting in a jail cell. And now I'm in a limousine, headed to NBC to appear on national television. Isn't that the craziest thing?"

At the moment, I thought, yes, that's the craziest thing. I had no idea how much crazier it was about to get.

Eight

▥

Ever since high school, I've been fascinated by Japan. I think it began when I saw a documentary on the bright lights and kimono-clad women of the Ginza; Tokyo always held a magical allure for me. When I finished up at Bucknell, I enrolled in the U.S. Navy's Officer Candidate School in Newport, Rhode Island, and, after I graduated, hit the jackpot and was assigned to the Yokosuka naval base near Tokyo.

Elsewhere, my fellow officers were engaged in frightful combat in Vietnam, but here in Japan it was peacetime duty by day and long stretches of free time in the evenings. I was living the good life and loving it: For the first time, I felt like an adult in an adult world. I basked in the pleasure of changing into my civvies at the end of the day to stroll the streets of the Alley, Yokosuka's bustling bar district, taking in the sights and sounds and, to be frank, seeking out those women behind the colorful kimonos and mysterious smiles. And then, one night, it happened.

I was sitting with a fellow officer in a popular restaurant in the early hours of the morning when I spotted her. She was seated at a table nearby, and from the moment I saw her, I was smitten. She seemed petite and composed, her black hair done up in a neat bun in the back. But I was tantalized by her dark brown eyes, lively and mischievous, and when she spotted me staring at her, she boldly stared right back and smiled, and I was done for.

A little while later, when I was checking out, we happened to

My idealism as a newly commissioned naval officer in November 1964 faded fast, when I encountered the realities of the Vietnam War. *Courtesy of the author*

find ourselves next to each other at the register—okay, so maybe that wasn't just a coincidence on my part—and we started chatting. She was open and funny and had just a hint of the devil in her eye.

She told me her name was Yoshiko, and my heart jumped into my throat when I found out she worked at the post exchange—the retail store—at my navy base as a clerk in the electronics division.

"Maybe I'll see you there sometime?" she said, and I tried to discern if she was flirting or just being nice. I assumed the latter, but was hoping for the former. There was something about the way she presented herself—polite and mannered, but confident and assured—that made me feel like whatever was about to happen was as much in her control as in mine.

And so the next day I found myself in the electronics division of the PX, where I spotted her. She was just as lively and full of spirit as she'd been the night before.

"So," I finally said, working up my courage, "do you think you might like to go out to dinner this week?"

"I was hoping you'd ask," she said, and I assumed she meant: I knew you would.

For me, it was love at first sight, and I will be a little conceited and tell you that, as I found out soon enough, it was for her as well.

Very soon we were inseparable. I came to know her as a strong woman, very sweet but as stubborn as I was. And incredibly generous: One day she took my measurements, but wouldn't tell me why; a few weeks later she presented me with a beautiful suit, which her father, a tailor in Osaka, had made for me.

She wanted me to learn some Japanese: "*Dozo yoroshiku*" and "*Hajimemashite,*" I learned to say when meeting someone, and she could never hide her giggles at how bad my accent was. I never did get it right, but I think she loved that I was trying.

I saw her every chance I could. I remember one Saturday in early January when she took me on a day trip to Tokyo. We boarded the noon train and spent the hour's ride holding hands and putting our arms around each other. I could have just about died then and been a happy man.

It was a beautiful, sunny day; January is a little warmer in Japan than it is back home. As we strolled the Ginza, with its hundreds of bars and brilliant neon lights and big advertisements, to me it was like Times Square. And at the same time it was nothing like Times Square at all, like nothing I'd ever seen in my life.

I looked over at her, dressed for the holiday in a beautiful colorful kimono with a big obi sash and geta shoes, and I could see how enormously proud she was to show me the city that had so captured my fascination. I'd dreamed of the Ginza for so many years, and here I was, with a beautiful girl on my arm, the sun shining on my back, not a care in the world.

I took her out to a nice dinner at a fancy Chinese restaurant, and after a few hot sakes we were good and tipsy. I was a little sad afterward to get on the train back home, but then, when we got to her house, she told me she wanted to give me a traditional Japanese bath.

She helped me undress and led me to the *ofuro*, a wooden Japanese soaking tub. I felt a little odd at first, but she put my mind at ease.

"Please, Jim-san," she said. "This is our tradition. You like to show me your traditions and your ways. I want to show you ours."

"I've just never had anyone give me a bath since I was about two," I said.

She smiled. "You are in Japan now," she said. "It's important that you learn Japanese customs. This is how we do things. First you'll soak in the tub. Then I'll bathe you on that stool."

So I got into the bath and soaked for a while, and then, as she instructed me, I sat on the stool—and howled as she poured scalding water on my back. But she persisted, and the louder I screamed, the louder she laughed.

"Oh, come on," she said. "It's not that bad. Japanese can do it, you can do it."

It couldn't have been more than a few weeks later that I moved in with her. It was a dream: Some nights we would go out to dinner, but my favorites were the nights we'd stay in. We had dinner in the traditional style, sitting on the floor with our legs dangling into a pit that contained hot coals to keep our feet warm. She would make me hot tea, and we would sit and talk about our love and how lucky we were to have found each other so soon after I'd arrived in Japan.

Winter turned to spring, and when she told me she was scheduled to go to the United States on a short vacation, I was elated. I wrote to my parents, telling them I'd given her their names and phone number and had asked her to call them; I couldn't wait for them to meet her. "She said she would be in New York and if she wasn't scared or nervous she would call you," I wrote. "I told her she had nothing to fear because you would make her feel right at home. I sure hope she does contact you. I am so anxious for you to meet her and tell me what you think of her."

The night before she left for the States, I got a strange call from her. It was about ten o'clock, and she was clearly distraught. She was in Yokohama, where her ship was scheduled to depart from, and she pleaded with me to come see her right away. I was about to report for duty and couldn't find a replacement, so I told her I couldn't come. I assumed that she was just upset to be leaving me and wanted to see me one more time before she departed, so I assured her it would be fine and that our month apart would go quickly.

But as the weeks went by, and my parents hadn't heard from her—and neither had I—I became concerned. Had something terrible happened to her? I was getting more and more worried by the day. I went to a neighbor's house and asked if she'd heard from her. She directed me to the home of a girlfriend of Yoshiko's who might have had some news from her.

The friend invited me into her home, and when I told her about my apprehensions, because I knew Yoshiko had gone to the States on a brief tour but hadn't returned, she looked puzzled.

"A tour?" she said, speaking English fairly well—not as well as Yoshiko, but much better than many young women I'd met. "She did not go on a tour. Did you not know? She told me that she told you."

My heart was banging against my rib cage like it wanted to get out. I managed to form a question that I was not at all sure I wanted to hear the answer to.

"Told me?" I repeated. "Told me what?"

The young woman hesitated for a moment before replying. "She did not go on a tour," she said, finally. "She went there to be with her husband."

I thought I heard wrong at first. Or wanted to think so, anyway. I could not believe what this young woman was telling me. I asked her to repeat it, and she did. Then she filled in the details, although I was barely hearing what she said: Yoshiko's husband was a naval officer, like me. They'd met three years ago and married last August. He'd shipped out to the States, and now she had gone to join him. They were living, she told me, in Utah, where he was from.

I sat dumbfounded, the life drained out of me. I had a thousand questions swirling around in my mind. How could she have kept this from me all this time? And why? Did she really love me, as she said she did so many times? And if so, how could she just leave me forever, without a word of goodbye? And if not—

I stopped myself short, realizing the young woman was beginning to feel uncomfortable, sitting in the heavy silence that had fallen over us.

I stood up slowly and heaved a painful sigh.

"Please write to her for me," I said. "Tell her I know that she is married. Tell her I hope she has a happy life."

"I will," the young woman said, a sad smile on her face. I could tell how sorry she was, how surprised she was to learn that Yoshiko had kept me in the dark. I could tell how much she wanted to ease this moment for me, just as I knew that nothing possibly could.

So I thanked her and left, and wandered the city aimlessly, ending up on a hill overlooking Tokyo Bay, staring out to sea, wishing the ocean could just swallow me whole and put an end to my misery.

□

I served out the rest of my time in Japan in something of a daze. I went through the motions of life—working on the base by day, hitting the bars by night—but something fundamental had changed for me. There was a hole in my life, a big gaping hole, and I tried to find a way to fill it.

I took up with another Japanese woman, and we lived together, but it was a hollow life. Her name was Sachiko; she loved me, and we went through the trappings of a normal existence. My parents even came for a visit, and at the end my mom said she hoped I would bring Sachiko home with me, but I was incapable of that kind of commitment, that kind of belief in a sunny future. Sachiko became pregnant during the end of my tour and wanted to have the child and raise it with me, as a family, but my heart had turned to steel by this point. I insisted she have an abortion; she did, and shortly afterward I left the country. I have no idea whatever happened to her.

I tell you this with enormous shame. I know I was heartless and I know I broke her heart. Sachiko deserved so much more than I gave her, to say nothing of the child we conceived. The memory of what I did, and what I failed to do, continues to haunt me. I bring it up because, when I consider the chapters of my life that followed Japan, I can see how what binds them together was my need to fill the void that was left by Yoshiko's disappearance. Eventually, I do believe, my work and my faith became the things that made me whole again, that sustain me, emotionally and spiritually.

But it would not be the last detour I took on my path to earthly salvation.

Nine

▥

TEXAS, 1987

It was absolutely surreal, sitting on the set of *The Today Show* next to Nate Walker, waiting to be interviewed by Bryant Gumbel. We were hustled out there as soon as we got to the studio; a producer told us we were going to be in the 7:10 a.m. slot. I turned to Nate and said, "Holy cow! This is the number one slot! You are big news!" Nate got a grin on his face that was probably one-third joy and two-thirds holy terror.

We could see Gumbel nearby, reading, preparing for the interview. I don't know how people keep their composure in these moments, with the bright lights glaring down, and young people with headsets and clipboards rushing every which way, and some godlike voice of the producer coming over an unseen loudspeaker. But Gumbel was the picture of tranquility as he walked over and shook our hands and sat down. Nate and I were seated next to each other, with Gumbel facing us, and his easy demeanor helped me to relax.

Then he leaned in and said, "Now, Reverend McCloskey, let's stick to Nate's story in this interview. None of that religious stuff this morning, okay?"

I was aghast. I felt like letting him have it right then and there. But this was Nate's moment and I wasn't going to do anything to dampen that. I just said, "That was not my intention, Mr. Gumbel." And even though there was an edge in my voice, he got that radiant

TV smile on his face and said, "Good, good," and the godlike voice said, "Back in thirty," and then we were on.

And after that, nothing was ever the same.

Between the article in *The New York Times* and the interview with Bryant Gumbel, the whole world seemed to know, and to care, about Nate Walker and, to a small extent, about Jim McCloskey too. *Jet* and *Ebony* and *People* all came calling, and *60 Minutes* as well. It was amazing.

When I got back to Mrs. Yeatman's, I collapsed, exhausted and elated, the emotion of the last few days finally washing over me, the adrenaline draining from my body and leaving me spent. I must have slept sixteen hours that night.

When I woke up and went downstairs, Mrs. Yeatman had a look of incredulity on her face. "There's . . . some mail for you," she said tentatively.

I looked at the pile of letters on the table; there must have been twenty or thirty of them, from all over the country. I started opening them, and they were all the same: pleas from inmates and people whose loved ones were in prison, insisting on their innocence and begging me to help.

"That's a lot of requests," I said to Mrs. Yeatman. "I don't know how I'm going to sort through these."

I didn't know the tenth of it. In the coming days, dozens of letters kept pouring in. People convicted of murder and rape and all sorts of heinous crimes, all pleading their innocence and begging for my help. And then the phone started ringing, and didn't stop. All day long. It quickly became overwhelming. And then came what I can only believe—sorry, Mr. Gumbel—was a moment of divine providence.

It was the Monday after Thanksgiving. I had been to the seminary in the early morning and sat in the chapel asking God for guidance, praying that God would send someone to help me find my way through this rapidly growing forest of desperate letters and phone calls. It was peaceful to be there, but when I got back to Mrs. Yeatman's, the phone was already ringing, and by early afternoon I was feeling overwhelmed again.

I was reading a letter from another prisoner when the phone rang for the umpteenth time. Someone else saying something about needing help. "Give me a second," I said. "Let me grab a pad and paper. Okay, give me the information about the prisoner you're calling about." I tried not to sound too weary, but I'm afraid my exhaustion was giving me away. So much so that it took me a minute to understand what the woman on the other end was saying.

"No," she said, "I was saying that I saw your picture in *The New York Times,* and *you* look like you need some help. I'm calling because I want to help *you.*"

I pulled the receiver away from my ear and stared at it for a second. I couldn't believe what I was hearing. This just could be, quite literally, the answer to my prayers.

"I'm sorry," I said. "Tell me again what you said your name was?"

□

A few weeks later we met in the lobby of the InterContinental hotel in New York, a place I'd stayed often, back in my businessman days, and from the start I could tell this was a no-nonsense woman.

Her name was Kate Germond, a woman in her late thirties with close-cropped dark hair and a sly smile. I quickly got her back story: She'd been living something of a hippie existence with her husband in Mendocino, California, spending some time on what she called an "Old MacDonald" farm, but also running a bookkeeping operation helping various businesses get organized and stay solvent. Her husband had just been offered a job in New York City, so she followed him there and was looking for something productive to do when she saw that pathetic picture of me in the *Times,* sitting on my bed engulfed by mail, and decided, quite correctly, that I needed someone to organize my life. She had by this time already been offered a bookkeeping job by a small company in Manhattan, but she was stalling them, trying to get ahold of me.

"I'll be honest," she said. "I tried to call you for days, but I kept getting a busy signal. So over Thanksgiving I told my husband, when we get back to New York, I'm gonna try one more time, and if I don't get through, screw him. I gotta move on. I guess I just got lucky."

As we kept talking and I kept peppering her with questions—as is my nature—I quickly came to realize that I was the one who had gotten lucky here. Here was this funny, witty, smart woman who seemed to have a big heart and a passion for the work I was doing. Enough of the hippie to want to do right in the world, and enough of the bookkeeper to figure out how to get it done.

At one point I asked her, "Did you always want to do this kind of work? I mean, did you ever see yourself getting involved in the criminal justice system?"

"You know, it's funny," she said. "When I was young, I did want to be a criminal defense lawyer. But I had this high school guidance counselor who told me, 'Girls don't become lawyers.' And for all the rebelling I'd done in my life, I said, 'Oh, okay.' I don't know why I gave up so easily. Believe me, Jim, that's not my nature."

"I'm sorry that happened," I said.

"I'm not," she replied. "Because I don't think that's what I really wanted. You know what really interests me? I used to watch *Perry Mason* all the time. But what struck me—was it Paul Drake, his detective, or investigator, who is the one who always solved the cases? He brought whatever the key was to solving the crime to Perry Mason. That's what intrigues me now."

I couldn't believe my ears. It was like talking to myself. Finding someone with that kind of passion for getting to the truth—and someone who, from the sound of it, was going to help me find my way through that forest—was, well, not to put too fine a point on it (and not that I mentioned it to her at the time), nothing short of miraculous to me.

I felt, quite literally, like she was heaven-sent.

Pretty soon, she was taking the train down to Princeton a couple of days a week, although the first time she walked into my room at Mrs. Yeatman's, I was afraid it was going to be the last. Mrs. Yeatman had taken to living just on the first floor, so her housekeepers only occasionally came upstairs, and her old cat took to using the hallway as a litter box. Sometimes it was like walking through a minefield, and I was too busy and focused to clean it up myself. But if Kate was grossed out by it, or put off by the threadbare carpet, the fading wallpaper, the leaves blowing in through the fireplace, or the ragtag furniture in my room, she didn't show it. She just smiled and said, "Well, let's get to it," and sat down on my single bed and started going through the letters.

Within a few weeks she'd created a system of organization for the cases and case files and all the information pouring in. She figured out that she could get file folders and other supplies cheaper in New York than I could in Princeton, so she started schlepping all that stuff down on the train with her, and by early 1987 I started feeling like we had things under control. And thank heaven for that.

While she was focused on bringing order to the chaos, I was focused on only one thing. It was a case I heard about right after I was on *The Today Show,* and I couldn't get it out of my mind.

I'd gotten a call from a man named Ozell Brandley. His minister had seen me on the show and told him to call. Ozell's brother Clarence had been convicted of a murder in Texas that he swore he didn't commit. That wasn't what got my attention, though; I was already inundated by calls like that by the time I heard from Ozell. What he said next stopped me in my tracks.

"Mr. McCloskey," he said, "my brother is on death row. They already have an execution date. If you don't help us, my brother is gonna die."

Holy cow. Death row. In Texas of all places, the state most well known for its use of the death penalty. And to make matters worse, the execution date, March 26, 1987, was just a few months away.

I talked it over with Kate. We agreed it was impossible. There was no way we could get all the information and get down there and find something to exonerate him and get that information in front of a judge in time. It just couldn't be done.

We also agreed on another thing: We were going to do it.

□

On the plane down to Texas in February 1987, I went over the facts of the case for the thousandth time. The crime took place in late August 1980 at the high school in Conroe, about forty-five minutes north of Houston, a week before school was scheduled to start. There were janitors and students milling around, and the football team was having a scrimmage. In the gym, a girls' volleyball team from Bellville, a town about an hour away, was practicing. Around 9:00 a.m., Cheryl Fergeson, the manager of the volleyball team—pretty, blond, blue-eyed, all of sixteen years old—went looking for a bathroom. Two hours later, her body, nude except for her socks, was found by the janitors' supervisor, Clarence Brandley, and another janitor, in the auditorium loft under some plywood. She had been raped and strangled to death.

Panic, shock, and terror shot through the school, and soon through the town. It was just ten days before the start of the school year, and the panic soon morphed into something approaching mass hysteria. Many parents threatened to keep their daughters out of school until the killers were arrested. The pressure on the police to solve the crime, and fast, was intense.

Desperate to find a suspect, the police almost immediately focused on Clarence and one of the other janitors, Ickie Peace, because they were the ones who discovered the body.

And so a few days later, Clarence Brandley was arrested and charged with the murder. It's important to note that Clarence was the only black janitor—one was Hispanic and all the others were white—because as I leafed through the papers I had with me, I came back to what Ickie had said later: On the day of the crime, a white Conroe police officer was speaking to him and Clarence, and he told them, "One of you two is going to hang for this." Then, turning toward Brandley, he said, "Since you're the nigger, you're elected."

Soon afterward, a story emerged: The four other janitors had been in the area of the bathroom when Cheryl came by. Their stories all lined up: A few minutes after they'd directed the girl to the bathroom, Clarence showed up. They told Clarence not to go into the restroom because a girl was in there. Clarence, they said, sent them away to do work elsewhere but didn't go with them. About thirty minutes later, he showed up at the area where he'd sent the janitors. The inference was clear: He was the only one left near the restroom when the girl was murdered.

That the crime had clear racial overtones was nothing new for Conroe, a town with a long history of bigotry, prejudice, and hate. In 1923, a black man accused of raping a white woman was burned at the stake on the Conroe courthouse lawn. Fourteen years later, in 1937, a black man charged with raping a white woman was shot in the back of the head—in a Conroe courtroom—by the rape victim's husband, who was acquitted of that murder two weeks later.

There are those who said that that was all ancient history, that times had changed, and that Conroe was much more enlightened now. As I stepped off the plane into a cool gray Texas day, I wondered if that was true.

Ozell and his minister, the one who'd seen me on *The Today Show*, picked me up at the Houston airport. I spent some time with Ozell and his family, and they kept thanking me for showing interest in the case, but I said, "Ozell, I can't do anything for your brother until I meet his defense team. His lawyers might not want me coming in on this."

Ozell nodded slowly. "Well, then," he said, "let's go."

A few minutes later we were headed to the offices of one of the most famous lawyers in Texas, Percy Foreman, a flamboyant, larger-than-life character known for his fierce battles on behalf of high-profile defendants—among them James Earl Ray, the man who assassinated Martin Luther King. Foreman wasn't handling Clarence's case directly; a new member of the firm, a lawyer named Paul Nugent, was handling it. He'd come on about four months earlier, and this was his first case. In fact, on Paul's first day on the job, the senior lawyer in the firm, another famed attorney named Mike DeGeurin, had handed him the Brandley file and said, "Dig in. We've just got a few months before he's executed, and we have nothing. We have to come up with something."

I wasn't sure what Clarence's lawyers would make of me, this New Jersey minister in a white suit dropping out of the sky to offer to help them, and as we walked into their office, I was a little worried about how that first meeting was going to go. I didn't find out until later that Nugent took one look at me and decided that if Percy Foreman had seen me—a big bald Irishman talking intensely about how he'd uncovered conspiracies and prosecutorial misconduct in previous cases, and how he thought something fishy was going on in Clarence's case as well and wanted to work on it for free—he'd have decided I was some kind of kook and would have tossed me out on my can. So Nugent hustled me into a side office and we started talking.

As chance would have it, Nugent was another Jersey boy, which gave us a nice sense of connection. Still, he seemed pretty skeptical of me, so I knew I had to be persuasive, and quickly.

I laid out for him where I thought I saw a little daylight in the case: It had to do with the four other janitors. Especially one of them, a guy named John Henry Sessum. I thought that the perfectly aligned stories of the four janitors (a little too perfect, I would soon come to realize) were starting to diverge a bit, and maybe Sessum was the key. I had read all the transcripts of Clarence's trials: There were two, the first ending in a hung jury, as well as a 1986 post-trial hearing. At that last hearing, there were indications that maybe Sessum was starting to edge away from his original trial testimony. That was intriguing to me.

I told Paul about how I had already gotten several witnesses to recant false testimony, how I approached them, how I didn't judge them, how I allowed them to feel comfortable with me and then helped them release the guilt of hiding a lie year after year after year. And how my clerical collar didn't hurt. I could see a lightbulb going off over Paul's head as I talked about getting Sessum to recant, and after a while he pulled DeGeurin in on the conversation.

As much as I had come in with all my preconceived notions of what a famous Texas lawyer would be like—all bluster and braggadocio, loud and boorish and conceited—that's how much Mike DeGeurin proved me wrong. Like Paul, he was polite and easygoing, self-deprecating and modest. The three of us talked for another couple of hours, and by the end of it (and without telling Percy Foreman) they decided to bring me on board. They were all Don Quixotes, trying to do the impossible for all the right reasons, they told me, and they saw me as a kindred spirit.

"And just so we're clear," Mike said to me, "you really work for free?"

"Well, I need two things," I told them. "I need a car and I need a place to stay."

They looked at each other, and back at me, and that famous Texas hospitality broke through their skepticism.

"We have an apartment over the garage," Paul said. "You can stay there. And I just bought Mike's mother's old '78 Chevy Chevelle—Mike didn't want her driving anymore—so you can drive that."

"So how soon can you start?" Mike asked me.

I stood up and stretched my legs, weary from sitting for hours, reached out my hand to shake his, and said, "I think I just did."

□

The thing that really infuriated me from the get-go was that evidence had already emerged pointing the finger at two other men. One was a janitor named James Robinson, a young nerdy-looking guy (and not a very bright one at that), with a leftover Beatles haircut that was still popular at the time. He'd worked at the high school until about a month before the murder. At one point Richard Reyna, an investigator for Brandley's defense team, had persuaded Robinson to take a polygraph test; when asked if he killed the girl, he paused for four and a half minutes—four and a half minutes!—before answering, "Well, I could have done it and forgot," and then quickly added, "No, I couldn't have done it. I'm not that kind of person. I'm innocent."

But five years after Clarence's trial, a woman named Brenda Medina came forward to say that she'd been living with Robinson, back at the time of the crime, and he had confessed to her that he'd killed Cheryl. And she'd told the district attorney, Peter Speers, about it. And Speers proceeded, on the basis of this startling new evidence, to do absolutely nothing.

I was flabbergasted when I learned about this. I knew enough about law by now to know that after a conviction, if the prosecutors learn of new evidence that could benefit the defendant, they're required by law—to say nothing of simple human morality—to pass the information on to the defense. And here, a man is going to be executed and all the DA cares about is protecting his conviction, the truth be damned? It's beyond words to imagine how anyone could do that and live with himself. It's the ultimate in corruption, in my view of the world. I had already seen it before, and now I was seeing it again. Could this be how DAs everywhere behave? I shuddered to imagine that that was the case.

So that's what was going on with James Robinson. Meanwhile, suspicion had also fallen on another of those white janitors, Gary Acreman. I could see why: A lot of his testimony at Clarence's trial seemed strange to me. I was champing at the bit to go confront both of them, but I knew, from my experience in other cases, and from the gut I was learning to listen to, that they weren't the key. After all, if they were the real killers, chances were pretty slim they were just going to come out and admit it.

The key was another one of the white janitors, John Henry Sessum, the one whose story had been changing over the years. I thought maybe there were cracks in his testimony that led to something bigger.

But before I could talk to any of them, I had to talk to Clarence.

It was a chilling, somber feeling, visiting death row. You get a sense of your own mortality when you are among men facing theirs. I couldn't imagine how they dealt with it, each of them, and couldn't imagine the toll it was taking on Clarence Brandley, knowing he was facing imminent death for a crime he didn't commit.

We sat on either side of a wire-mesh cage, and from the beginning there was something about him that put me at ease, just as his lawyers had. He had the nice Texas drawl and the polite southern manners—"yes, sir," "no, sir"—of a man who'd retained his dignity despite the indignity he was facing. Beads of perspiration dotted his forehead, and he had the solid build of a guy who'd maybe played sports in high school. Whatever stress and anxiety he might be feeling, you wouldn't know it. He was self-contained and poised as we spoke, but he was reserved as well, and it took me a while to draw him out. When I finally did, he spoke clearly and forcefully, with the conviction of a man telling the truth.

"Look, all I can tell you is I don't know who did this," he said to me. "I don't know if Acreman did it. I don't know if Robinson did it. I didn't see Robinson there that day myself, but I was told he was there. I know I didn't do this. I had nothing to do with it, and I just want to make that very clear to you."

That's what impressed me the most: There was already suspicion of those other two janitors, and Clarence could have tried to point the finger at them as well. But he didn't. Here was a man wrongly accused, a man about to die, who refused to accuse someone else just to save his own skin.

I looked at him through that wire mesh and tried to imagine how he was holding up so well, with death staring him in the face.

"It's because I'm not alone in this, Mr. McCloskey," he said. "I don't know what I'd do without my family. They've stuck by me. They believe in me. They believe me that I'm innocent. That I had nothing to do with this."

There was a question hanging in that warm, still air, and Clarence was too polite to ask it, but I answered it anyway.

"I believe it too, Clarence," I said. "I believe that you're innocent. That's why I'm here."

□

It wasn't until the end of February that I was able to get back to Texas to start preparing, and not until March 5 that I could begin the field investigation. Paul and Mike were getting a little concerned as the days ticked by. If I was going to find new evidence to clear Clarence Brandley, I had exactly twenty-one days to do it, or he was a dead man.

It wasn't long before I came face to face with John Henry Sessum. John, by now, was working for the county parks and recreation department, cleaning trash off the streets and highways. Every day he'd ride his bicycle ten miles along the flat roads from his shack to the county yard, and each day he'd buy a twelve-pack of beer and put it in his bicycle basket for the ride home. More often than not it was half gone by the time he got there.

He had just ridden into his yard around dusk that evening when I pulled up. Richard Reyna, the defense team investigator, had come with me. John had a little brown dog, a mangy mutt if ever there was one, that growled at us until John called it off. We explained why we were there, and the three of us stood around talking. The more John drank, the more comfortable he became.

He was a tall, blond man with a thin mustache, with the same Texas drawl and polite manners that Clarence had. Sessum had the habit of closing his eyes as he spoke and then popping them open as he finished, which became a kind of emphasis at the end of a sentence, and the things he was saying were blowing my mind.

He told us that yes, indeed, he'd seen Gary Acreman, one of the other white janitors, talking to the girl on the steps leading to the restroom. He'd heard the girl say "No." He saw another man on the steps as well, and when we showed him a picture of James Robinson, he said that yes, that was the guy on the landing with Acreman and the girl.

He told us something else startling: A few days after the murder, a Texas Ranger named Wesley Styles had the three other janitors—Sessum, Acreman, and Sam Martinez—come to the high school for a "walk-through" so they could "get their stories straight." Styles had actually worked out a way for them all to have an alibi—even Acreman—and to point the finger at Clarence. At one point, John told me, he started correcting the series of events that Styles was spinning, and Styles barked at him, "Shut up. I know what I'm doing."

After telling us that, John went silent. When he spoke again, he had a strange look on his face, as though he was struggling to say something and not say it at the same time.

"I don't know, sir," he said, closing his eyes. "I don't know. This gives me nightmares, I can tell you that. I can tell you that." His eyes popped open. "Every time I have a bad night, Gary is in it." He closed his eyes again. "I know you're here to help Clarence," he said. "He's a nigger and I have no love for niggers, but I'll try and help him out."

He opened his eyes and looked at us, and for the moment there was nothing more to say.

☐

Over the next week, John took us on a roller-coaster ride. He surprised us by suggesting we take him back to the scene of the crime, thinking that maybe it would jog his memory. I was really excited that Sunday and couldn't wait for Monday to roll around. But when we got to the steps to the restroom, he froze in fear. "I can't do it. I can't do it," he said, and, frustrated, we drove him home.

On Tuesday, we went by his shack again, with the pressure of time weighing heavily on us; it was now March 10, execution day minus 16. This time, he actually seemed pleased to see us. It was clear that he'd been through a six-pack or so, and maybe that gave him the courage to do what he did next; I'll never know. But I do know that—to my shock and amazement—he told us the complete story of what had actually happened on the day of the murder.

"Here's how it happened," he said, closing his eyes. He told us that he and Sam Martinez, another school janitor, were down by a watercooler near the steps that led to the girls' restroom. They had seen Robinson and Acreman go upstairs, and they heard them dragging the girl toward the bathroom. "We heard her yelling for help," he said. He told us Sam had stopped him from going up the stairs. His eyes opened. "I heard her yell for help," he said, a wave of sadness washing over him. His voice got quieter. "I was the one who caused her death. I could have saved her if I went up there."

He paused and picked up another beer. "That's what's been eating at me all these years. I could have saved her if I went up there."

I proceeded cautiously. "Was Clarence there?" I asked.

"Clarence didn't come by but maybe ten minutes later," he responded.

My heart raced. I knew what I said next was vitally important.

"It wasn't your fault," I said. "You didn't kill that girl. Nobody here is judging you, John. But you do know there is something you can do to redeem yourself. Completely. If you would—"

He cut me off in mid-sentence, sounding angry at me, though I know his anger was directed inward. "I let one innocent girl go to her death. I'm not going to let an innocent man go to his. What do you want me to do?"

The hairs on my neck stood up.

"Will you come to Clarence's lawyers' office in Houston and tell him what you told us? We'll need a sworn statement. Will you do that?"

"Yes, sir. You have my word."

He took my hand and shook it firmly, and I was convinced that we had not only just saved Clarence's life but ended John's nightmares as well.

"This is your time to redeem yourself in the eyes of God," I said to John. "He is looking down on us, and Cheryl Fergeson is looking down on us, and she's praying that God gives you the strength to tell the truth. You can get right with God," I told him.

A beautiful smile came over his face, and he pointed to heaven. "God is with us on this," he said.

I smiled back. "Yes," I told him. "God is with us on this."

But a few days later, I wondered if God had abandoned me. And Clarence, too.

We had wanted to go to the attorneys' office right away, but John had insisted on waiting until that Sunday—five days later, which is an eternity when a man's life is on the line. And then, when the day finally rolled around, John was nowhere to be found. Richard and I drove around for a while and spotted John along a desolate roadside. I said, as casually as I could, "Yo, John, what's up? Time to go to Houston."

"Get the hell out of here. I ain't goin'," he snapped.

We tried to persuade him to change his mind, but the more we talked, the angrier he became. We rode off in silence. Neither of us said it, but we both thought the same thing: Without John, Clarence is a dead man.

It was clear to me that John was wrestling with himself and the demons that had haunted him every day since Cheryl's murder. He seemed to me to be a good and honest man, trying to muster the courage to do the right thing, but his fears of physical retribution by the killers, and being jailed for perjury by the law enforcement officials who had forced him to tell their lies, were very powerful forces for him to contend with, let alone overcome.

Richard and I went back to his shack the next day, March 16, this time with Clarence's attorney Mike DeGeurin in tow. John was in a foul mood, but he invited us in. It was the first time we'd been inside. The place reeked of urine, and John's dog came running up and bit Richard on the ankle. John didn't seem to care; he went into the kitchen to get a beer.

And emerged wielding a butcher knife.

"I don't ever want to see you fucking guys again. Now get the fuck out of here!" he shouted. It seemed like a prudent idea, so we got the fuck out of there.

I was devastated as we drove away in silence. The question arose in me, not for the first time and not for the last: Where is God in all of this? Clarence is going to die. How can God allow this to happen? I searched my mind for a line of scripture that would give me some kind of reassurance. For the moment, it eluded me.

☐

At one point Reyna and I tried to get ahold of James Robinson. We flew to Greenville, South Carolina, and in the wee hours of the morning we went to the textile factory where he worked. We found him up on a scaffolding, pouring dye into a vat. I had the collar on, and he already knew Reyna, so it was pretty clear from the get-go why we were there.

"Look," he said, "I can't talk to you here. When I get off my shift, why don't you come over to my house and we'll talk."

It was a miserable rainy night, and we sat in the car in the parking lot for a few minutes, discussing whether we thought Robinson was actually going to talk to us, when, suddenly, we got our answer. Because here comes Robinson, running out the front of the factory like a frightened jackrabbit, jumping into his car, and taking off.

We followed him for a while, careening down rain-slicked two-lane roads at breakneck speed, following his red taillights as best we could. Reyna was at the wheel and doing a pretty good job of it, but then I told him, "Look, I think he's made it pretty clear he doesn't want to talk to us. This might not be the best idea we've had."

In the darkness I could see Reyna purse his lips and shake his head; he gunned the engine for a few more seconds, took one more tight turn, and then eased up on the gas. We pulled over and sat by the side of the road, listening to the windshield wipers and knowing that long wet road in front of us was just one more dead end.

☐

Paul and I visited Clarence several times through all of this, and through it all he remained as composed as the first time I met him. At one point, he mentioned that he had quit smoking on death row.

"Really?" Paul asked him. "I'd think there are so few pleasures on death row, I'd smoke a pack a day, if I could afford it."

Clarence gazed at him serenely. "I have no control over my life in here," he said. "The warden and the guards control every aspect of my life. I needed to take control of something. This is one thing I can control."

I was impressed, both that Clarence could be so philosophical while confronted by the dehumanizing quality of death row and at how resilient he was. And how gracious.

"I know you're doing your best, Mr. McCloskey," Clarence said to me, more than once, and I couldn't believe that a man facing imminent death was trying to reassure me, instead of the other way around.

I walked away from our last visit that week thinking of a line from that Dylan song about Rubin Carter—

Rubin sits like Buddha in a ten-foot cell
An innocent man in a living hell

—and I thought, that's Clarence. Serene as Buddha, with death just days away.

The day after John Henry Sessum chased us away with a butcher knife was St. Patrick's Day. Through all our visits, we'd gotten to know his neighbor Mattie Johnson, a very sweet and upright woman in her forties whose trailer was as neat and tidy as John's was disgusting. Within an hour after John's chasing us with the knife, we called her up to tell her what happened. She'd been sympathetic to us all along, but I couldn't have anticipated what she said next.

"You come by my place around four tomorrow," she said. "I'll have John ready to talk to you."

We all showed up—me, Nugent, DeGeurin, Reyna, and a reporter from the *Dallas Times Herald*—and brought a video camera just in case John was really there and ready to talk. I was not overly optimistic going in, so I was relieved when we walked into her trailer and saw John sitting there, meekly, on the couch, greeting us like we were old friends, not people he'd most recently waved a large knife at. Without a moment's hesitation he agreed to talk and be taped.

We turned on the camera, and Mike DeGeurin, the lawyer, asked him to tell us what happened that day. He proceeded to tell us everything.

He said that he, Acreman, and Martinez were sitting at the bottom of the steps leading up to the restroom, waiting for their boss, Clarence Brandley, to come back and give them their next work detail. That's when Cheryl Fergeson showed up, asking for directions to the restroom. After she started up the stairs, they saw Acreman go up after her, and they heard something going on between them. But, instead of intervening, John and Martinez walked downstairs to the water fountain. That's when James Robinson came sprinting out of nowhere, up the stairs to where Acreman and the girl were. John heard her begging for help. He heard her being dragged into the bathroom. He heard her screams. And then he heard silence.

The interview went on for about thirty minutes; we contained our enthusiasm—Mike was the perfect even-tempered lawyer, quietly questioning a witness—but when it was all done and we packed up and drove away, we were elated.

What I was thinking was, God does care. God is real. This is unbelievable. I believe God has intervened in this. What I said was, "Gentlemen, we just fucking saved Clarence's life."

We drove for a while and then decided, what the hell, let's go for broke. We called a number we had for Gary Acreman and decided we'd confront him with what John had just told us. We left a message, and glory be, he called back and agreed to meet with us.

Reyna and I drove the 145 miles to Corsicana, Texas, immediately. We met up with Gary at a Holiday Inn in Corsicana, and he was shaking so badly he had to sit on his hands to keep them still. I offered him a cigarette and had to light it and put it in his mouth for him.

"Look, we know what happened," I told him, repeating John's story.

"No, no, no! It wasn't me! It was Robinson!" he said. And that didn't matter one whit to me, because they were both confirming what we needed to know. It wasn't Clarence.

"Well, you're going to have to give us a statement to back that up," Reyna told him. Gary stared at the video camera and puffed at the cigarette, and suddenly his shaking stopped.

"Okay, okay," he said. "All right. Okay. I'll do it."

Other than painting himself as a witness to the crime, not a participant, he confirmed every detail that John had given us. Clarence was nowhere to be seen through the entire incident, he said. He didn't come by until ten or fifteen minutes later.

We drove back to Conroe, and you can't imagine what a high we were on. It had been a helluva St. Patrick's Day, that's for sure. I called Mike and Paul, and they were thrilled. Not one but two of the janitors who'd been present had exonerated Clarence. We felt really sure we were going to at least get a stay and save Clarence's life.

Paul Nugent was waiting up for me when I got back to his home in Houston. We had a nightcap of bourbon, or maybe two, to celebrate our great good fortune and raise a toast to Saint Patrick.

Later, when I returned to my room, I picked up my dog-eared

Bible and held it for a long time before opening it. I reflected back on how shaken my faith was when John had chased us away. I knew that there would be times again when my faith would waver. But in this moment, I felt not in the least bit alone. I thought of John Henry Sessum, pointing to heaven. And I could hear his words in my head: "God is with us on this."

□

The new statements we'd gotten out of Sessum and Acreman were enough to get us a stay of execution for Clarence on March 20, just six days prior to his execution date. It was an incredible, wonderful, emotional day for us, a fantastic victory. But we knew it was just step one.

Things started happening fast and furious after that. Patti Hassler, a producer from *60 Minutes,* was already working on a profile of me, and now she was on her way down to Texas, ready to switch the focus of the story to Brandley. A week later I was in her hotel room with John Sessum, trying to persuade him to go on air and talk to CBS journalist Harry Reasoner, to tell the world what he'd told us.

I knew it would take an abundance of courage for him to tell the truth—to admit that he let an innocent girl go to her death and sent an innocent man to death row in front of millions of people. I didn't expect the one caveat he put forth.

"I'll do it," he said. "But I gotta ask my brother first."

His brother Robert was sixteen years older, and the leader of their rural family in Mississippi. I asked him why he had to call Robert, and he said, without blinking an eye, "If my family ever heard I was helping a nigger, they'd never speak to me again." I caught my breath, picked up the hotel phone, and told him to call his brother, then and there.

Patti and I sat in stunned silence as John dialed the phone. He talked for a few minutes, then handed the receiver to me. "He wants to talk to you," he said.

I got on the phone, and explained to John's brother who I was and what I was doing, and why it was so important for John to do the interview. Then I handed the phone back to John, and all we heard him say was, "Yes, sir," and again, "Yes, sir," and a third time, "Yes, sir." He put down the phone, looked at us, and closed his eyes.

"He told me," he said, and opened his eyes again, "to do the right thing."

Lo and behold, he did it.

The *60 Minutes* story with Harry Reasoner aired just two weeks after that phone call, and suddenly public opinion began to swing Clarence's way. A flood of new witnesses started coming forward, and huge public protests were being planned. I spoke at one of them—standing before a sea of faces, mostly black, and though I'd never done anything like this before, I didn't give it a second thought. I was flush with the thrill, the rightness, of what we were doing.

After talking for a few minutes, I put my lips close to the microphone, with hundreds of faces looking up at me in anticipation. I said, "I don't believe Clarence Brandley is innocent." I paused, watching the puzzled looks appear on their faces, then concluded, as loud as I could, *"I know he's innocent!"*

At that the crowd erupted, and I let their joy wash over me. And in that moment, I felt a great certainty wash over me as well. I felt certain that I was right, certain that what I was doing was important, and certain that this is what God wanted me to do.

I have to believe the momentum we'd gained from all that publicity contributed to what came next: On June 30, Texas's highest court ordered an evidentiary hearing in Clarence's case and assigned an independent West Texas judge to hear the case. We were granted a change of venue to Galveston, a city far away from the toxic environment of Conroe and one where we believed Clarence would get a fair shake. The hearing happened in September, with a parade of forty-six witnesses in ten days tearing down the lies that had been built up by the DA in Conroe and Ranger Styles.

We didn't even have to wait for his written opinion. At the end of the hearing, Judge Perry Pickett said, "The litany of events graphically described by the witnesses, some of it chilling and shocking, leads me to the conclusion the pervasive shadow of darkness has obscured the light of fundamental justice. I shall recommend a new trial for the defendant."

With that the courtroom erupted with shouts of joy. For a judge to say what his recommendation will be at the end of the actual hearing, rather than waiting to review the record and consider the law before rendering his opinion, is unheard of. To me it was testimony to the depth of corruption in this case and the power of the truth to bring light into the darkest corners of an unjust system.

On November 19, 1987, Judge Pickett issued his formal opinion. In it he stated that "the testimony at the evidentiary hearing unequivocally establishes that Gary Acreman and James Dexter Robinson are prime suspects and probably were responsible for the death of Cheryl Dee Fergeson."

And in his conclusion, he stated, "In the thirty years this court has presided over matters in the judicial system, no case has presented a more shocking scenario of the effects of racial prejudice, perjured testimony, witness intimidation, an investigation, the outcome of which was predetermined, and public officials who, for whatever motives, lost sight of what is right and just. The continued incarceration of Clarence Lee Brandley under these circumstances is an affront to the basic notions of fairness and justice."

He ended by saying, "The Court respectfully recommends that Clarence Lee Brandley be granted a new trial."

It took another two years before the Texas Court of Criminal Appeals, in a 6–3 vote on December 13, 1989, published their decision supporting Judge Pickett's findings of fact and reversed Clarence's conviction. The DA appealed to the U.S. Supreme Court, but they refused to hear the case, and soon afterward the DA dropped all charges.

And so it came to be that on January 23, 1990, Mike DeGeurin, Paul Nugent, Richard Reyna, and I climbed into Mike's old Jeep

Clarence Brandley takes his first step to freedom after nine years on death row. *Paul Nugent*

Wagoneer and drove up to Huntsville, Texas, to bring Clarence Brandley home.

We arrived at the Ellis 1 Unit near Huntsville, where a bunch of mostly black prisoners in white outfits were hoeing a field, like a scene out of an old prison movie about the 1940s. There was a big redbrick tower, and a guard lowered a bucket down on a rope and yelled for us to put our IDs in it. He hauled them up, gave them a once-over, and opened the gate.

We sat in the lobby for what seemed like an eternity, looking around at what's called the "piddling"—arts and crafts made by prisoners. Boats made out of matchsticks, a charcoal sketch of a horse, that sort of thing. Finally we were ushered into the warden's office. I didn't know what to expect from him, but he couldn't have been nicer—telling us what a model prisoner Clarence was, congratulating us on our good work, and promising us that they'd get Clarence up there as soon as possible.

Sure enough, a few minutes later, Clarence came walking in,

slowly, a dazed look on his face. I realized this was the first time I'd seen him without a wire cage between us, and I think he must have realized the same, because without a word we put our arms around each other. Clarence just kept thanking us; I was gleeful and jubilant, and Clarence was struggling to grasp the reality of the moment. He had a glazed look in his eyes, as though he were floating in an unfamiliar world.

The warden gave him an old onion bag to carry the few possessions he had amassed on death row. We laughed, and then we left.

The media swarm in the parking lot was beyond anything I'd ever seen. Cameras and reporters were everywhere; there were even helicopters flying overhead. Mike took the lead and said a few words to the reporters; then we climbed into the Wagoneer. Clarence said he wanted a Coke—he hadn't had one in all his years on death row—so we stopped at a convenience store, then headed to the church where Clarence's family was waiting.

There was another huge crowd there, supporters and civil rights activists and tons more media. Clarence and Mike were in the middle of it all. I kind of slipped aside and sat in the back pew, taking a moment to myself.

I bowed my head and said a prayer of thanks.

Thanks for the miracle of helping John Henry Sessum to come forward. The miracle of everything that came afterward. The miracle of showing a simple man like me that there was another way to live.

It was fitting, I thought, that this story was ending in a church. Because in a very real way, for me, it was also in a church where the story began. Or more specifically, on a Saturday night before church, the night I made the decision to go to the seminary. As I sat there, in that pew, I reflected back on the winding path that led me to that fateful night. A path that was something of a miracle in itself.

Ten

||||

I was not a hippie in the sixties. I was, however, an idealist. I believed in the domino theory, I believed in stemming the flow of communism in Southeast Asia, and I believed in personal responsibility. I wrote in a letter to my parents when I was still in Japan, reeling from my breakup with Yoshiko, "I feel that duty in S. Vietnam is a personal responsibility of everyone in the service, especially young unmarried men like myself. I firmly believe that we should be there fighting for the freedom, independence, and right of self-determination of the South Vietnamese people.... I figure it is about time I gave of myself and sacrificed my own personal comfort for something I really believe."

Now, you may say my idealism came at a fortunate time for me, a way of distracting me from the heartache I'd just suffered. Maybe I was so depressed I just didn't care what happened to me. I can't argue one way or the other. Maybe I was just bored with my work in Japan and wanted to be where the action was. All I know is that I volunteered, and off to war I went.

And so my disillusionment began.

It started that summer, in a three-month training program in California. One part of this training involved a twenty-four-hour period where all 125 of us were held in a mock North Vietnamese prisoner of war camp, with Navy SEALs posing as our North Vietnamese captors. Each of us was forced to climb into a black box with the lid shut tight; our guards banged on the box and threatened not to let us out until we signed a document declaring the U.S. war effort to be morally wrong.

Even though they'd told us we would not be in the box more than fifteen minutes, twenty-five of my fellow mock POWs signed that confession. It was the first time I learned how easily the human spirit can be broken, how easily you can convince innocent people to confess to crimes they didn't commit. It would not be the last. But that disillusionment paled in comparison to what happened next.

A few months later I got the job I dreamed of when I volunteered. I was assigned to be an advisor to a Vietnamese naval junk fleet, to live on a base with my South Vietnamese counterpart and scores of South Vietnamese sailors. We had as our primary area of responsibility Go Cong Province in the northeastern part of the delta and the rivers leading up to Saigon. We were to intercept Viet Cong supply boats and assist the South Vietnamese Army in its land operations, which included conducting our own search-and-destroy missions.

I thought it was my dream job anyway. It turned out to be a nightmare. What I witnessed horrified me: Viet Cong prisoners summarily executed, with American advisors showing not the slightest hint of concern. Vietnam villagers decapitated for the crime of being suspected members of the Viet Cong, their heads tossed into the nearest rice paddy.

"Grow up," the West Point graduate army major, who was the advisor to those ordering the executions, told me when I protested. "Stop being so naive. This is war. You better get used to it."

Corruption was everywhere. I saw my American navy superior blatantly fabricating reports detailing Viet Cong killed and weapons captured, all to impress senior officials in Saigon, who in turn, I suspected, inflated their reports to those above them in Washington. One of my Vietnamese officer counterparts spent more time running a whorehouse than running patrol missions. And I saw Vietnamese and American officials turning a blind eye.

So later, when I found myself facing rampant corruption

throughout the U.S. justice system, watching officers of the law lie and force others to lie, and watching officers of the court turn a blind eye, it wouldn't be the first time. I can't say Vietnam prepared me; I was, as you've seen, still pretty green when I started. But perhaps it steeled me for what was to come.

"I'm really disgusted with everything," I wrote to my parents a year later, just before I left Vietnam, "starting with the Vietnamese officers right on up to the way the whole war is being waged. If the province I work in is any criteria, the U.S. will be here indefinitely.

"It'll be a long, long time before this conflict is even close to a settlement," I wrote. "I don't think we should have gotten involved over here. I don't think the loss of one American life is worth the 'freedom of South Vietnam.'"

I came home from Vietnam disheartened and disoriented. I separated from the navy and set my sights on a business career in Tokyo. Ever since I'd left Japan for Vietnam, the stirrings to return had gnawed at me, and they only grew stronger as time went by. Even after the heartbreak it had offered me, the city of Tokyo—and the dream of becoming a businessman there—were still where my heart lay.

□

After Vietnam, I enrolled in the Thunderbird Graduate School for International Management in Glendale, Arizona, with one goal in mind, and that was to get trained to become a consultant in Tokyo, working with Western firms wanting to do business in Japan.

As soon as I graduated, I borrowed $1,200 from my folks and struck out for Tokyo. I didn't have a single job prospect, but, hey, Geronimo, here I go. I did have the name of one prospective employer, a Harvard Business School graduate named Bud Ingoldsby who ran a firm called Coral Inc., performing market research for American corporations exploring entry into the Japanese market. I knocked on his door, and I was surprised—and delighted—when he hired me, right on the spot. I learned later that he had probably seen a little of himself in me: He too, ten years earlier, had come to Tokyo with no job, just a dream of success in Japan, where he too had served in the military. I thought that with my previous experience in Japan and my newfound business training, I would be the perfect candidate to consult with Western firms that wanted to do business in Japan.

I learned a very important lesson from the many Japanese business executives I dealt with in those years—one that would serve me so well later. Take the long view. Patience and perseverance will win the day. One Japanese executive put it this way: "Americans want to get things done too fast. They're always pushing for and expecting immediate results. In the race between the turtle and the hare, the turtle will win in the end. The hare will exhaust himself and get discouraged in a long race. We are the turtle and you Americans are the hare."

I learned something else valuable from my market research work. I remember being sent from Tokyo to Korea to do a major-market analysis for the First National City Bank of New York. Its Tokyo headquarters had hired our small consulting firm to go to Korea to learn and describe the leasing market there. I didn't think it would be that hard: I'd find the expert in Korean leasing, take him out to dinner, wrap it up easy. Thank goodness a fellow by the name of Mark Mobius came with me to get me started and set me straight. He told me as we were flying to Seoul, "Now look, Jim. The way this works, don't expect to find a central source of information who's going to tell you how the whole market is. You have to go and interview many different people, get their little piece, and put the pieces together in a puzzle."

It was a lesson I'd learn again and again, in Japan and beyond: You don't get the answer right away. You go piece by piece, and when you get all the pieces together, however many there are, you put those pieces into the puzzle, and you see the whole picture. Criminal investigation turned out to be no different. You have to interview scores, sometimes hundreds, of people, and then you put the case together, piece by piece.

And so the people I've helped to free from prison have a lot of people to thank, but certainly my mentors in Japan were among them. They taught me to take the long view. They taught me to put the pieces together. And they taught me to wait.

☐

I had waited years to make the phone call I was about to make, and this time my patience was wearing out. As you might have guessed, business wasn't the only thing that had drawn me back to Japan. There was also the matter of Yoshiko. And a piece of paper in my wallet.

Before I'd left for Japan, I did one of the dumbest things I think I've ever done. That friend of Yoshiko's I'd met in Japan had told me where her husband lived, and so, just before my classes started at business school, I got in my yellow Camaro and drove 550 miles from Arizona to Mount Pleasant, Utah, on the wild hope of tracking her down. I know how crazy that sounds; that's exactly how crazy I still was about Yoshiko, even years later.

I went to the only bar in town and chatted up the bartender, managing to eke out the information that there was exactly one Japanese person living in town. Her name, it so happened, was Yoshiko. I concocted a story: I said I had promised a friend of hers from Japan that I would do my best to find her current address and phone number. The next thing I knew, the bartender had Yoshiko's mother-in-law on the phone. I gave her the same story I had told the bartender, and what she told me broke my heart all over again. Yoshiko had gotten so homesick for Japan that her husband rejoined the navy and had gotten transferred there so they could return.

My pulse pounding in my ears, I asked for her phone number in Japan to pass along to the friend I'd invented. She gave it to me.

I got the hell out of town, thinking—as I should have on the way there, if I'd had any sense—that if Yoshiko had been in town, my visit could have caused all sorts of trouble between her and her husband. But that didn't stop me from slipping that piece of paper with her phone number into my wallet.

Now here I was back in Japan. Trying to work up the courage to dial that number. At this point I was living a pretty decent life, working hard by day, going to bars and trying to meet girls by night. But at the end of every night, I looked at that phone number. Month after month I thought of calling, and didn't. But on New Year's Eve 1969—fortified by a few cups of hot sake—I finally worked up the courage to make that call.

My hands were shaking as I dialed her number. I had decided to just hang up if her husband answered.

He didn't.

Eleven

TEXAS, 1988

Sometimes—actually, a lot of times—I hear voices in my head.

They are the voices of the innocent.

I've stayed in touch with many of them over the years: the folks we've managed to free, the once-imprisoned, now-exonerated men and women who have found a second life, after their first was shattered by lying police officers and false testimony and just downright evil. Sometimes, what I remember are their descriptions of the hell that they lived through.

"When I entered the Missouri state prison," Darryl Burton once told me, "there was a banner that read, 'Welcome to Missouri State Penitentiary. Leave all your hope, family and dreams behind.'" Darryl spent twenty-four years in prison, wrongly convicted of the murder of a man at a St. Louis gas station, based on the false testimony of two people who claimed to be eyewitnesses, along with some shoddy police work. I worked with two attorneys, Cheryl Pilate and Charlie Rogers, and an investigator named Dan Clark, and we managed to get him out of prison. It took us eight years, but he was exonerated and freed in 2008.

"*Time* magazine described it as the bloodiest forty-seven acres in America, and it was," Darryl told me. "I witnessed such violence. Heard such unbelievable screams. I mean I never heard men scream like that before. Somebody was attacking a man; two or three men were assaulting him in a sexual way. You see guys get their head busted. You see guys get stabbed. The first day I was put in the unit, day number one, they lock these big old gates, and within ten feet, me and this other guy are walking, we heard rumbling and turned and looked around and two guys were getting stabbed. That was day number one. And the very day that I was released from the prison, they was rushing a man to the prison infirmary. Someone had cut his throat from ear to ear, tried to decapitate him. And I saw so much more. In the dining rooms, in the housing units, everywhere."

I can't imagine that kind of hell. But I have been lucky enough to witness, time and again, what it's like to be freed from that hell. I remember Lamonte McIntyre—just seventeen years old when he was framed for a double murder in Kansas City, Kansas—telling me about the moment he first hugged his wife as a free man.

They had met in prison. His mother was visiting him; the young woman was visiting her brother. "And I seen her, she seen me, I spoke to her, and she told me her name was Corisha, and she was the prettiest, man, and I was going through my appeal process and I was thinking I was going to get out, and I looked at her and I said, 'Okay, this is gonna be my future wife.'"

In fact, Lamonte did marry Corisha when he was still in prison, but when his appeals were denied, his heart was broken, and he told her to forget about him. "She was just twenty years old," Lamonte told me later, "and she had her whole life ahead of her. I didn't want to drag her along, because I was suffering and I didn't want her to suffer with me."

So they divorced, over her objections, but their romance rekindled a few years later while I was working his case. Again working with attorney Cheryl Pilate, I managed to get two drug lords to come clean and name the real killer, and together we found a slew of new evidence on top of that. Lamonte was set free after twenty-three years in prison.

"When I walked out of that gate," he said, "before I went in the street, she was in the lobby of the courthouse, and she hugged me, and I hugged her for the first time as a free man. And I knew I didn't have to let her go. When I was in prison, we only had one minute to hug each other and that was it. So when I hugged her when I was a free man, I knew I didn't have to let her go. And it felt so good. It felt so good."

Lamonte's voice is one of those that comes through to me loudest and clearest, in those quiet moments. Because he was so articulate about the depths of pain and despair he had fallen to, and how he had climbed out of that place.

"The one thing I wish someone would have told me when I was in my darkest moment was, 'It's only dark right now, and it gets better even when it don't seem like it will, especially if you look forward to it getting better.' The moment I started to wake up in the morning realizing it could be better, that's hope," Lamonte told me. "So I developed hope. So as long as we know that hope is alive and is well, we can survive. Because hope will keep you alive, and hope kept me alive. I knew that one day I would get free. I knew that one day these things would change. So I developed hope and I never let go of it."

But the most amazing thing, when I think back on what these men and women have told me—what I am struck by, so often—is how little anger I hear in those voices.

"I can't waste any more time being angry," Darryl told me once. "Anger is just another prison.

"The anger wasn't getting anything in return," he went on. "I had to let that go. I wanted to be free, not just physically, but mentally and spiritually free. Free from all of what has happened to me. And the only way I could be free is to let it go and just move forward with the time I have left."

I was so moved when Darryl told me that. I am moved by all of these men and women, when they speak from their hearts about their unimaginable suffering. But there is one person whose words were forever seared on my heart.

Her name was Joyce Ann Brown.

☐

In late 1987, I was still living in Mrs. Yeatman's beautiful if somewhat neglected house on Library Place, but the burden of having all this going on under her roof, and having tons of mail coming to her home from so many prisoners throughout the nation, was too much for poor Mrs. Yeatman. She never said anything to me, but apparently she talked to my new partner in crime Kate about it—"When is he leaving, Kate?" she would ask, unbeknownst to me—and Kate kept hinting to me that maybe we should look for an office. "No, no, Mrs. Yeatman loves having me here," I told her. Years later, Kate told me, "I didn't have the heart to tell you she wanted you out."

So on her own, Kate found us a little office on Nassau Street in downtown Princeton and convinced me to move the operation there. I still lived in Mrs. Yeatman's home for a while, but she passed away shortly after we got the new office. When I left, to rent a room in a house on the outskirts of Princeton, it was a little bit like leaving your childhood home. This is where Centurion was born, where it took its first steps. I remember looking around the place wistfully, one last time, and thinking of how much Mrs. Yeatman had given me, just by her strong presence, her easy wit, her civil manner. She had given me a place to watch my creation grow up, and now it was time to see where it would take me next.

It had been a roller coaster of a year for me. And not without incredible heartache. Because while I was working on Clarence Brandley's case, I had taken on another death row case as well, that of Jimmy Wingo. Jimmy—along with another man, Jimmy Glass—was convicted of breaking into the home of a couple on Christmas Eve 1982 and murdering them. It was a horrendous crime.

The night of the murder, both men were on the lam, having walked out of a small northwestern Louisiana parish jail. At their separate trials, Glass admitted that he was the shooter, but he testified, "Wingo made me do it." From the get-go Wingo insisted he had split from Glass after the jailbreak and tried to hitchhike home in the rain; that he was never in that house; and that about an hour after they separated, he reluctantly accepted a ride from Glass when he pulled up in a stolen car.

I was bouncing back and forth between the Brandley case and Wingo's, and so I wasn't able to start on the Wingo investigation until June 2, 1987—just two weeks before his scheduled execution date. It was extremely stressful, dealing with these death row cases simultaneously.

The star witness for the prosecution was Wingo's girlfriend, who had testified that Wingo said he'd been in the victims' house while the murder took place. It was a story that was becoming all too familiar to me: She later admitted, in a video affidavit she gave me, that the story was a lie. She had been threatened by a deputy sheriff, who told her he'd put her in jail and take away her children if she didn't incriminate Jimmy. And, she said, the deputy forced her to have sex with him for good measure.

I presented all my evidence to the parole board several days before Jimmy was to be put to death, but they refused our request to stay the execution. I stayed with Jimmy for an hour or so on the afternoon of his execution. It was an incredibly difficult visit for me, but Jimmy was accepting of his fate. Jimmy died in the electric chair just after midnight on the morning of June 16, 1987; his last words were "I am an innocent man. You are murdering me this day. I do still love you all in Christ. God bless you all."

The headline in the Baton Rouge *Advocate* the next day was "McCloskey's First Failure." It was more than that for me. It was a painful and tragic loss of life. I was absolutely convinced of Jimmy's innocence.

Now, looking back and closely reviewing the case, I have to admit that I'm not so sure. There are questions—legitimate questions—as to whether Jimmy Wingo was in the house that night. In my view you don't execute a man in any event, but especially when there is reasonable doubt about his guilt. The question of whether Jimmy Wingo was ever in that house still gnaws at me to this day.

So, sadder but wiser, I hit the road again. Kate had put together a list of six or seven prospective inmate clients in the South and West for me to visit, so I headed for Louisiana, Texas, and California.

By this time, I had almost a decade under my belt of doing this work. I'd encountered all manner of people on both sides of the law. I'd met some good cops and prosecutors, and too many dishonest ones. I'd walked into many prisons and met all sorts of inmates, some whose guilt was without question and some whose innocence was just as clear.

But I had never met anyone like Joyce Ann Brown.

□

I met her in prison in Gatesville, Texas, in the spring of 1988. We were separated by a glass barrier, with a little round grate we could talk through. From the moment I sat down, I was struck by her. An African American woman in her early forties, she had a broad face and piercing eyes, and she spoke in a southern drawl with the rhythms of a preacher and the power and dignity of a woman who refused to be broken. I started by going over the facts of her case with her and telling her why I was there. It was just a preliminary meeting—for me. But for her, it became quickly apparent, it was much, much more.

"Mr. McCloskey," she said, after we'd been talking for not more than a few minutes, "you cannot imagine—you cannot *imagine*— what I have gone through. You cannot imagine how easy it would be for me to lose my mind in here. But I will not let that happen to me. I have been locked up for eight years, one month, and seven days. But I will not believe that I am destined to stay in here for the rest of my life. That cannot be my destiny, Mr. McCloskey. That can *not* be my destiny."

I noticed that tears had started to slide down her cheeks, yet there was no hint of a sob in her voice, no sign of weakness in her face. She continued to stare straight at me with those piercing eyes as she told me of the toll that being falsely imprisoned had taken on her family.

"They took my daughter away from me, Mr. McCloskey," she said. "And my stepson"—at this her voiced wavered, just for a moment, before she continued more quietly—"my stepson committed suicide."

I was taken aback. I wasn't sure what to say, other than to offer my sympathy. As though she could read my mind, she answered the question I was thinking, but didn't dare ask.

"I don't know if he committed suicide because I was in here," she said to me, the tears flowing freely now. "But I do know this. If I were home—if I had been there . . ." She shook her head, working up the strength to finish the thought. "If I had been there, I know, *I know,* this would not have happened."

She continued to stare at me, through me, as though to burn that thought into my head, as though there were nothing more important than having me understand the truth, and the importance, of what she had just said. And perhaps nothing was.

"They will not defeat me, Mr. McCloskey," she said. "I will see this put right."

It was as though I was in the presence of a powerful spirit, a power greater than myself. I was so shaken I couldn't continue.

"Joyce, you're going to have to give me a moment," I said.

I got up, walked away from her, and stared at the door leading out of the interview room. In a short while I would walk out that door. Something in me knew that I would not stop until one day Joyce had walked out of it as well. A decision had been made, somehow, before I knew I was making it. I sat back down.

"Joyce," I said, "Kate and I agreed that on this trip I would visit a handful of prospective clients and then go back to Princeton and discuss them in full before we decide which ones I would take on. But I'm throwing that plan out the window. I already know which case I'm going to take on. It is yours."

She looked at me, incredulous. Her voice trembled as she asked if I was saying what she thought I was saying.

"I do not have a scintilla of doubt that you are an innocent woman," I said. Her ironclad alibi had convinced me of that before I arrived; her honest, straightforward demeanor only confirmed it. "I am here to tell you here and now that I will do all in my power to free you."

A look crossed her face that I can describe only as a blend of love, peace, and grace. "I am looking at you now, Mr. McCloskey," she said. "And I know I am looking at the man who is going to set me free."

"This is like a marriage, Joyce," I said. "You and Centurion Ministries are together until death us do part—or at least until we bring you home to your mama and daughter. I've never made this kind of promise before, but I promise you. We will free you."

As I was leaving, I was told the warden wanted to see me. I couldn't figure out what I had done wrong. But when I got to her office, she told me that she just wanted to wish me well. "Everyone knows Joyce is not good for this," she said. "What can I do to help you in your efforts?"

I was taken aback. I asked if Joyce would be allowed to call me once every two weeks—outside the parameters of the prison at the time.

"Consider it done," she said. "And good luck."

"Thanks," I said. "We're going to need it."

□

When I got back to the office, I was a little anxious about breaking the news to Kate; she'd come up with this system for vetting our cases, and here I'd broken the plan the first time I walked out the door. Turns out it wouldn't be the last.

Kate was fine with it, though. "I was already in love with the Joyce Ann Brown case," she told me later. "I was deliriously happy when you took it on because I thought she was absolutely innocent."

When you look at the facts of the case, that's pretty clear. In fact, you can't even believe that Joyce was sent to prison to begin with.

Here's what happened. On May 6, 1980, two armed African American women, one wearing pink pants and the other a navy blue jogging outfit, robbed Fine Furs by Rubin in Dallas, a shop owned by two Holocaust survivors, Rubin and Ala Danzinger. For no apparent reason, the woman in pink shot Rubin as he begged them to spare his life and his wife's. She then fired another shot that went through the window, missing Mrs. Danzinger. Ala told the shooter she was dying of cancer and had only a few weeks to live—a lie she made up on the spot, desperately trying to save herself. It worked.

"We'll just let you suffer, then," said the woman in pink.

And with that the two bandits walked away with thirty-five furs stuffed in a black plastic trash bag. They drove off in a brown 1980 Datsun.

The car was found the next day, and police learned it was rented by someone named Joyce Ann Brown. They knew that name. Joyce had not lived the straightest life. She'd been arrested for prostitution in the past, but she'd cleaned up her act since, working now, by sheer coincidence, as the receptionist at another fur store.

That was enough for the detectives. They took Joyce's photo to Ala Danzinger, already in a horrible emotional state as her husband clung to life at the hospital. During their visit she got the phone call she'd dreaded: Her husband had just died. Despite her unimaginable shock and grief, the police went ahead and showed her their photo lineup, and in that overwhelmingly emotional moment she pointed to Joyce's photo, identifying her as the woman in blue, the shooter's accomplice.

The homicide investigators' case began to unravel immediately. For starters, they learned they had the wrong Joyce Ann Brown; the car had been rented to a different woman by the same name, from Denver. *That* Joyce Ann Brown told them she lent the rent-a-car to a friend named Rene Taylor, and when they searched Rene's apartment in Dallas, they found all the goods: the murder weapon, a few of the stolen furs, a pink jogging outfit, even a yellow pages phonebook turned to Fine Furs by Rubin.

Beyond that, my Joyce Ann Brown had a rock-solid alibi; her time cards and co-workers made it clear that she'd been at work on the day of the murder, except for a thirty-six-minute lunch break. And no physical evidence ever tied her to the crime scene, unlike Rene, whose fingerprint was found on a coat hanger in the rented car.

But the police stuck to their story. They put forward the scenario, defying credulity, that Joyce took a quick lunch break, changed clothes, drove three miles through heavy lunchtime traffic, committed the robbery, drove the three miles back to work, changed clothes again, and went back to work at the reception desk, chatting with co-workers like nothing had happened. They threw Joyce in jail— with bail posted at a million bucks, no less—and despite all the holes in their case they went forward to trial.

So how did they make it stick? Take a guess.

Yep, you got it. Another surprise witness, with another miraculous jailhouse confession.

The woman's name was Martha Jean Bruce. While Joyce was awaiting trial, they threw her in a cell at the Dallas County Jail with Martha Jean, who was serving time for attempted murder. Martha Jean testified that for some reason, again defying all credulity, Joyce confessed to her that she'd committed the robbery.

Of course, the DA also had Ala Danzinger's ID of Joyce, shaky though that was. And it didn't help that when Mrs. Danzinger concluded her testimony and was leaving the courtroom, she shouted at Joyce, "Why did you do it? You ruined my life! You took my husband's life!" That outburst couldn't have been anything but terribly prejudicial to the jury.

Joyce was convicted of the crime. Flash forward four years: Her lawyer, Kerry Fitzgerald, managed to get a post-conviction hearing. By this time, Rene Taylor has pleaded guilty to the Danzinger murder and been sentenced to life in prison, swearing in an affidavit that Joyce Ann Brown was *not* her accomplice. She wouldn't say who was, but she made it clear that it wasn't Joyce. Fitzgerald also produced letters showing that even though Martha Jean Bruce said no promises had been made to her in exchange for her testimony, the DA had engineered a reduction of her sentence, enabling her to return home on parole after serving only thirteen months of a five-year sentence for attempted murder.

So here was a judge at the post-conviction hearing, with the woman who shot Mr. Danzinger saying that Joyce wasn't her accomplice and with letters showing that the woman who got the miraculous jailhouse confession was rewarded right after Joyce's trial with a get-out-of-jail-free card. And what did the judge do? Did he recommend to the Court of Criminal Appeals that her conviction be thrown out, as you would assume anyone confronted with all this evidence would have?

No. He referred the case to the CCA without comment or recommendation. And the appeals court ruled, for whatever reason, that they didn't find Rene Taylor's testimony believable enough and therefore Joyce wasn't eligible for a new trial. Once again, truth and justice had no place in the discussion. Joyce's innocence didn't matter. They decided there was no flaw in the case worthy of reversal, and for that Joyce could wallow in prison.

I couldn't, for the life of me, understand that. But it wasn't my job to understand it. My job was to keep my promise to Joyce Ann Brown. And luckily, I knew right where to start.

□

Martha Jean Bruce lived in a long, two-story public housing complex in an impoverished part of South Dallas. I knocked on her door and found it ajar, so I pushed it open a bit and called out, "Martha Jean, it's Jim, can I come in?"—like she would know who I was—and to my surprise a voice called out, "Come on in."

There was a woman sitting in the dark, and I said, "I'm looking for Martha Jean," and the woman said, "She just stepped out. She'll be back in a few minutes."

So I stepped out and came back fifteen minutes later, and there was Martha Jean. It took only minutes for her to begin telling me everything. She told me that people from the DA's office had fed her facts that she would weave into her story. And that the DA promised her he'd help her get an early release so she could get home to her children.

"I'm sorry for what I done to that woman," she said, her voice full of emotion. "But they were gonna send me away for five years. I had to get home to my children. I was desperate. I have to think of my kids."

I felt anger well up in me—not at her so much but at the DA. I had to let it pass. As always, I tried not to judge her.

"My God, that's a tough choice, Martha Jean," I said. "I can certainly understand why you chose that particular fork in the road. But I want you to think about Joyce. She's a mother too. She's been taken away from her daughter for all these years. She doesn't hold any bad feelings for you. She just wants to go home, just like you did."

At that, I could see her soften. I didn't attempt to "close" her then, in business-speak, just gave her all the information I had about why I knew Joyce was innocent. I asked her to think about giving me some kind of statement.

She said she would, and I left with my fingers crossed.

□

Through the whole process I stayed in touch with Joyce. The warden let her call me pretty much as often as she wanted to, and I visited her whenever I could. That was mostly to keep her informed, of course, but it was also for me: I just found her inspiring to talk to. It lifted my spirits to be in her presence or to talk to her on the phone. The power of her belief helped fuel my own.

She would sometimes tell me about her life in prison. Living among thieves and murderers and baby killers and con artists and extortionists wasn't the worst of it, she would tell me. The physical conditions—the awful smell, the tiny cells, spending your days sitting on iron benches—that wasn't even the worst of it either.

"It's all so degrading, Jim," she would say. "The guards tell you, right to your face, that you are the 'property of the Texas Department of Corrections.' That you are no better than an animal. They just want to break your spirit and dehumanize you."

The most common way that prisoners would bring contraband into their cells was by "legging it," she told me—putting it in their underwear or up between their legs. So the guards, regularly, would just come up to the prisoners, reach their hands between their legs, and give them a hard chop to the crotch, pretending to look for illegal merchandise. "And all the while grinning in your face, as if to say, 'I own you, and there isn't anything you can do about it.'"

She told me about one prisoner that everyone called Granny, a little old black woman in her seventies, convicted of killing her children and some grandchildren as well. Granny pretty much had the run of the prison, but talking about her made Joyce despondent.

"I have these nightmares," she would say. "Nightmares that I'm going to wind up like her. A little old lady, spending the rest of her life in this place."

Other times, our conversation was lighter. She would regale me with stories from the life she'd left behind, including tales of some of the stranger customers she'd had when she was a prostitute. One was a judge who didn't ask her for sexual intercourse; he just wanted her to powder him with baby powder, then put him in a diaper. Another was a big steel executive from Pittsburgh who'd come to see her every time he was in Dallas. They met at a high-end hotel bar—that's where Joyce met most of her customers—and he went from being a regular customer to being something of a long-term friend. In fact, she told me, he was supporting her while she was in prison, sending her money and getting to know her family. That might sound strange to you, but it was actually kind of familiar to me—for reasons, again, that will become obvious.

One time, though, our visit turned very serious.

"Joyce," I said to her, "I have to ask you something. It's not going to be easy for you, but it's important."

Her eyes flared, and she stared at me intently, without a word.

"I know Rene Taylor is in this prison with you," I said. "I need to talk to her. And I need you to ask her if she'll talk to me."

Joyce remained silent, her gaze unchanged.

"I know you've told me that you avoid her like the plague in here," I said. "And I know she makes you sick to your stomach." I could understand it: Even though Rene had told the judge back in 1984 that Joyce wasn't her accomplice, Rene's act of robbery and murder—and her silence at the time of Joyce's trial—were the reason Joyce was here, and might remain here for the rest of her born days.

"Joyce," I continued, "I need to find out who her accomplice was. I need to just ask her, flat out. I don't know if she'll tell me, but I need to try. Which means I need you to try. Will you do it?"

We sat in silence for the longest time. It was agony for me. I'm sure it was much more agonizing for her. Finally, she spoke.

"All right," she said. "I'll do it. I don't know if she'll listen to me. But I'll do it."

□

Joyce came through, just as I hoped she would. And a little while later, our request to visit with Rene Taylor was approved. Richard Reyna, the investigator who worked with me on the Brandley case, had come on board for Joyce as well. He came with me to meet Rene.

I knew from the record, which no one had followed up on, that Rene and an accomplice had been wanted for the 1978 robbery of Lloyd's Furriers in Albuquerque, New Mexico. I thought that maybe her partner in that crime was the same person who joined her in the Danzinger caper.

And that's just what Rene told us.

"My associate in Albuquerque was my associate in Dallas," she said flat out.

It was an electrifying moment, and I tried to push it a little further. "What was her name?" I asked.

Rene looked away for a moment, then looked back.

"I'm not giving you that," she said.

But no matter. She had given us enough. Richard and I tracked down the lead Albuquerque police detective on the 1978 fur store robbery. When we went to visit him, he was the chief of police in the small town of Bernalillo, about twenty minutes north of Albuquerque, and he got us the original police file on their robbery.

There it was, in black and white, the name of Rene's alleged accomplice: Lorraine Germany. She had worn a navy blue jogging outfit, just like the one in the Danzinger robbery.

Her photo was in there, too, and when I looked at it, I couldn't believe my eyes. She was a dead ringer for Joyce Ann Brown.

I made a beeline for Denver, where I knew Lorraine was now based. A really sympathetic Denver detective, J. C. Tyus, located her for me—she was doing time in the Colorado state prison for another armed robbery—and arranged for me to meet with her the next day.

I nearly jumped out of my shoes when she walked into the visiting room; she was, indeed, the spitting image of Joyce Ann Brown. She was friendly at first, proudly admitting that she beat the rap on the Albuquerque fur store robbery. But when I started bringing up the similarities to the Danzinger case—and mentioned that Rene told me her accomplices in Albuquerque and Dallas were one and the same—she clammed up, screaming at me, "You're a fucking liar! We're through! Guard!"

But it didn't matter, because I knew I had solved this puzzle. Rene and her accomplice, whom Rene had basically identified for me as Lorraine Germany, had gotten in a car rented by the other

Joyce Ann Brown—the one from Denver. They'd robbed the store, and Rene shot and killed the owner. The distraught survivor, Ala Danzinger, had seen that accomplice and mistaken her for my Joyce. Poor Joyce had the misfortune of having the same name as one of the people involved, and almost the same face as the other most likely suspect. And because the case was so flimsy, the DA had concocted a phony jailhouse confession to win his trumped-up, no-good conviction.

I had it all pieced together. Now I just had to prove it.

While I was in Denver, Detective Tyus set me up to meet with a guy known as the Black Godfather of Denver—a sharply dressed man named Selmon Fletcher. Tyus had told me he ran a lot of the illegal activity throughout the Midwest and Southwest. Fletcher was like a venture capitalist of crime: He would front people the money to do their illegal activities, then take a healthy share of the profits. Rene, Detective Tyus said, was one of the criminals under his wing.

Selmon met me in a nondescript, run-down joint called the Quorum Club. He came with the other Joyce Ann Brown in tow. And, after frisking me to make sure I wasn't wearing a wire, he was surprisingly friendly, claiming to be a recent born-again Christian himself. He confirmed for me that I was on the right track, and to my surprise he agreed to give me a note to give to Rene, telling her to help me free my Joyce Ann Brown.

But it was all for naught. When I went back to see Rene, she denied ever telling us that her Albuquerque and Dallas accomplices were the same person. I showed her the note from the Black Godfather of Denver. "Yeah, right. Selmon's found Jesus," Rene said, tossing the note back at me. "Not me. We're done here. There's nothing left to discuss."

☐

My ace in the hole, unfortunately, didn't pan out either. When I went back to see Martha Jean Bruce, she went south on me.

"Listen, Mr. McCloskey, I appreciate what you're doing," she said. "But if I give you a statement, I know exactly what's gonna happen. That man, the DA, Mr. Kinne, he's going to come after me again and take me away from my kids and send me to prison for perjury. And I ain't going there." After that day, she disappeared. I never found her again.

But while I was striking out on that front, Richard Reyna was about to hit one out of the park. Reyna had gone down to the Dallas Courthouse to check on Martha Jean Bruce's criminal history. And lo and behold, he discovered that on March 13, 1980—six months before Joyce's trial—she had pleaded guilty to lying to a police officer.

Bells went off in my head. At Joyce's trial, Martha Jean had been asked if she had any other convictions besides shoplifting and burglary, and she said no. Because the Dallas DA's office had convicted her of that charge of lying to a cop, Joyce's trial prosecutor, Norman Kinne, *had* to have had that information. Meaning not only was Martha Jean a liar, which wasn't disclosed to the jury, but the DA had suborned that lie. And *that* was the flaw in the case—the pinhole that, with any luck, we could drive a truck through.

Which is exactly what we did. We managed to track down several of the jurors at Joyce's trial, who said they definitely would have voted differently if they'd known the star witness had a prior conviction for lying to a police officer.

I reached out to *Dallas Morning News* reporter Steve McGonigle, who had covered Joyce's trial. I gave him everything Reyna and I had gathered; he ran with the story, and suddenly Joyce's cause was front-page news.

I pitched the story to *60 Minutes*, and they jumped on it too. Before I knew it, Joyce was ushered into the same visiting room where I often met her, with an avuncular, craggy-faced man with an easy smile sitting opposite her saying, "Hello, I'm Morley Safer."

She was powerful, and compelling, as she sat and talked to the famed correspondent, again with tears on her cheeks but not a hint of a catch or a sob in her voice. She told him plainly why she was there.

"They needed a conviction," she said. "They needed the pressure off. Two blacks? In Texas? In broad daylight? Shot and killed a businessman? Somebody was going to pay. I became that somebody."

Safer seemed genuinely moved by Joyce, as is everyone who comes into her presence. "Joyce," he said, "if as you say you didn't do it, and you tell it very convincingly, how do you get through every day in this place?"

"I keep going day for day," she told him, "because I want the world to know I'm not guilty of this crime. And to break, or lose my mind—I will remain here for the rest of my life. I have a family that supports me. I have a daughter that needs me. And I'm guilt-free. I can lay down at night and sleep. I don't have to dream about a crime—I don't have to dream about a man shot down like a dog—because I wasn't there."

What Joyce told Morley Safer echoed one of the most powerful lessons I learned from so many of our exonerees: Their closest friend in prison, the ally that gives them the strength to endure, even in the depths of their despair, is their absolute knowledge of the truth of their innocence. It is the truth, the honest, unwavering bedrock of truth, upon which they stand, day after cruel, heartbreaking day. And, when discovered, it is an irrepressible force with the full redemptive power to set them free.

And it is what inspires me, year after year after year, to work diligently on their behalf.

□

Joyce's words echoed across the nation: The power of that broadcast, as well as the continuing coverage in *The Dallas Morning News*, meant the DA's office could no longer ignore the irrefutable evidence we were presenting. In short, they caved.

It happened like lightning: Kerry Fitzgerald, Joyce's trial attorney, who had continued to fight for her ever since the trial, filed a writ of habeas corpus that demanded Joyce's case be brought before a judge and that laid out the new evidence Richard and I had developed. The DA agreed that Joyce deserved a new trial. The Texas Court of Criminal Appeals set her conviction aside. The DA agreed not to retry the case.

And just like that, it was all over.

It was just a few weeks before Thanksgiving 1989 that Joyce walked out of that prison and into the arms of her mother and daughter, for the most joyful reunion you can imagine. The scene was absolute chaos—cameras and reporters everywhere, jostling to get close to the woman whom the whole nation had been rooting for—but within the chaos I felt utter joy, and immense gratification, because I had kept my promise to Joyce that I would free her. And we did.

I became aware once again of the redemptive power of the truth, of knowing that for one moment—for this moment at least—the universe was kind and just. That the truth won out against those who fought ferociously against it. That freedom had come to a woman who deserved nothing less.

☐

In the years that followed, Joyce put her life back together—but much more than just that. She became a powerful advocate for Centurion, helping us raise significant funds. More important, she became a tireless advocate for the wrongly convicted. Joyce formed a nonprofit organization called MASS—Mothers for the Advancement of Social Systems—to help women behind bars, and to help them reintegrate into society when they are released. She traveled the nation, telling her story and those of many other innocent people in prisons throughout the country. Often she spoke to law students,

Joyce in 2013. She used to call herself
"Mrs. Joyce Ann Brown McCloskey."
I was always so touched by that.
Diane Bladecki

knowing that they could become the people to change the very system that had caused her such torment and pain.

"The nine years, five months, and twenty-four days that I was in prison, nobody has ever paid me for that time," she told one rapt group of students, her voice carrying the powerful rhythms of a preacher. "But I ain't *angry* about that. 'Cause *you* can make my nine years, five months, and twenty-four days worth it. Because if *you* become a lawyer, if *you* become a judge, or *you* are one of my legislators, or if *you* are in any decision-making position, that's going to affect a person's life, and you think about Joyce Brown." And then her voice went quiet as she continued: "And you think about all those innocent people when you are making a decision on somebody's life, then my nine years, five months, and twenty-four days won't be in vain."

You could have heard a pin drop in that room.

A few months after she was released, Joyce wrote an incredibly powerful article in *D* magazine, a monthly in the Dallas–Fort Worth area. In it she described the horrors of prison life and the hatred that she felt when she was first imprisoned. She described how, for the sake of her daughter, she had to learn to let go of her anger.

"There is a poem that best describes my years in prison," she wrote, "and it goes, 'Two prisoners looked through bars/One saw mud, the other saw stars.'

"I never stopped looking at the stars."

☐

Throughout the time I was working on Joyce Ann Brown's case, I was still knee-deep in what had become the longest siege of my short career—the first case to truly test the lessons of patience I'd learned in Japan.

When we freed Joyce Ann Brown, on November 3, 1989, we were also on the verge—I thought—of finally claiming victory, and justice, in the Monmouth County, New Jersey, case of Damaso Vega. It was a significant one in my life for two reasons.

One is that it took us five years to get Damaso freed. The other is that it was the only time I had a gun stuck in my stomach.

I had tracked down a witness to another violent crime who I thought might have some information on this one. I showed up at her job, and she said she'd meet with me at home that night so her husband could be with her. So at seven o'clock on a warm New Jersey night in a nice, tidy suburban neighborhood, dressed in my clerical collar and with a big smile on my face, I knocked on her door.

I was not greeted by my witness; I was greeted by her husband. In one hand he was holding a leash, which barely restrained a snarling German shepherd. In the other he held a handgun. "Get the fuck in the house," he said in a low, furious growl.

He didn't have to tell me twice.

Time froze for me. My travels in this work had taken me to the most dangerous corners of many cities, and I'd confronted some pretty threatening characters, but this was the first time I'd had a gun pointed at my gut. And it was by a guy who seemed to be deciding whether to use it.

"Now you listen to me, you fuck," he said. "I don't care if you are a priest."

I decided not to take that moment to point out that I was, in fact, not.

"Who the fuck are you to show up and bring up shit my wife don't have no need to be reminded of? Now, she don't know nothing about any of this shit you're asking about, but I can tell you what I know. I know that if you ever—if you *ever*—show your face around here again, you won't live to see another day."

You'd think I'd become a little more careful after that about showing up at people's doors while I was investigating crimes. I never did. Never gave it a second thought. I just kept doing it, because I knew that in the long run it was the best way to go about the work I was trying to do.

In any case, Paul Casteleiro and I did compile enough evidence to get the case back before a judge; it took forever, but finally the judge announced his ruling from the bench.

"There are aspects of this case that terrify me, that these things can still occur. It shakes you right to the bottom of your beliefs in the justice system," he said. "Plain and simple, I guess we made a mistake. My apology to Mr. Vega."

□

It had been a wonderful month—Joyce was freed on November 3, 1989, Damaso just twelve days later—and the beginning of an incredible stretch of success for Centurion Ministries. From the middle of 1989 until the spring of 1992, Centurion freed nine innocent inmates from all across North America—including our first Canadian exoneree, David Milgaard of Saskatoon.

One of the nine was our first DNA exoneration, in 1991. Kate handled that one. Using DNA in this way was still in its infancy. The first case had occurred less than two years earlier, and the Innocence Project, pioneers of this kind of work, was still a year away from its formation. In our case, in August 1991, DNA tests proved that Charles Dabbs was innocent of a 1982 sexual assault in Westchester County, New York.

Centurion's finances were a roller-coaster ride during this stretch. In 1989—partly thanks to the publicity our successes were garnering—several foundations came forward to help, and our annual budget swelled to $178,000. But being a rookie at this, I had no idea how temporary that support would be, and in 1990 our income plummeted to less than half that.

I want to take a moment to highlight the lone foundation that stayed with us then (and that has stuck with us to this day), the Prospect Hill Foundation, started by Bill Beinecke and now run by his family. Because of it, and the other benefactors who came forward as our successes started to grow and get noticed, we were able to climb out of that financial hole and regain our modest financial health. By 1992 our income had increased to close to $200,000, and we were starting to take on the semblance of a real organization, with three staff members and a small army of volunteers, mostly retired folks from different walks of life.

Which is a good thing, because the requests for Centurion's help were ballooning. We had five hundred requests a year in 1989 and 1990; the next year, that number doubled.

Something else began to happen, too. We started getting noticed in Hollywood. It's not every day you pick up the phone and hear, "Jim? This is Marlon Brando." Brando was interested in getting the rights to the life story of Geronimo Pratt, the leader of the Los Angeles Black Panther Party, whom we had freed from prison just one week earlier. And he wasn't the first person to reach out.

But each new project was more offensive than the last.

First, Lorimar Television wanted to produce a TV series about Centurion. I agreed, on the condition that they didn't change the facts, but wouldn't you know it, their first script turned me into a district attorney who saw the light and went over to the other side, to defend the innocent. So, even though we really could have used the money, I gave back the $10,000 advance they'd given me.

Next came Abby Mann, the famed producer and Oscar-winning screenwriter. He brought me out to his home in Beverly Hills to start working on a screenplay for a feature film that Warner Bros. contracted him to write. I have to admit that it was a big ego boost to get that kind of attention. It was fun—until it wasn't. Abby Mann's script—at the insistence of the producer at Warner, he told me—had me going in my clerical garb to interview a witness and minutes later ripping my collar off and having sex with her.

I was dumbfounded and disgusted. It was all so far from the truth. I decided that unless someone wanted to tell a story that was true—the story as I'm telling it to you now—it wasn't worth it.

So I gave up on Hollywood and just went back to work. It was a good moment for us: We'd freed a lot of innocent people, the press respected us, the public was on our side, and the judicial system was starting to pay attention.

I could not have been less prepared for what was about to happen next.

Twelve

||||

Yoshiko answered on the first ring, and although she recognized my voice immediately, I could tell she was apprehensive. I told her I'd been in Japan for a few months, and that it had taken me a long time to work up the courage to call her, but now that I had, it was good to hear her voice. She seemed reluctant and unsure that she wanted to talk to me, but I pressed on.

I held my breath and asked her to come to Tokyo for an afternoon, from her home in Yokohama, just so we could put closure to what had happened between us. She was hesitant, but finally agreed.

I will never forget the moment I saw her again, standing on that train platform, looking exactly as she had five years before, wearing a beautiful kimono, catching my eye, and smiling.

We stood together awkwardly for a few minutes, smiling at each other, not knowing quite what to say. My heart was pounding. Finally, I managed to find some words.

"Yoshiko," I said, "it is five years almost to the day when we first came to Tokyo and ate at that Chinese restaurant. Do you remember that?"

She nodded with a smile, and said, "Jim-san, I am nervous. I didn't think this day would ever come."

Those words made my heart swell. We talked, catching up on all we'd missed. I was surprised to find out that she was the mother of a young boy. Our day lasted long into the evening, and I almost made her miss the last train back to Yokohama. I rode with her for a few stops, trying desperately to convince her to see me again; at each stop she said no, and then, as the last stop in Tokyo was approaching, where I had to get off, I asked her one more time. The sound of that "yes" will stay with me forever.

As the weeks went on, she admitted that she had never lost her love for me, and we settled into the affair I knew I had come to Tokyo for. It was heaven. It was bliss.

One day, she called and asked me to come down to Yokohama for lunch. We met at a nice restaurant downtown; she'd arrived before me. As I approached, I saw her sitting there with someone next to her. It took me a moment to realize it was her son.

"This is Andrew," she said, gesturing to the boy and then turning to him. "Andrew, this is Mr. McCloskey." She offered no explanation to him of who I was—perhaps she'd told him something about me beforehand, perhaps not—and she offered me no explanation of why she'd brought him along. It seemed like a reckless move. What if he mentioned something to his father about the nice man he and Mommy had lunch with that day? But I didn't ask any questions. We chatted about everything and nothing, and the boy sat quietly. It wasn't until I was walking back to the train home that it hit me.

The boy I just met, Yoshiko's son, was about five years old. That means he was conceived . . . when she and I were first together.

How could I have been so naive? Did she bring him as some kind of signal to me? Was that boy my son?

As the weeks turned into months, I wondered, but never had the courage to ask. Our love affair lasted two more years. We would see each other only when her husband was away at sea, which, thankfully, was often enough. She would get a babysitter and I would go down to Yokohama. The days were a dream for me; I like to think they were for her, too. I kept pushing her to leave her husband and marry me. But something in me knew it was never to be.

One day she called and said she had something important to tell me. I could have guessed what it was. We met at my apartment in Tokyo, where she told me that her husband had been assigned back to the United States. She was leaving me—again.

"Yoshiko," I begged. "You are the love of my life. And I am the love of your life. I'm pleading with you. Divorce your husband and marry me, and we'll live here, in Japan, together, with your son, for the rest of our lives."

She looked away, out the window, and then looked back at me.

"Jim-san," she said. "I want to. And I can't. You know I can't."

We talked for a long time, but she kept coming back to the same thing: She could not bring herself to destroy her family, could not face the guilt or the shame.

And so, in the end, she left me, as she had left me before.

I was bereft. As I look back now, nearly fifty years later, and consider the path that led me to the seminary, and to the work that has become my life's mission, I often see God's hand guiding me. But I see Yoshiko's, too. The devastation of losing her again—this time for good—left a yawning hole in my soul that I spent years trying to fill.

Many of those years I spent trying to fill it in exactly the wrong ways, until I found the right one.

I stayed in Japan for a while afterward, but it had lost its magic for me. I tried to focus on the other dream that had brought me to Japan—to become a successful American expatriate advising Western firms in Japan. But then I was dealt another blow: The small consulting company I was working for, Coral Inc., was secretly sold by Bud Ingoldsby, its founder and president—the guy who hired me and who'd become my mentor—to a large Japanese bank. I couldn't believe he did this behind my back, without a shred of warning. We'd talked often of our dreams to build Coral into the go-to consulting firm used by Western corporations hell-bent on entering the Japanese markets, and even spreading our wings throughout Asia. But with the sale, that dream vanished as well. I knew enough to know that there was no future for an American in that corporate culture.

So, feeling betrayed and humiliated, I resigned. I returned home, once again searching for meaning and a way to put together the pieces of a shattered life.

Thirteen

||||

VIRGINIA, 1988

Have you ever found yourself wading through a stream in a small coal-mining town, your pants taped to your boots the way coal miners do to keep the coal dust out, trying to see whether the water came all the way up to your crotch or stopped about a foot above your ankles?

Probably not.

But I did.

I mean, when you're trying to re-create the movements of your client on the night a gruesome murder was committed, to see if it's possible that he committed the crime, you do whatever you need to do.

It can be pretty chilly, in a hollow in western Virginia, wading through fast-moving water in the middle of the morning. But I wasn't feeling the cold. I wasn't even thinking, what the hell am I doing, wading through a stream in a coal-mining town in the heart of the Appalachians?

I was thinking, I'm soaking wet. And that's great news. Because it means my client is innocent.

□

I had met Roger Coleman a few days before. He was a simple man, tall and pale, reserved and serious, but very polite, with huge glasses that made him look more the college professor than the coal miner he had been before he was sent to death row. Roger stood accused of raping and murdering his sister-in-law, Wanda McCoy. I'd already reviewed the primitive forensic evidence against him, and it seemed pretty unconvincing. After talking to him, I decided that nothing in the state's case added up.

I didn't think it did, anyway. But of course, I had to go figure it out for myself.

So the very same afternoon that I met Roger, I left the Mecklenburg Correctional Center and made the three-hundred-mile drive down one back road after another, headed for Grundy, Virginia. The scene of the crime.

Grundy is tucked away in the southwestern corner of Virginia, with a population of about seven hundred on a good day. I drove into town past an old-fashioned-looking filling station where, I knew from the files, someone had put up a big lighted sign, right before Roger's trial, that said, "Time for a new hanging tree in Grundy."

This was not going to be a friendly place.

I pulled into the parking lot of the area's one motel. The clerk noticed I was from New Jersey and asked me, in a friendly way, "What brings you all the way down here?"

I told her the reason, just to see what her reaction would be. "I'm researching Roger Coleman's claims of innocence," I said, and suddenly her warm smile turned into a cold frown. "In that case it is not a good idea for you to stay here," she said. "Law enforcement folks like our coffee shop, and they wouldn't appreciate it none if I gave you a room, bein' as how they have some pretty strong feelings about what that boy did to the McCoy girl." So I headed to the trailer at the address Roger had given me for his uncle and wound up staying there with him and his wife, Geneva, for a month.

For all the sketchy neighborhoods I've walked into on this job, I have usually felt safe, even when I probably had no right to.

But something about Grundy made me feel ill at ease.

□

I didn't usually call Kate very often from the road, but for some reason I found myself checking in with her by phone a lot. Ostensibly, I was going over the case with her, but really I think I was just trying to keep one foot in reality, because what I was living through down there in the backwoods, ten miles from nowhere, felt pretty surreal.

Not that the people were hostile, mind you. Just the opposite, in fact. People talk about southern hospitality; you don't hear as much about Appalachian hospitality. But that's what I encountered, almost everywhere I went (that first motel clerk notwithstanding). Folks couldn't have been nicer. Still, I was lonely and disoriented. Somehow the coal mines and hollows and trailer parks felt too alien to a city dweller like me. The only way through it, I decided, was to just do what I do. Focus on the facts of the case and try to unravel them, one by one.

The facts of the murder itself were fairly straightforward. On Tuesday, March 10, 1981, at around 11:15 p.m., Brad McCoy, having finished his shift as a parts clerk in the United Coal Company's repair shop, arrived home, where he discovered Wanda McCoy, his nineteen-year-old wife, spread-eagle on the floor. There was a horrific slash wound across her neck that severed her carotid artery and went deep, almost to her spinal cord. The coroner put the time of death at somewhere between 10:30 and 11:00 p.m. and found that she had not only been raped and sodomized but stabbed twice after she was already dead, once in the heart and once in the liver. This was brutal overkill, the work of someone in a crazed, frenzied fury.

Wanda McCoy was, as *The New York Times* would put it, a victim out of American folklore. Her husband was a member of the hillbilly clan of McCoys that had battled the Hatfields in the nineteenth century. There was immediate pressure in the town to find her killer.

The police determined—wrongly, I think—that Wanda had let her assailant in. They asked Brad whom she might be that friendly with. He said she was shy, only that comfortable with a few people.

And one of the people he named was her sister's husband, Roger Coleman.

By now, you know how this goes: Community pressure to solve a case often causes the police to focus with tunnel vision on the first likely suspect. And Roger had the great misfortune to be that guy.

It was that simple.

Nothing about the case, beyond that, was simple by any means.

No DNA test was done, of course; they weren't available then. The blood and hair samples that seemed to put Roger at the scene were inconclusive at best. And, of course, desperate for a conviction, the prosecution brought in a despicable criminal with multiple felonies on his record—including charges for assaulting and threatening to kill another inmate for refusing to perform fellatio on him—who claimed that Roger confessed to him in the Buchanan County jail. But what really intrigued me, the more I looked into the case, were not the forensic details but Roger's movements on the night of the crime.

Here's what's undisputed. Roger, driving his pickup truck, had reported for the night shift at a coal mine, up a mountain three miles north of Grundy, at 9:45. He talked to a shift foreman, who told him his shift had been laid off.

On his way down the mountain he ran into a friend, Philip Van Dyke, and they chatted for a while. Philip puts the time Roger left him at about 10:30, because he clocked into his job at a different coal company a quarter mile away at 10:41.

Roger then drove past Wanda's neighborhood, along Slate Creek Road, to a trailer park to see a friend, who wasn't home. He then walked to another trailer, talked with a couple he knew there for a minute or two, then left.

Then—according to the prosecution—Roger drove his pickup back toward Wanda's neighborhood, about three miles away, parked it on the shoulder of the heavily traveled highway, waded through a fast-moving creek, walked through a crowded neighborhood (with the hope of going unnoticed by nosy neighbors and barking dogs), gained entrance to Wanda's, raped her, killed her—all without leaving any coal dust from his dirty work clothes or a drop of water from the creek in her house—then retraced his steps, went back through the creek, got in his truck, went to a bathhouse to clean up, and then drove home.

He got there, according to his wife, Tricia, by 11:05 p.m.

It just didn't make any sense to me. I interviewed everyone involved—Philip Van Dyke, the couple at the trailer park, everyone. I measured the time and distances from one point to another, all along the route from when Roger left the coal mine until he got home. It seemed like you'd have to be a ninja to do what the prosecution was saying Roger had done. I just couldn't see how Roger could have possibly committed the crime.

So that's why I tried retracing his steps myself. I went to the spot where Roger and Philip had talked on the night of the crime. Indeed, it was a few minutes from where Philip had clocked in to work. Conservatively, I assumed that Roger had left that spot at 10:25 p.m.

I then drove to that highway and waded through the creek, trying as hard as I could not to splash the water. That's when I got soaking wet. Which just confirmed for me the absurdity of the commonwealth's theory of the case.

Here's why. The prosecution had made a big point of showing that Roger's pants were wet, up to about twelve inches from the bottom. They said that proved he had waded through the creek to murder Wanda. Even though his socks and long johns were dry as a bone.

After I waded through that stream, my socks were soaked. My pants were soaked. And the prosecution's case, I realized, was all wet, too.

□

When I finished my little experiment in the water, I kept going, up toward Wanda's house, just to see if the timing made sense. It didn't.

Not by any stretch. But something else caught my eye. It was a big, looming house on the hill just above Wanda's place. There was something about it that seemed ominous—like the house looming over the Bates Motel in *Psycho*. I made a mental note to go and see who lived there, and a few days later I followed up.

The Ramey family—Mama Helen, Daddy Bobby, and two of their kids, both in their twenties—were home when I paid a call. Like everyone else, they were polite and pleasant. But I had the distinct feeling they were hiding something. The dad just sat and stared out the window, down at Wanda McCoy's house, the entire time I was there. His son Donnie—or "Trouble," the name I later found out he was known by—did most of the talking. He was a wiry guy with a scraggly beard and a way of not exactly looking at you when he talked to you. Everything about him made me suspicious.

Donnie told me that at 9:30 on the night of the murder, he and his younger brother, Michael, were returning from the movies when he'd seen Roger's pickup parked outside the McCoy house. That made no sense, of course, because Roger would have just been reporting for work then. And then they told me that the whole family had gone to bed by about 10:30. That seemed a little unlikely, too; the whole "goodnight, John-Boy" scene seemed a little too pat.

There was so much about this case that wasn't adding up. The three things you look for in a suspect are means, motive, and opportunity. We've already established that Roger didn't have means or opportunity, and as for motive there was never a hint that he had anything but a very cordial relationship with Wanda and her family. No motivation whatsoever. Remember that Wanda's husband told police that Roger was one of the very few people she would let into the house.

The more I talked to the good people of Grundy, the more I felt that the law had just had it in for Roger from the start and overlooked other obvious potential suspects.

Like, maybe, one of the Ramey brothers.

For example, from the minute Roger was arrested, the county

was abuzz about articles in the local papers with accounts of Roger's prior conviction on a charge of attempted rape. That case had taken place about a month after Roger graduated from high school; his accuser was the mayor's daughter, and Roger had spent twenty months in jail for it. I'm not sure if Roger was really guilty of that crime, mainly due to the testimony of the school superintendent, who said that Roger was with him at the high school at the time, as it turned out, that the victim said the assault occurred.

But I will tell you this: The former husband of the victim in that case was the guy who put up the "hanging tree" sign in Grundy. He was one of the people I talked to.

And even he had doubts about whether Roger murdered Wanda McCoy.

□

But beliefs are beliefs and facts are facts, and I still hadn't come up with the first thing that would get Roger out of prison. I needed something new. So I told Roger I needed him to give me a DNA sample, to prove that he wasn't the person whose sperm was found in the victim. And to my consternation, Roger refused.

"I'm sorry, Jim," he said. When I asked him why, he hesitated and then said, looking me straight in the eye through those great big glasses of his, "You see, I had sex with a female jail employee before the trial. And I think she was a plant."

No sentence any client ever said to me ever made less sense than that. I asked him what the hell he was talking about.

"I think they wanted to get my sperm and put it in Wanda so it would look like I did it."

I just stared at him. I couldn't believe my ears. "What are you talking about!" I said, my voice rising. "That's ridiculous."

"Well," he said, "you never know what these people down here are gonna do."

"Well, they're not gonna do that!" I said, standing up. "But I'll tell you what I'm gonna do." I took a breath, to regain my composure. "This gives me some cause for concern with regard to your case. I'm wondering if you might be afraid to get it done because maybe it *is* your semen in her. I don't know that, but your explanation for not getting it done is not sound at all. It smacks of being afraid to get it done for whatever reasons. So, I'm pulling out until you decide to get DNA done."

And for the first time, I walked out on a case.

□

In September 1990, several things happened that brought me back in. Roger's new attorney, Kitty Behan, was a breath of fresh air. She brought new energy to the case. She succeeded where I'd failed, convincing Roger to authorize the DNA test.

She also did something that Roger suggested: She placed an ad in the Grundy weekly newspaper, *The Virginia Mountaineer,* asking if anyone had any new information about Wanda's murder. And guess what? A woman named Teresa Horn said a man had attempted to rape her in 1987, and he told her during the attack that if she didn't shut up, "he was going to do me like he did that girl on Slate Creek." That "girl on Slate Creek," of course, was Wanda McCoy. And that man was none other than the one who had given me the creeps in the house above Wanda's, Donald "Trouble" Ramey.

Teresa inspired other women to come forward with their own accounts of how Donnie attacked them as well. One name led to another, and pretty soon three more women gave us statements that when they were in their teens, Donnie sexually assaulted them.

I developed other evidence that pointed the finger at Donnie Ramey. His common-law wife confided to her best friend that once, when she and Donnie were having a terrible fight, he threatened her, saying, "I'll do to you what I did to Wanda McCoy." Helen Ramey, Donnie's mother, shaking with fear, told a good friend that on the night of the murder her two sons had a violent fight with their drunken father. The boys then left the house, and when they returned, Helen said, she could feel "murder in the air." Another good friend of the Rameys' told me that Donnie told him he and his brother were high on LSD the night Wanda was killed. And then at a party, as he and some folks were passing around a joint, Donnie let it slip that he "had a hand in the incident at Slate Creek."

So now we had a lot to go on. We had a woman who was saying— and who would soon give me a sworn affidavit—that someone else had confessed to the crime. We also had the DNA test that Roger had agreed to. When Roger's semen was compared with the semen from the victim's vaginal swab, we discovered something startling: There were not one but two semen samples present in the victim. Meaning it was entirely possible that two people had committed this crime. Meaning the state's case held even less water than it had before: Their argument had stipulated that Roger was alone at the time of the crime.

Unfortunately, the DNA test did not conclusively rule Roger out (although, in those still-early days of DNA testing, it couldn't really prove much of anything with real certainty). The state argued that the results showed that one of the sperm samples found in Wanda could belong to only a small percentage of the population, of which Roger was a member.

But Kitty didn't give up. She found other experts who said the mixed sperm sample made an accurate reading very difficult and certainly open to question. And that the studies the state was quoting, to indicate what percentage of the populace was ruled out by the DNA test, were flawed. Based on all the accumulating evidence casting doubt on Roger's guilt, Kitty filed an extensive new petition to reopen the case. We were optimistic about the possibilities.

And devastated by the result.

Without a hearing, the judge summarily dismissed the petition. He set May 20, 1992, as the date that Roger Coleman would die.

□

Up until this point, every state and federal court had denied Roger's appeals, based on a very narrow technicality: His original appeals lawyer had filed the notice of appeal one day late. But jazzed with all our new evidence, we were very hopeful that our appeal to the U.S. Supreme Court would yield a different result.

It didn't. On June 24, 1991, the court ruled, 6–3, that the lower courts were correct, and because Roger was a day late in filing his claim, he was procedurally banned from having his appeal heard.

I can't begin to tell you how insane I think that is. That we would condemn a man to death for an error so petty, so minor—it was inhumane. This wasn't a game of volleyball we were playing, where a line judge rules a ball in or out of play. This was a man's life.

Roger's life.

It felt, in those last weeks leading up to the execution date, that the entire nation was on our side. *Newsweek* ran a huge spread on the case headlined "Hung on a Technicality." ABC's *Primetime Live* devoted half an hour to the case. On May 11, Roger was on the cover of *Time* magazine with the headline "This Man Might Be Innocent." The *Los Angeles Times* reported that "startling new evidence" had emerged—referring to Teresa Horn's allegations about Ramey. Around that same time Teresa died, reportedly of a drug overdose but possibly by more nefarious means, and suspicion about the case went through the roof.

Roger, piped in remotely from prison, went on all the shows making his case—*The Today Show, Larry King, Phil Donahue*. He was mesmerizing. "There's a lot of anger," he told Larry King. "There's a lot of bitterness, and a lot of frustration." He said that when he first went to death row, "I had a tremendous amount of hate, and it was consuming me. I had to deal with it, and I did a pretty good job of getting a handle on it. But now those feelings are back, and they're multiplied by a factor of ten."

In what veered beyond simple reporting into pure exploitation, *The Today Show* asked if Coleman would come on the show along with Brad McCoy, Wanda's husband. Desperate to keep people listening to his story, Roger agreed. But while he had remained calm on all those other TV shows, now he lost it. "I did not kill Wanda, Brad!" he yelled. "I didn't have anything to do with it! And if you'd open your eyes and look at the evidence we have now, evidence that the state has withheld—I mean, you just listened to what they said, and you bought their theory, and you just closed your mind to everything that we've uncovered!"

But in the end, while the media were convinced of Roger's innocence, the courts were not. Eight days before the execution, a federal judge—without even conducting a hearing—denied Roger's final appeal.

□

The concrete floor outside Roger's cell was cold and smelled of stale disinfectant. We sat and talked for a while, Kitty and I on one side of the bars, Roger on the other. I had spent the last two weeks desperately traveling the state, trying to find any new evidence I could, and meeting with the staff of Virginia's governor, Doug Wilder, hoping against hope that he could be convinced to grant either a stay of execution or clemency. Even Mother Teresa intervened, calling Walter McFarlane, the governor's executive counsel, to say, "Mr. McFarlane, this is Mother Teresa. I'm calling about Roger Coleman. I'm not telling you what to do. Just do what Jesus would do."

And still the governor refused to intervene. McFarlane did say that if Roger took and passed a polygraph test, he might reconsider. Roger took it, on the day he was to be executed, and failed. Before you jump to any conclusions, let me say this: A polygraph test records signs of stress exhibited by the subject. Can you imagine taking a test, knowing that if you fail you will die? Do you think you might exhibit stress?

But that was our last, best Hail Mary. Our prayer went unanswered. And so now we sat on that concrete floor, in a room with three empty cells and Roger in a fourth, and the execution room at the end of the corridor.

We split a cold pizza that Roger tore into slices by hand, and we talked about everything and nothing, how unbelievable it was that Roger was going to die on a technicality, for filing a motion a day late, how inspiring it was to have everyone from Bryant Gumbel to Mother Teresa on your side, how incredibly well Roger had advocated for himself.

"You were so strong and clear on *Larry King*," I said. "No one could have been a better advocate for himself. I just want you to know that."

"Well, I did my best," he said humbly. He turned and looked at the TV that was playing on the wall behind me and Kitty. *Wheel of Fortune* was on, and someone had just solved a puzzle. "Look," Roger said, smiling. Kitty and I turned around and saw the letters Vanna White had turned around. They spelled, "MISCARRIAGE OF JUSTICE."

Throughout the evening he remained calm, as he always did; it was, once again, as though he were trying to ease this moment for us, instead of the other way around. There was an air of grace that was palpable, unmistakable. He showed as much courage and equanimity as you could imagine for someone who was about to die in an electric chair.

It was then that I realized something: There are people who teach you how to live. Roger was teaching me how to die.

□

At about 9:00 p.m. they prepared Roger for execution—shaving his head, taking his big glasses away, and putting a thin white sheet over his nude body. He looked like a Buddhist monk, sitting in his cell awaiting his time.

Just before they took us away, Roger wrote something on a

paper towel and handed it to me, telling me that those were the last words he would speak. I copied them onto another piece of paper and looked into his eyes. I told him that I would never stop fighting to prove that he was innocent, that they had put an innocent man to death.

He thanked me for all we had done; astonishingly, even in the moments before death, he was gentlemanly and polite.

At that, Kitty and I were transported back to the administration building to await the inevitable.

I read later in *The New York Times* that at a dinner party at the Canadian embassy in Washington that night Chief Justice William H. Rehnquist and Associate Justice Anthony M. Kennedy were repeatedly called from the table, presumably discussing the possibility of a stay on the telephone with the other justices.

But at midnight, Kitty was called into another room in the administration building to take a call. She came back, her face ashen.

"We're denied," was all she could say.

I hugged her, trying to reassure her that she had done more than anyone could have. There was nothing more to say.

We waited until the deed was done; then, numbly, I walked out to the front of the building, where a massive horde of reporters was waiting—maybe fifty cameras, from all around the world. There, I read the final words of Roger Coleman. Here's what he wrote:

> An innocent man is going to be murdered tonight. When my innocence is proven, I hope all Americans will realize the injustice of the death penalty as all other civilized countries have.

I remembered, in that moment, the vow I had made to Roger—that I would never stop fighting to prove his innocence. It would take another fourteen years, but we would finally, finally get to the truth.

And it was nothing any of us expected.

Fourteen

The first thing I noticed when I came home from Japan was that there was something wrong with my dad. He seemed diminished and depressed. I'd walk into a room and realize he'd been crying. It was hard, at first, to get him to tell me what was going on; he kept saying he didn't want to trouble me. But when he finally told me the story, it was like a punch to the gut.

A few years earlier, in the fall of 1969, right around the time I was headed back to Japan for my momentous reunion with Yoshiko, my dad was going through the best, and worst, time of his life. McCloskey and Co. had been awarded the contract to build Veterans Stadium. It was a huge deal in Philadelphia, and my dad was riding high, until Arlen Specter, the DA in Philadelphia at the time, stepped in. He accused my dad—falsely—of substituting cheaper building materials than those specified in the contract. It was splashed across the front page of *The Philadelphia Inquirer*—"Jury Indicts McCloskey Firm, Charges 'Cheating' on Stadium." My dad, as executive vice president of the firm, was named in the indictment.

We were sure this was political payback: My great-uncle Matthew McCloskey, the founder of the company and the man who inspired my youthful nickname, was a key supporter of Mayor James Tate, the guy Specter had run against for mayor and lost in a very bitter campaign.

Whenever we would touch on this subject, my dad would be on the verge of tears. I had never seen him cry before. My heart went out to him. I felt guilty for not having been there for him when all of this was taking place. Mom told me that the notoriety made Dad look like a cheat. Dad was worried that all his friends and associates would think he was a crook. Even though he was innocent, he was ashamed to go out in public, fearful that everyone would believe what they'd read in the papers about him.

Eventually, the indictment was quashed by a Philadelphia judge; the DA's office had used illegal methods of obtaining it. This came as a great relief, as did the support of all those who stood by my father through this period. But I don't think he ever got over it.

I don't think I ever did, either. When I look back on it now, watching my dad live through the horror of being falsely accused of a crime he didn't commit must have stayed with me. Granted, what my father was accused of doesn't compare in any way with what Centurion's clients faced years later, but witnessing the pain my father endured, I am sure, carried me forth to the decisions I would make about my path in life.

But that was still a ways away.

I had a lot of wrong turns to make first.

☐

My brother was going through a divorce at the time that I returned from Japan, so we got together and rented a two-bedroom apartment out in the western suburbs of Philadelphia. I didn't have two dimes to rub together, but I'd developed a degree of expertise about Japanese business, so I tried to find a consulting firm that might have use for a guy like me. I wrote to twenty-five companies and got rejected by twenty-four of them. Luckily, a firm called Hay Associates, which had a strong reputation as an international consulting firm but had not yet made any inroads in Asia, was looking to establish itself in Japan. They decided I was the guy for them. The plan was for me to build our business with Japanese subsidiaries in the United States and use these relationships as the foundation for setting up the Hay office in Tokyo.

And just like that, I was in Fat City. Here I was, a member of a respected consulting firm, reporting to the two top partners, who were giving me the freedom to think and act without anyone watching over my shoulder—complete freedom to build the business, and a hefty salary to go along with it. It was just the career path I had been looking for.

What no one at the firm knew was I was living a double life. I was working in New York two or three days a week, knocking on the doors of Japanese executives to try to sell Hay's services. I stayed at the InterContinental hotel at Forty-Eighth and Lexington, which was convenient for two reasons. One was that by day I could walk to a lot of the midtown offices where I had meetings. And two was that by night I could walk to Times Square.

To pick up hookers.

For those who don't remember Times Square back in the day, it has changed tremendously since the 1970s. Where today it's all Disney characters and chain stores, then it was all prostitutes and adult movie theaters and drug dealers and addicts. No M&M's store, that's for sure. So I found myself, sometimes, upon a lonely night, following a prostitute up a dark staircase in a seedy hotel that rented rooms by the hour.

I knew that all I was doing was trying to fill the hole in my heart left by Yoshiko. I also knew that it was reckless and self-destructive behavior that could get me killed. But I did it anyhow. From the distance of all these years, I can see why I descended into the world of Times Square prostitutes: It was emotionally uncomplicated. I could come and go as I pleased, engaging and disengaging without the danger of abandonment, without the fear of being hurt.

I never even went back to the same prostitute twice. That is, until one night in the early spring of 1977.

I first spotted her in front of a place called the Roxy Burlesk, which offered "live burlesk" and "bizarre action" for twenty-five cents. She was wearing a very short silk dress, very low cut, and was beautiful, with short, dark hair and light brown skin, and she gave me a big smile as I walked by. I stopped, and we started to chat.

She said her name was Brandy and she was twenty-five, from Montreal. Before long $50 had changed hands and we were up in her apartment. When it was all over, she gave me her phone number and told me to call her the next time I was in New York.

Which I did, of course, the very next week, and before I knew it, she wasn't charging me. We were getting together and having sex and having dinner and having the time of our lives, chatting and hanging out like old friends.

Once she even took me home to Montreal to meet her parents. Which was strange enough. And stranger still, because back home I was dating another woman—a married woman, no less; separated, but still legally married. So maybe I was living a triple life. And it was about to become even more complicated.

□

Between my work at Hay Associates and my secret life—or lives—a need began to grow in me. Here I was, living what to all comers looked like the good life. I had a great job, and I had not one but two lovers on the side. But I realized that something very important to me was missing.

My personal conduct was reaching rock bottom; I could see that I was betraying something vital within myself. I also realized that the seeds that had been planted in me all those years ago and had lain dormant for so long had started to grow and that they were what I desperately needed and wanted to reclaim.

And so I went back to the church.

I know how hypocritical it was, to be sleeping with a Times Square prostitute and cheating on her with a married woman—or maybe the other way around—and then sitting home reading scripture on Saturday nights. And believe me, I felt about as phony as you probably think I deserved to feel.

But there was something in me that was aching to reclaim the simplicity and authenticity of my boyhood faith. I met often with my pastor, Dick Streeter, at the Paoli Presbyterian Church and talked to him about it. He didn't judge me or tell me what to do. He just gently and persuasively guided me to passages of the Gospel that he thought would be of help.

I started reading the scriptures voraciously. They became my meat and drink. Dick's constant theme in his preaching was that we are to follow Christ's model of washing the feet of the poor, that a life well led is one that serves the needs of others. Over time this started to plague my conscience. Who was I serving? No one but myself, and Hay, my corporate god. To the extent that I was washing anyone's feet, it was theirs, as I engaged in making money for them and for me.

It was getting harder and harder to look at myself in the mirror. In addition to the hypocrisy of it, I felt that I was leading a shallow and selfish life, one that I feared was not at all pleasing to God. It was beginning to wear me out. I had one foot planted in the sacred world and the other in the secular, with all of its seductions. And so far the secular world was winning. I kept up with my scripture, and I kept up with my carousing, and no one at the firm, none of my friends, no one but Pastor Streeter, knew I was living this triple life.

It was rapidly spinning out of control.

In New York, when Brandy wasn't around, I'd occasionally pick up other prostitutes. I woke up in a hotel room on one of those nights to find that the hooker I had picked up was gone. So was my wallet. I'd fallen asleep and she'd rolled me.

That was the moment I got up, looked in the mirror, and finally said to myself, what the hell way is this to live your life?

The answer was about to come to me, on a cold and lonely Saturday night.

Fifteen

||||

Linda Jo Edwards was hard to miss.

Big and striking, Linda Jo had the kind of beautiful brown eyes and vivacious personality that light up a room. She grew up in the tiny town of Bullard, Texas, a little railroad crossing of a place, population five hundred. Linda Jo stood six feet tall and weighed two hundred pounds, a strong and powerful farm girl who was the star of the Bullard High basketball team. She got married a few months out of high school, but it was a bad match: For a small-town farm girl she had big aspirations, yearning for a lifestyle that was out of her reach.

Out of her reach, that is, until she met James Mayfield. The minute he hired her to work for him as a periodical clerk at the library at Texas Eastern University in Tyler, Texas, Mayfield set his sights on wooing her. It wasn't hard: As dean of the university library he carried a measure of prestige, and as an avid tennis player he had the strong, trim body and powerful physique of someone half his age.

In other words, someone just about Linda Jo's age.

Even though he was twenty-two years her senior, the man with graying hair at his temples, a forceful, strident personality, and a dutiful wife at home managed to seduce the impressionable young girl. By Christmas 1975 they had started a torrid affair.

From the start, Mayfield began remaking Linda Jo in the image of the woman he wanted her to be. He put her on a strict diet and exercise regimen, fed her diet pills daily, taught her to play tennis and racquetball. Their sex life was passionate and varied; she took pleasure in satisfying every facet of his voracious appetites. By that summer she was down to 150 pounds. Mayfield convinced her to get a divorce and move into his home, where he continued the affair, right under his long-suffering wife's nose.

The affair did not go unnoticed by Elfriede, who stood by her husband even though he demeaned and abused her, ordering her around and demanding that she cater to his every domestic whim, while Linda Jo took care of the rest.

The affair did not go unnoticed by their adopted daughter, Louella, either; she despised the young woman who was causing her mother untold sorrow. Her fury added to the tension in their home, nestled in the otherwise peaceful, serene community of Lake Palestine. More than once she confronted Linda Jo and threatened to kill her.

Louella was not the family member most prone to violent outbursts, however. That title was reserved for Mayfield himself. Friends said the hot-tempered head librarian was like an electrical capacitor, building up a charge and then letting it go like lightning. One said he would "shake with red-hot glassy rage" when his temper got the best of him. At Midwestern University in Wichita Falls, Texas, where he had worked before coming to Texas Eastern, seven women signed a petition asking the university's president to fire him because of his abusive behavior and hot temper.

It was no surprise, then, that when his relationship with Linda Jo started to unravel, in the spring of 1977, he didn't handle it very well.

Things had started out on an upbeat note for Linda Jo: That May, after twenty-three years of marriage, Mayfield walked out on Elfriede and moved in with Linda Jo. She had dreams of them getting married and starting a new life together. But the honeymoon lasted barely a week. On Elfriede's forty-second birthday, she begged Mayfield to move back home; he did, and that very night Linda Jo attempted suicide, downing ten sleeping pills.

When the university president got wind of the whole thing—the scandalous affair with a university employee half his age, the suicide attempt—he fired Mayfield on the spot. Mayfield was devastated. This was his dream job, the job he believed he would work at for the rest of his life. He blamed his woes on Linda Jo.

And yet, somehow, the two star-crossed lovers, one sexually addicted to the girl he had sculpted in his image, the other infatuated with the domineering figure who promised her the world, somehow got back together for a few tumultuous weeks. After leaving the hospital, Linda Jo moved in with a co-worker, back at the same apartment complex she'd been living in with Mayfield, the Embarcadero. She returned to work, telling co-workers she was determined to win Mayfield back. But while their sexual relationship continued, she began seeing other men, casually. She had developed the habit, some young men in her apartment complex noticed, of parading nude in front of a window to show off the body she had become so proud of. One of those men introduced himself to her at the pool in early June, and she invited him back to her apartment. He slid the patio door closed behind them, and they had a furious make-out session on the couch. He left with the souvenirs of a few hickeys on his neck and a smile on his face.

Mayfield grew more and more jealous, and more and more furious, as he started to hear rumors that Linda Jo was seeing other men. In a rare moment of clarity and strength, he made the decision to move with Elfriede to Houston, to try to resurrect a life from the charred ruins of his career. They planned to relocate sometime that summer. But Linda Jo told him she too was planning to move to Houston, and he feared that if she were still in close proximity, the affair he blamed for destroying his life would all but certainly consume him again.

It was still consuming him on June 8, 1977, his forty-fourth birthday, when he visited her and they had sex; it was still consuming him the next day, June 9, when he saw her at least five times. And it was likely consuming him that same evening at 8:00, when Linda Jo visited him at his house and told him she was indeed dating other men. After leaving him, she visited some neighbors, telling them Mayfield had become upset with her. She then visited another neighbor, whom she told she was having trouble with her jealous married boyfriend and was going to leave him. She seemed nervous and distracted, her legs shaking. The friend said she kept looking at her watch and finally got up to go at 10:30 p.m.

About two hours later, her roommate, Paula Rudolph, came home, opened the front door, and stepped into the darkened foyer. She looked into Linda Jo's room, just fifteen feet away from where she stood; the lights were on in the room, and she saw a man whirl around and face her for a second or two, then quickly walk over and shut the bedroom door. She thought it was her boss, Linda Jo's married boyfriend Jim Mayfield. So she called out, "It's okay, it's only me. I'm going to bed."

She would say later that while she was going to bed, she was feeling angry at Mayfield. "That son of a bitch," she remembers thinking. "Why can't he leave her alone?" A few minutes later she heard the patio door open and close; she read for a few minutes, then fell asleep.

The next morning, she didn't hear Linda Jo stirring, so she opened her bedroom door. What she saw would haunt her for the rest of her life.

Linda Jo Edwards, the beautiful farm girl, the naive library assistant, lay on her back on the floor, nude, covered in blood, her limbs outstretched, her eyes staring lifelessly ahead. Paula stuffed her fist in her mouth, backed out of the room, and called the police.

They arrived to discover a scene of immense overkill. Linda Jo's face and head had been smashed with a five-pound statue from a credenza in the living room. She'd been stabbed in the neck nine times with a scissors. Her mouth was cut with a vegetable knife from the kitchen. The killer had stabbed her vagina over and over, cut her right breast, plunged the knife into her chest, rolled her over, and thrust the knife into her back three times.

It was clearly a horribly violent, frantic act, and yet there was no sign of struggle in the tiny eleven-by-twelve-foot bedroom, no indication that Linda Jo fought back. The iron was on and upright on the ironing board, the bed was made, her fingernails were intact—all signs indicating that the killer might have been someone she knew and let into her bedroom.

You would think that suspicion would fall on Linda Jo's jealous ex-lover, the man prone to violent outbursts of rage, the man who blamed her for the loss of his job, the man obsessed with her and unable to leave her, who matched the description Paula gave to the police of the man she'd seen in Linda Jo's room on the night of the murder: silver hair cut in a medium length touching the ears, wearing white tennis shorts, with a dark tan, about five feet eight inches tall and about 140 pounds, a slender man with wide shoulders. You would think he'd be the main suspect in fact. And that the police and prosecutors, this time, would have no reason to fabricate evidence against anyone else.

You would think that, wouldn't you?

Now who's being naive.

☐

In the days that followed, Paula told several people that the man she saw in Linda Jo's room that night was Mayfield. And he certainly wasn't acting like the grieving lover. The morning after the murder, an employee at the library told Mayfield that Linda Jo had been beaten badly and offered to drive him to her apartment. They sat in a car outside the Embarcadero Apartments, where the library employee suggested that Linda Jo might be dead. She said Mayfield started to cry, but his mood abruptly changed to fury, obsessing once again over the fact that "she ruined my life and cost me my job." That afternoon he went to the police, telling them he knew he'd be a suspect. He told them about his affair with Linda Jo. He agreed to take a polygraph the following Monday.

That's when it all went south. A few days later he popped into the office of a psychology professor at the college, who happened to have a state-of-the-art polygraph machine in his office, and asked him how to beat the machine. Later that day, his lawyer—Buck Files, the best defense attorney in Tyler—announced that Mayfield was not going to take the polygraph after all, and instructed the police never to contact Mayfield or his family without asking Buck's permission first.

From that point on, the police never again spoke to Mayfield, his wife, or anyone at the university. Mayfield hid behind his alibi: His dutiful wife and the daughter who hated Linda Jo both said he was home with them, and the police accepted it. They turned their attention to finding another suspect.

For Sergeant Eddie Clark, the man in charge of the investigation, finding Linda Jo's killer was personal. He'd grown up in Bullard like she had, knew her family very well, and felt he owed it to them to bring in her killer. A lot of pressure on a brand-new twenty-six-year-old homicide investigator.

He knew Mayfield had motive and opportunity, but he just couldn't believe that the university's library dean could be capable of such a savage murder. He was convinced that the key to solving this murder lay somewhere else in the Embarcadero apartment complex. He spent most of June and July knocking on the doors of two hundred of Linda Jo's neighbors and had countless male residents polygraphed.

But there was something else, too: While dusting for fingerprints at the crime scene, investigators had found two prints on the patio door that they couldn't account for. The fingerprint investigator, Doug Collard, told Clark, "When you find the man whose prints are on the sliding patio door, you will have your killer." Those words were a kind of mantra for Clark, a subliminal suggestion. He focused intently on finding the man whose prints were on the sliding patio door. It didn't take him long.

□

Kerry Max Cook was tending bar at the Holiday Club in Port Arthur, Texas, in the summer of 1977, a place he described later as a suit-and-tie haunt where businessmen would listen to soft rock like Lionel Richie's "Easy." He'd worked there since he left Tyler a few months earlier; the hickeys he'd gotten from the girl he met at the pool of the Embarcadero Apartments had long since faded, along with most memories of his brief afternoon fling with her. But that was all about to come rushing back.

On the afternoon of August 5, 1977, two men he'd never seen before came in and ordered a couple of beers. A few minutes later, he was summoned to the office by his manager, where the two men swooped in and, before he knew it, had manacled his hands with a pair of handcuffs.

"My name is Detective Eddie Clark," one of them said. "I am from Tyler, Texas. Kerry Max Cook, you are under arrest for the rape and murder of Linda Jo Edwards."

Kerry was dumbfounded. At the local police station, he later recalled, officers screamed furiously at him: "We know you killed her, you son of a bitch!" The interrogation was relentless: They pushed his head into the toilet and flushed it, demanding that he confess. Finally, he passed out and woke up on the floor of a cell.

He was flown back to Tyler and thrown in a cell with a steel bunk. Alone, freezing, and craving sleep, Kerry was terrified, until his parents came. Kerry was close with his family, and he begged them to help him. His father asked if he knew the girl who was murdered. He leaned in and whispered that he did, but his father cut him off. As Kerry recounted the story to me later, his father told him, "Kerry, don't tell anyone you were inside that apartment. If they ever place you there, they're going to pin that murder on you. Promise me you will keep your mouth shut."

Kerry promised. And thus began his horrible march toward death row.

□

After I finished the Joyce Ann Brown case in 1989, I was getting ready to go back to New Jersey when I ran into David Hanners, a Pulitzer Prize–winning reporter for *The Dallas Morning News*. His colleagues had done terrific work, exposing the evils of the prosecutors in the Brown case for all the world to see. The publicity they'd given us was invaluable, and I thanked him for all that his paper had done.

"Thanks, Jim," he said. "But I think you're leaving another one behind." He started to tell me about another case he'd been working on, but I cut him off cold.

"David, first of all, we got other cases going on here," I said. "It's not just Brown. I mean, we're snowed. We've got, literally, hundreds of requests coming in. We're trying our best to vet the cases. When I go back to Jersey, I've got, I don't know, seven or eight cases I'm working on. I'm sorry, David. That's just the way it is."

I should have known that a dogged reporter like David wouldn't give up that easily. Over the following months, he'd check in every once in a while, telling me a little more about this guy Kerry Max Cook, who he was sure was innocent. But I was swamped. Centurion was growing, but only slowly, and we could barely keep up with the cases we were working on, to say nothing of the nearly five hundred requests that were coming in each year.

David never gave up. He kept pestering me to look at all the articles he'd written on the Cook case. Finally, in exasperation as much as anything, I told him to send me the files. I also wrote to Kerry himself, asking him to write me a letter spelling it all out—his life story, his case, everything. I mentioned that another prisoner had written me a letter that was sixty pages long.

When Kerry's came, it was sixty-one. "You see," he wrote, "I'm one page more innocent than that other guy."

I settled down one afternoon to read Kerry's letter and David's articles. And when I read them, I could barely believe my eyes. Kerry's trial had been a circus of lies, half-truths, and misinformation. The prosecutors presented Kerry's fingerprints from Linda Jo's patio door as their main piece of physical evidence, and they got the fingerprint officer, Doug Collard—the one who said, "When you find the man whose prints are on the sliding patio door, you will have your killer"—to testify that the prints were just six to twelve hours old when he lifted them on the morning of the murder, which would have put Kerry in her apartment at the time of her death.

Even though every fingerprint expert in America knows you can't age a fingerprint.

Paula Rudolph, the roommate who saw the killer on the night of the murder—and who told everyone afterward that it was Linda Jo's lover Mayfield—had now changed her story. She testified that she couldn't really see clearly who was in that room, that all she could see were "shadows and planes on a shape, a figure." But when asked for the first time if the man she saw was Kerry Max Cook, she replied, "Yes, he fits."

The prosecutors did everything they could to paint Kerry as a deranged, homicidal maniac. They also, falsely, painted him as a secret homosexual, as a way to tilt the conservative jury against him. Their star witness was a friend of Kerry's, Robert Hoehn, who said he'd spent part of that night with Kerry and concocted a story that they'd had oral and anal sex and watched a movie—*The Sailor Who Fell from Grace with the Sea*—with scenes in it that had sexually aroused Kerry greatly. The prosecution presented to jurors the most inflammatory images they could, leaving the impression that Kerry had cut out Linda Jo's vagina, rolled it up in one of her missing stockings, and taken it away as a souvenir— even implying that he had eaten it.

And of course, there was the requisite jailhouse confession. A murder suspect named Edward "Shyster" Jackson testified that he was in a cell with Kerry and that Kerry had confessed to the murder. The prosecutor insisted that no deal was ever made with Jackson. He went so far as to say in his closing statement, "I will be yelling for Edward Jackson's head right before this rail of justice," just as he was calling for Kerry's head now. "I don't make deals with killers," he said.

Except, of course, that he had. One month after Kerry was convicted and sent to death row, Shyster was allowed to plead down to involuntary manslaughter from his murder rap, with a sentence of time served. A *Dallas Morning News* reporter tracked down Shyster Jackson a few weeks later. He admitted that he'd made up the whole Kerry confession in exchange for the deal with the prosecutors that got him out of prison.

It's worth noting that Shyster had served only two years on a first-degree murder charge (in a county jail, no less, allowing him to avoid the dreaded Texas state prison system). It's also worth noting that when he got out, he went to Missouri and committed *another* murder.

I believe that blood is on the hands of Smith County district attorney A. D. Clark, who cut that rotten deal. But that outrage would have to wait for another day. The outrage before me was the one I had to deal with now. As I pored over Kerry's letter and the trial transcripts that had been provided to me by David, it became clear to me: I was headed back to Texas.

□

Kerry Max Cook was the most exhausting man I ever met. The minute I sat down with him, across a steel mesh in the death row visiting room, he thanked me for considering his case. I said, "You're welcome, Kerry." Those were the last words I spoke for about an hour.

Kerry was a human volcano of words, a constant eruption of ideas and anger and thoughts and information and argument, his ideas flowing from one subject to the next without pause, a soliloquy that knew no bounds. His knees bounced up and down as he spoke, his arms flying about, gesticulating madly to emphasize his points. He was clearly very articulate and intelligent, and he had a stunning memory for facts and dates. But his engine seemed to only run in fifth gear.

I was taking notes furiously as he spoke, but finally I'd had enough. I tried to interject a few times, politely, but it didn't stop the train, didn't even slow it down. Finally, exasperated, I said, "Kerry, goddamn it, let me say something. You've talked for what seems like an hour or two hours. I've got something to say here, and I have some questions I want to ask you. Take a fucking breath, and let me interject something here."

I thought he'd get offended, once those words were out of my mouth. But at that moment, I had no idea of the ordeal he had been through these last thirteen years. The torment and abuse he'd suffered, day in and day out. Given all that, being cursed at across a prison visitation room divider hardly merited a blip on his radar. He quieted down and listened.

I began, in my methodical way, to go over some of the points of his case. Kerry was now the intense, focused individual I needed him to be, meticulously pointing out flaws in the government's case, clearly and concisely making a case for his own innocence. At one point, I told him, "Kerry, there's one thing I have a problem with. How did your fingerprints get on that patio door?"

He hesitated and looked away for just a second. "Oh, well, Jim, you know, yeah, I don't know, it must have been when I was window peeping at her. I saw her nude from the sidewalk and went up to get a closer look."

I wasn't 100 percent satisfied with that, but I let it go for now. One thing I was 100 percent satisfied with, though: This man was innocent. Innocent and railroaded. The DA had clearly set his sights on Kerry and done everything in his considerable power to make a case against him. I had no doubt that DA Clark had coached Shyster Jackson, and that he had persuaded the roommate, Paula, that she hadn't seen what she saw. I put no stock in the story of that witness who said he'd had sex with Kerry just before the murder. Or that the movie *The Sailor Who Fell from Grace with the Sea* was somehow crude enough to entice a man to rape and murder.

"I'm going to go talk to your attorneys," I told him. "And then we'll make a decision. But I'll tell you what I tell everybody, Kerry," I said, looking him straight in the eye. "If I ever catch you lying, man, I'm out of here. I'm going back to Jersey. We got a lot of work back there. I don't need you. You need us or somebody like us, but I don't need you."

"You have my word, Jim," he said.

A week later, after doing some checking up on some of what he told me, I was back in that room. I told him we were going to take on his case and waited a moment for that to sink in.

"This part is over, Kerry," I said. "Now I have some work to do."

□

From the beginning, I was obsessed with the facts of the case that pointed to James Mayfield. I began by seeking out the people who knew him—neighbors, colleagues, faculty members, old associates from his distant past. One by one I tracked them down: in person, by phone, however I could. Remember that this was before email, so there was no easy way to do this. I just had to methodically, ploddingly, put one foot in front of the other. I spent weeks at a time in Tyler and traveled to Mayfield's hometown of Coffeyville, Kansas, finding everyone I could who could tell me anything.

Here's what they *didn't* tell me: Not a single person I talked to said, "Oh, Jim would never do anything like that." One after another, they said, "This is a man with an explosive temper. I wouldn't put anything past him."

I also spent a lot of time digging into the world of Linda Jo Edwards, talking with her friends and colleagues, learning about her relationship with Mayfield. My heart ached for her, and for her family. I knew they deserved justice, and I knew they thought they'd achieved it with the conviction of Kerry Max Cook. I also knew that justice had eluded everyone involved in the case. It had eluded the Edwards family as surely as it had eluded Kerry and his family.

My job was to get Kerry out of jail, which did not, as I've said before, necessarily entail finding out who really killed Linda Jo. But the more I heard about her, the more I wanted to solve the case. Everybody I talked to loved Linda Jo. She had a beautiful personality, they told me. She was kind and sweet and brought joy to everyone around her.

It wasn't difficult for me to get people to talk. When I visit them, I'm the most unintimidating guy you can imagine. This friendly, paunchy guy with a sense of humor and a smile on his face walks up with his little clerical collar on, and people just naturally let their guard down. Plus, these people wanted to talk. I can't tell you how many of them said, "You're the first person that has shown any interest in this case. The police never talked to me."

The police never talked to them. That's what galled me. That's one of the dirtiest secrets of the corrupt criminal justice system—the tunnel vision of homicide detectives in these wrongful convictions. Once the police home in on a suspect, they don't *want* to hear anything about anyone else. It'll just gum up their case when they get to court. So they investigate their suspect and ignore all the other facts and suspects that are staring them in the face.

I couldn't ignore any of it. I suppose that after six months, when I'd talked to more than thirty people, I could have decided I had enough information. But I could never leave a stone unturned. Because you never know where the truth is hiding, unless you look everywhere.

Which is what I did. Which is what I do. Which is what you have to do. I think I interviewed seventy-five people by the time it was all said and done. I worked seven days a week in Tyler.

Sometimes, on Sunday mornings, I'd knock on doors, but no one would be home, because they were all quite religious Baptists. When I came back in the afternoon and said, "I'm sorry I missed you this morning," they'd say, "What? You came by this morning? I thought you were a minister. Didn't you go to church this morning?"

I'd laugh and say, "Hey, look, I just like to think I'm doing God's work on Sunday." I hoped that maybe I was.

I also found one other thing in my travels: a book that Mayfield had gotten in trouble for having in the school library. It was called *The Sexual Criminal: A Psychoanalytical Study*, a 1949 book containing lurid photos and descriptions of sexually mutilated female victims. When I compared the photos in the book with the photos of Linda Jo at the crime scene, I was shocked: Linda Jo's wounds and the position of the body were almost identical to some of the pictures in the book.

If you were looking for a way to stage a crime scene to make it look like the work of a deranged serial sex maniac, this was your manual. Is that what had happened here? I sure had my suspicions. I just had to figure out how to prove them.

□

I visited Kerry whenever I could, and for the most part those meetings were strictly business. I'd fill him in on what I'd done—when I could get a word in edgewise—and he'd go over every detail of his defense.

But sometimes, I would ask Kerry how life was going for him on death row. What he told me I can only describe as the worst hell a person could ever imagine. From the moment he'd arrived there, the bogus reputation he'd been branded with by the prosecution—a crazed homosexual sex killer who cut out a woman's vagina and ate it—preceded him. For days, he was kept in isolation and given food too rancid to eat. When he had the gall to ask for something as simple as a shower, they gave it to him—in their own way: A blanket was thrown over his head and inmates showered him with punches until he passed out.

It got much worse. At one point early on, he told me, a group of inmates cornered him. One of them had some kind of metal shard with white tape at its base. "Bitch, take off your clothes," he ordered. Kerry pleaded with the man to leave him alone. The man responded, "What's it gonna be, bitch, blood on my knife or shit on my dick?" The prisoner raped Kerry, then carved the words "good pussy" into his buttocks.

That wasn't the end of it. Once you're labeled a "punk" in prison—someone who is raped and doesn't retaliate—other inmates all try to make you their "bitch" too. Kerry was raped more than once. Beaten more than once. He refused to fight back because he believed that keeping his record clean was an important part of mounting his defense. But the more he refused to fight back, the more he was branded as weak, and the more furious and disgusting the attacks became.

The horrors visited upon him in prison were matched only by the cruel indifference of the criminal justice system that put him there. Kerry's lawyer appealed the case to the Court of Criminal Appeals, the highest court for criminal cases in Texas. The appeal languished for nine long and tortuous years, the longest period for an appeals court to rule on a death row inmate's appeal in American history. And so year after year, Kerry waited, enduring one dehumanizing, disgusting, horrible attack after another.

Overwhelmed, Kerry came to feel that he needed to get off death row any way he could. And so one day he snuck the blade out of a razor he'd been given to shave with and cut himself severely. Was he just trying to get into the infirmary? Was it an actual suicide attempt? I guess at first I thought it was a little of both. It would not be his last suicide attempt.

One day when I visited him, some weeks later, he seemed more shaken than usual. The torrent of words was gone; he seemed diminished, weak. When he told me what had happened, I became dizzy. I nearly passed out myself. He told me that in anguish he had written a suicide note, taken a full pack of prescription Dimetapp, then run a razor down his arms and legs. And then attempted to sever his penis.

I thanked the Lord his attempts at suicide were unsuccessful. I begged him to hold on, to find the strength and patience to endure. And I said a silent prayer myself, a prayer for my own fortitude and patience as well. A prayer that I would find a way to bring Kerry Max Cook out of this hell.

□

In December 1987, Kerry's nine-year wait for a decision from the Court of Criminal Appeals finally ended—the wrong way. After all that time, they denied his appeal. It was almost too much to bear. But then, to the surprise of everyone, and thanks to the doggedness of Kerry's new public defender, Scott Howe—just eleven days before Kerry was scheduled to die in June 1988—the U.S. Supreme Court issued a stay of execution.

Another victory followed, though it would take three more years. Scott, in a brilliant legal maneuver, went back to the Texas Court of Criminal Appeals—the very same one that had denied Kerry—and convinced them to reverse Kerry's conviction. They ordered a new trial, based on what Scott had come up with: a legal technicality that occurred in the punishment phase of his trial.

Here's what it was: Dr. James Grigson—known in the Texas press as "Doctor Death"—was a Texas forensic psychiatrist who testified in 167 capital trials, nearly all of which resulted in death sentences. He would interview the defendants and invariably say they were a danger to society and, if convicted, deserved the death penalty.

Only problem was, when he interviewed Kerry, he didn't bother to mention that he was representing the state and that anything Kerry said might be—and of course was—used against him in a court of law. And so, because he failed to read Kerry the *Miranda* rights, those phrases that anyone who's ever watched a cop show on TV knows by heart, Kerry's rights had been violated, the Court of Criminal Appeals ruled.

I was ecstatic, and so was Kerry. He was confident that with all the information I'd gathered—plus more that had been uncovered by David Hanners at *The Dallas Morning News*—the second trial was going to go differently. He was moved off death row, to the Smith County Jail. I'd never seen his spirits so high.

I didn't want to dampen those spirits, but privately I knew his case was far from a slam dunk. I had a lot more work to do. For starters, I needed to hire Kerry the best lawyer I could. Scott Howe was excellent, but he was an appeals lawyer, and I needed someone who could take this all the way through another trial. The problem was, I had spent a good deal of Centurion's meager budget on the case already. I knew I'd have to find someone kind and dedicated enough to take on the case for free.

I knew just the guy. Paul Nugent, the lawyer I'd worked with to free Clarence Brandley, is a great listener. When you start telling him a story, it's like you're the only person on earth. And the more he heard about Kerry Max Cook's story, the more interested he became.

"There's only one problem," I told him. "I can't pay you a cent."

"Well, you didn't pay me for Brandley, so I guess that's my standard fee now with you," Paul said with a grin. "Don't worry, Jim. I'm in."

I thanked him and later thanked his partner Mike DeGeurin, too, because Paul couldn't have done it without Mike's consent. We talked for a while about what it would be like to deal with a death penalty case, especially in Texas. I learned how deeply Paul believed that the death penalty was not only unfair but immoral.

"There's churches all over the place in Texas," he said to me. "People like to tell you how Christian they are. Well, one of the commandments, I think, is 'thou shalt not kill.' It doesn't have an asterisk that says it's okay in Texas if it's done by lethal injection."

So just like that, Paul became Kerry's pro bono defender. Paul Nugent was, in so many ways, an answer to my prayers. Personally, he was a pleasure to work with. After the Brandley case I'd stayed friendly with him and his wife, Mary, who's a delightful woman, and I enjoyed spending time around their six kids. I even became godfather to their daughter Dorothy. It was a big Irish Catholic family, and I felt like a friendly uncle who used to stay in the room above the garage.

Professionally, he was everything I could ask for. He's one of those lawyers who's not in it just for the money. I mean, he needs to work and pay the mortgage and put his kids through college like anyone else, but he passionately believes in justice and fairness and is the kind of guy who gets on a case like this and becomes consumed, doing whatever he can to save his client's life.

The first time Kerry met him, he liked Paul right away, too—partly because, against all rules and risking all sorts of punishment, Paul smuggled in a cheeseburger and a soda for Kerry in his briefcase. For someone living on prison food, a cheeseburger can be like a gift from the gods. Kerry thought, hey, this guy's got game; first meeting and he's bringing in contraband. This guy's gonna be okay.

By the end of that first meeting, Paul's reaction to Kerry was the same as mine had been. He was impressed by his intelligence and understanding of the facts, but Paul was so overwhelmed by the avalanche of information, thoughts, ideas, theories, legal citations, and fury that was Kerry Max Cook that he wondered if he'd made a mistake. I promised him that whenever possible, I'd be the one to meet with Kerry, without Paul. We would divide and, with any luck, conquer.

And so the clock started ticking for Kerry's retrial. Paul and I went at it.

□

The first success was mine. I had a series of meetings with the man who would be the lead trial prosecutor, David Dobbs. It was a calculated move: I gave him memos I had written detailing all of my investigation, everything I had that pointed to Mayfield as the killer.

In exchange, he gave me police statements and grand jury testimony that Kerry's defense had never received. I hoped that there would be enough in those documents to warrant showing the opposition my hand.

Holy shit. Included among the papers was the grand jury testimony of Robert Hoehn, the guy who was with Kerry in his Embarcadero apartment on the night of the murder and who was the basis of all those theories about the crazed homosexual killer worked up into a frenzy by scenes in a movie.

First off, Hoehn had told the grand jury that he had had dinner with Kerry three days before the murder and noticed all these hickeys on Kerry's neck. He testified that Kerry told him that he'd gotten them from none other than Linda Jo Edwards, a girl he'd met at the swimming pool after seeing her parade around the apartment nude. That they'd made out in her apartment.

I couldn't believe what I was reading! Here, in my hands, was proof not only that the district attorney at the time, A. D. Clark, knew how Kerry's prints got on that patio door but that he'd suppressed the evidence. Hoehn also told the grand jury that he'd dropped Kerry off at his apartment at about 12:30 a.m. on the night of the murder—about the same time Linda Jo's roommate was coming home. That Kerry had invited him in, but he didn't go. And that Kerry was wearing blue satin shorts that night, not the white shorts Paula had seen on the man in her roommate's room. All of which would make it inconceivable that Kerry had switched clothes, run over to Linda Jo's apartment, and committed the murder.

Hoehn also testified before the grand jury that earlier that night Kerry was paying no attention to the movie that was playing; that they didn't have sex; and that Kerry was neither frustrated, angry, nor upset. In other words, not one whit of what he testified to at Kerry's trial was true. All of that had to have been made up later—at the insistence of Smith County district attorney A. D. Clark, was my guess.

There was more: Two other young men who were hanging out

with Hoehn and Kerry testified before the grand jury that Kerry had bragged to them about his exploits with Linda Jo as well. So there were three separate corroborating statements indicating how Kerry's fingerprints got on that door. All of which were suppressed by the district attorney. None of it came out at trial.

I was ecstatic. And I was pissed. Ecstatic because I'd found a smoking gun. And pissed that Kerry had lied to me; he'd been in her apartment after all, not just peeping through her window as he'd claimed.

It was confirmed for me when I took forensic fingerprint expert George Bonebrake, the retired director of the FBI's fingerprint division, out to the apartment where Linda Jo was killed. He had a copy of a photo showing Kerry's fingerprints on the door. He showed me how, based on the angle of the prints, Kerry must have been *inside* the apartment when he touched that door, closing it behind him.

The next day, I visited Kerry at the county jail in Tyler, loaded for bear. As nice as I can be when I'm wearing my collar and playing the avuncular Irishman, I can be just as furious when someone crosses me.

Before I could get a word out, Kerry said he had something important to tell me.

"Well, it better be pretty damned good because what I have to say is pretty damned important too, my friend," I said through gritted teeth. "So start talking."

Kerry proceeded to tell me everything. That he'd lied about not knowing Linda Jo. That he'd been in her apartment, making out, three days before the murder, and that that's how his fingerprints got on the door. He told me about his father saying he should never admit to knowing the girl, how he idolized his father and did exactly what his father had said.

"I'm sorry, Jim, I'm so sorry. I know I should have told you about this a long time ago. But with the trial coming up, I had to come clean. I know you're angry."

"Angry?" I exploded. "Motherfucker! You don't know angry.

Kerry, I didn't sleep last night because I was so pissed off. I want you to know that this is why I came here today—to confront you about this. I figured it out. And I was trying to decide if I should do exactly what I told you I'd do if you ever lied to me."

That thought hung in the air. Kerry's eyes were wide. He had the look of a man whose life hung in the balance, which of course it did. I stood up and took a deep, deep breath.

"Okay, man. Look, I'm glad you fessed up. I guess that's something."

It wasn't hard to imagine why, of course. A man doesn't stay silent about a detail like this for fifteen years and then suddenly come clean, one minute before the bell rings. I had told him I was taking a fingerprint expert out to the scene. Kerry's a smart guy; he must have put two and two together. He must have decided to try to beat me to the punch, which he had, by about two seconds.

But I didn't bother telling him any of that. I saw the fear in his eyes, and I saw the remorse. I said the only thing I could say.

"I'm not gonna drop the case, Kerry. But you fucking better not ever, ever, *ever* lie to me again. Are we clear?"

"We're clear, Jim," he said, in a voice that sounded like a vow, and a prayer.

"Okay. Now let's get back to work."

☐

The next success belonged to Paul Nugent. He also paid a visit to David Dobbs, the prosecutor, and while they were talking, Dobbs pulled some paper out of a box on his desk. Paul looked into the box and noticed a binder. "What's this?" he said. Dobbs pulled it out. "Oh, that's just Collard's report," he said, Collard being the fingerprint expert Doug Collard, of course—the one who testified that the prints on the patio door were less than twelve hours old.

Paul literally snatched it out of his hands. "This is very critical," he said. "We need this."

A sheepish Dobbs made a copy for Paul, who couldn't wait to read it. Halfway home his curiosity got the better of him, so he pulled over to the side of the road and started reading.

Paul couldn't believe his eyes. He discovered, in the binder, a thirteen-page memo written by Collard admitting that there's absolutely no way you can age a print. Seems there's a group called the International Association for Identification that was alarmed when they read about his testimony; in response, he admitted that he knew you cannot determine the age of a fingerprint. In his defense, he said that District Attorney Clark had insisted that he do so.

So now we had proof that not only did the DA's office fail to turn over things they should have; they had actually suppressed and hidden exculpatory evidence that would have helped an accused man avoid the death penalty.

Paul couldn't contain himself. He drove to the nearest pay phone to call me and tell me what he'd found. All I could say was, "Those fucking bastards."

□

The final success belonged to both of us. We went to see Shyster Jackson in the Missouri State Penitentiary, where he was doing life for the murder he committed in that state, and we got him to admit, on the record, to what he'd told the Dallas paper: that he'd totally made up Kerry's supposed jailhouse confession. At a pretrial hearing soon afterward, he told the judge that not only had DA Clark cooked up the idea, but he showed Jackson crime scene photos to help him craft his testimony against Cook. And as the icing on the cake, he said that the DA had made a secret deal to drop murder charges against Jackson, even though at Kerry's trial they insisted that no such deal was ever made.

So we thought we were sitting pretty when the trial date was approaching in late 1992. That's when we ran smack up against Judge Joe Tunnell.

Because of the enormous publicity surrounding the case, the venue had been changed to Georgetown, Texas—now a fairly hip suburb of Austin, but back then an excruciatingly conservative town with a painfully hostile judge sitting in the courtroom. From the start, every ruling by Judge Tunnell was as unfair as it was destructive to our case. He refused to allow any of the grand jury testimony to be entered into evidence—testimony that showed Kerry had been in Linda Jo's apartment days before the murder, thus explaining the fingerprints on the door. He disallowed Shyster Jackson's recantation. And beyond all credulity, he disallowed the memo in which the fingerprint expert admitted lying about how he aged the fingerprints.

While we did manage to get the judge to disallow the idea that the fingerprints were just six to twelve hours old, he somehow allowed the fingerprint expert to say that the prints were "fresh," which amounted to the same thing.

While the judge didn't permit us to bring Shyster Jackson in to recant his testimony, at least we wouldn't have a phony jailhouse confession to deal with this time around—or so I thought. Because lo and behold, out of nowhere, a former Smith County reserve deputy sheriff stepped into the breach and filed an affidavit saying that he had escorted Kerry in an elevator during jury selection at his first trial. Kerry, the deputy said, for reasons unknown, turned to him in the elevator and blurted out, "I killed her and I don't give a shit what they do to me."

Why on earth hadn't he come forward saying as much *for fourteen years*? And why on earth was he suddenly coming forward now? It was beyond unbelievable to me. And yet this testimony, the judge ruled, would be admissible.

Kerry, seated between me and Paul at the defense table, could barely hide his outrage as ruling after ruling went against us. "Jim," he hissed at me. "Can you fucking believe this? We're getting set up! This is a setup!"

"Not now, Kerry," I pleaded with him. "You have to contain yourself."

But in the bullpen afterward, I let him vent to me, and I probably vented back to him more than I should have. "This is an outrage, Kerry," I told him. "Oh my God. This judge is just hamstringing us. We can't do anything. This is ridiculous."

I saw his shoulders sag, and I was sorry I'd said that. But it was just an out-of-body experience, watching the judge making these rulings. Once again it seemed like truth had no place in the court of law, and as much as I should have become inured to that idea by now, I still couldn't fathom the depths of deceit and dishonesty being paraded before the jury.

"Look, we got our work cut out for us," I told Kerry, trying to buck him up. "But we still got a chance. We got Mayfield. We got a great case. Wait till we put our defense on. When we bring in all those Mayfield witnesses. Then things will turn our way."

But they didn't. The judge severely restricted what those witnesses could say about Mayfield, and again it stopped us from making our case. One after another, his rulings did everything to help the prosecution preserve their phony narrative. I was stuck somewhere between outraged and numb.

I think the most galling moment came when prosecutor Jack Skeen gave his closing argument, telling the jury, "Ladies and gentlemen, you have not heard one piece of evidence that in any way indicates that Mr. Cook was in that apartment prior to the night of the murder." Well, true, technically—they had not heard it, because the judge had excluded it from the trial! I think if I had any shred of faith left in the honesty and integrity of the system, it was crushed at that very moment. A moment I will, sadly, remember for the rest of my life.

There was one more shock to come. The jury, during deliberations, asked to see the jeans that Linda Jo was wearing that night. They unrolled them, and out fell her stocking, the one that Kerry had, according to the DA, wrapped Linda Jo's body parts up in to take away as souvenirs. The cops had never even bothered to look at the evidence, much less examine it for clues.

But in the end, it didn't matter. Paul had fought as hard as he could, and he seemed to have made some headway: The jury deliberated for five days and came back hopelessly deadlocked, 6–6. Paul couldn't win this one, but had battled the prosecutors to a draw. The judge declared a mistrial. It certainly wasn't the outcome we were hoping for. But given all the evidence that had been excluded, it felt like something of a moral victory, anyway.

The state decided to try Kerry a third time, and in 1994 we went to trial again. But it was new judge, same old story. Judge Robert Jones made the same rulings that Judge Tunnell had made, and once again we were terribly hamstrung in trying to make our case.

This time there was a new outrage: Judge Jones allowed the prosecution to bring in an FBI "expert," David Gomez, who had just completed his two-year training as a violent crimes analyst. He testified that the facts of the crime led him to conclude that this was a "lust" murder committed by a stranger. But our own expert, Robert Ressler—one of the founders of the FBI's behavioral science unit and its director for sixteen years, who has co-written two "bibles" on the subject of violent homicide (which, in fact, Gomez admitted under cross-examination were the primary references in his training)—was, astonishingly, barred from testifying by Judge Jones, who seemed hell-bent on subverting us.

Ressler was prepared to explain why it was so obvious that this was a "domestic homicide" committed by someone the victim knew—partly because there was no sign of a struggle, largely because that kind of fury and overkill is often seen in murder by a lover or spouse. But the jury never got to hear a word of it. Even though by law and common practice it is perfectly acceptable for expert witnesses to receive such material, Jones claimed that the defense should not have given Gomez's testimony to Ressler to review, prior to Ressler's testifying.

It was an outrage, and it harmed us immeasurably. At the end of the trial, Paul and I sat with Kerry and tried to keep his spirits up.

"It doesn't look good, does it, Jim?" he said to me.

"Kerry," I told him, "we need to pray here. Take my hand."

He held my hand and closed his eyes.

My prayer was short and sweet. "Dear Heavenly Father," I said. "Please give the jury the wisdom and insight to see through this mountain of lies offered by the witnesses for the prosecution. Help them see that Kerry is an innocent man and that he truly is a lamb among wolves. And provide those who see this sham of a trial for what it is the courage to speak up and make their views known. We ask this in Christ's name."

Just then, a tap on the windowpane cut me off. It was one of the prison guards.

"There's a note," he said. "A verdict."

Kerry opened his eyes and stared at me with a look of peace, of acceptance, as though he already knew his fate.

"Whatever happens," he said to Paul and me, "thank you for fighting so hard for me. I love you both."

Well, here's what happened. After three days of deliberations, the jury had asked that Agent Gomez's testimony be read back to them—the testimony saying this was a lust crime, which we were never allowed to rebut with our own expert. Within thirty-nine minutes of hearing that, they came back with their verdict.

Guilty.

Another unanswered prayer.

I'm not sure what happened after that. My head was spinning. I might have even blacked out for a few seconds. I don't remember talking to Paul or saying goodbye to Kerry. I remember seeing him led out of the courtroom, and I remember him looking back at me. It was like watching him tossed overboard, slowly drifting away to sea, drowning, and I was helpless to save him.

The next days were a blur as well. During the punishment phase, Kerry stood before the judge and said, "With respect to the court, and with respect to the jury, and with respect to the victim's family, I am an innocent man. God forgive them, they know not what they do."

Judge Jones sentenced him to death.

I was disconsolate as Paul and I stood with Kerry in the finger-print room afterward. Kerry, remarkable soul that he is, took the moment to thank Paul and me again for all we had done.

"This isn't over, Kerry," I said, grabbing his shoulders. "This isn't over. I will never stop fighting until I walk you out of here a free man."

"It's over, Jim," he said to me. "Get on that elevator and walk away and don't look back. There is nothing more that can be done. You have to let me go."

Tears fell from his eyes.

"I will never let you go, Kerry," I said. "There is always something more that can be done. I promise you. I will find it. Never give up hope."

But as I got on that elevator and thought about what I just said—there is always something more that can be done—I wondered, for the first time, if maybe that wasn't true.

☐

I flew home overcome by waves of fury and sadness. I went over it all again and again: You see those witnesses up there, lying. You know they're lying. You absolutely know it. You know the prosecutor knows they're lying. And then you have that fucking hostile judge, Robert Jones, ten times worse than Judge Tunnell, who preceded him.

The words floated to the front of my consciousness, once again, and they refused to leave: *Where is God in all this?*

The minute I landed, I called Kate. I must have ranted at her for half an hour. She let me talk. "I don't know how you've endured all this so far," she said. "I don't know how you could have done this. You did all you could. It wasn't your fault."

"Then whose fault is it? Is this God's fault?" I cried. "You know, Kate, at this point, I don't even know if God exists."

At that Kate fell silent. She was not one to talk about religion with me, but she knew how much my faith had guided me to that point. She must have known that without that faith, I was like a man on a crumbling ledge, hovering over the abyss.

And so I was.

With nowhere else to turn, I called Dick Streeter, the minister at my church, who had helped me find my way to the seminary in the first place. I told him about how profoundly, painfully, my faith had been shaken. There was a Catholic retreat center right across the street from the church; he urged me to think about spending some time there, searching my soul—and the Bible—for answers.

And so I found myself, a few nights later, in a spartan room with a single bed, sitting at a small desk with a lamp, reading scripture, trying to find my way home. I prayed, fervently, but at the same time found myself seriously questioning the power of prayer. Prayer is my way of speaking to God, and scripture is the way I believe that God speaks to me. As I prayed, I became keenly aware of my own doubts that God was listening. And so instead I buried myself in scripture, because it was there, and only there, that I could hear his voice.

On the third night, while reading Jesus's Sermon on the Mount in the Gospel of Matthew, I came across a passage that jolted me. It was like Jesus was talking directly to me himself. In the passage, he was saying, "Love your enemies, so that you may be sons of the Father, for he makes his sun rise on the evil and on the good, and sends rain on the just and the unjust."

I bet I'd read those words a thousand times before, but they'd never hit me like they did that night. I stared at the passage, realizing I'd found my answer. It was a bewildering one, and it frustrated the hell out of me.

"Really?" I thought to myself. "Is that your answer to what goes on down here? You don't intercede at all? You sit back and watch what we human beings do to each other?"

And then, inexplicably, a sense of deep understanding pervaded me. I realized that it was Jesus's way of speaking to me—directly, to me—to tell me that this is just the way it is.

It rains on the just, and it rains on the unjust.

There is nothing I can do to change that.

It said to me that there will never be a time when justice reigns unfettered. I'm going to win some and I'm going to lose some. The unjust will be punished sometimes, but the just will be punished sometimes, too.

And then I thought, yeah, but not if I can help it.

It was a revelation, not one I particularly enjoyed, but a true one: Sometimes, the truth *won't* set you free. I was certain that God wanted justice to prevail. But just as certainly, I realized that it was up to us humans to make that happen.

And so, in the days that followed, as I prepared to leave the retreat and get back to work, I knew I would have to grapple with two conflicting feelings: the presence of an enduring faith, and the places in me where that faith was absent. After that, I spoke to God less often; mostly I let God speak to me, through scripture, as God had spoken to me that week at the retreat center. As God had on another fateful night, fifteen years earlier.

Sixteen

▥

I came back from New York after I'd been rolled by that Times Square prostitute feeling pretty low. It was a few weeks after New Year's, and that Saturday night I was home reading scripture as usual. But something felt different this time. This time, I was reading it like my life depended on it.

I came across a passage in which a young rich man comes up to Christ and says, What must I do to inherit eternal life? And, in the passage that follows, Jesus says, Sell all that you have, and come follow me. The young rich man walks away in sorrow because he knows he can't do that.

But I looked back again at the words Christ spoke: In essence, he was telling the young man, Give up your life. Come, follow me.

The words haunted me. I don't know why. Maybe it was the strain of living a double, triple, quadruple life; maybe it was the shame of all the things I'd been hiding. But I felt like I was the man in that story, as though Christ was telling *me* to sell everything and follow him. As though I might turn the page and see my name printed right there. It scared the hell out of me.

I came across another passage in which Jesus is telling his disciples that if you save your life, you will lose it, but if you lose your life for my sake, you'll find a new one. And I thought, well, the life I'm living now is deteriorating anyway. (I swayed for a moment into the Gospel According to Bob Dylan: When you ain't got nothing, you got nothing to lose.) I read on, and more and more whatever I read felt like it was written precisely for me. It was scary, yes, but it was thrilling, too.

When I'd joined Hay, I had wanted to work hard, find new business, and eventually become a senior partner. After three or four years of working there, I'd lost that hunger. It just didn't matter to me anymore. Whatever purpose it had offered me had dissipated. I yearned in that moment for a more authentic life. I've always thought of that as meaning that regardless of your station in life, you look after the interests of others just as much as, if not more than, your own. It's about doing what's good and right; namely, as the prophet Micah says, "To do justice, love kindness, and walk humbly with your God."

And perhaps that's why all the running around and carousing I had been doing had lost whatever thrill it used to inspire in me. I had bottomed out. Getting robbed might have been the moment that opened my eyes, but now I could see more clearly that the life I'd been living had been only an illusion of happiness, a mirage.

I went back and read the passage again: *If you lose your life for my sake, you'll find a new one.* Inside me, I could feel that new life emerging.

The next day, after church, I talked to the minister, Dick Streeter, about an idea that had started to form in my mind throughout this process and that had become a bit firmer the night before.

I said, Dick, I'm thinking of going to the seminary, and I have to ask you a question: Am I crazy?

I talked to him about how he was touching people's hearts and souls, and all I was touching was their pocketbooks. I said, I know I'm thirty-seven years old and I'll be way older than all the other seminarians, but my life is turning to dust before my eyes and I need something more.

Dick smiled at me and told me that God works in mysterious ways. He didn't preach to me or tell me what to do. He told me to keep reading scripture; the answer will come to you.

□

It was a few Saturdays later, a cold February night. I picked up my dog-eared maroon leather-covered Bible and randomly turned to the last chapter in the Gospel of John, where the resurrected Christ is speaking to Peter. He tells him, When you were young, you girded yourself and walked where you would. But when you are older, you will stretch out your hands and another will gird you and carry you where you do not wish to go. And then he said, "Follow me."

And somehow, once again, I felt like it was speaking directly to me. That somehow Christ was telling me that when I was young, I did whatever the hell I wanted to, but now I'm older, and I have to give myself up and let some force outside myself lead me where I don't want to go.

That did it. I knew what I wanted to do. What I had to do. What I was going to do.

I was overcome with a feeling of relief, like water pouring into a parched valley. I looked out the window and a gentle snow had started falling, and the wind was whipping it against the window, but inside it was bright and warm. I turned my gaze away from the window and back to the page of the Bible in my lap. Out loud, I heard myself say, "Thank you, Lord," and it made me laugh.

The following Monday morning, I walked into the office of my boss, Bill Dinsmore, and told him I was resigning. "I know you're going to have a hard time believing this," I said, "but I'm going to join the seminary to become a pastor."

"Seminary?" he said. "I didn't even know you went to church!"

I smiled. "There's a lot of things you don't know, my friend. But we'll save that for another time."

Bill and I agreed that I would stay on for a while—turned out to be half a year—to finish up some of the work I'd started. But my life was changed from that day forth. I never saw Brandy again, or any of those hookers in Times Square. I was done with all of that (well, except for the stripper at my going-away party. One step at a time, I guess).

I thought back on how, when I was younger, I girded myself and walked where I would. And now I was prepared, truly prepared, to stretch out my hands and let another carry me where I did not wish to go. Had you told me then that that place would be a prison cell in Trenton, talking to a junkie named Chiefie, and spending the rest of my life fighting for him and others like him, I would have had only one response.

Surely, God works in mysterious ways.

Seventeen

TEXAS, AUGUST 2000

The day I left the retreat, after my defeat in the Kerry Max Cook case, I took stock of where Centurion had been and where we were going.

Certainly, there was an upside to the renown we were beginning to garner. All of those stories on *60 Minutes* and *48 Hours* and in national and local papers hadn't gone unnoticed. By 1993 we had 825 benefactors from all across the nation, who had given us upwards of $300,000 per year.

My foray into Hollywood hadn't gone unnoticed, either; out of nowhere, celebrities of all stripes were rallying to the cause. Suddenly Tony Bennett was performing at a fund-raiser for Centurion in Bel-Air. Brian Dennehy and Richard Dreyfuss started speaking at our events as well. Politicians too: Former U.S. senator Bill Bradley got involved; former Texas governor John Connally (who was shot along with President Kennedy) reached out to me to discuss a case. Johnnie Cochran, the flamboyant and controversial lawyer from the O. J. Simpson case, spoke on our behalf—right in the middle of O. J.'s trial!

The funding kept me from having to take any restaurant jobs, and I'm thankful for that, but more important, it allowed us to increase our caseload and deal with the nearly twelve hundred new requests that our staff and six volunteers were drowning in. We were able to spend money more freely on the cases we were working on.

We were handling ten cases a year by then and had added two full-time staff members besides Kate and me.

We kept on growing. By 1995, we were up to a thousand benefactors and a total income of just a hair under $400,000; by the next year our caseload had increased to fifteen. I could hardly catch my breath for how overwhelmed I was by the kindness of strangers.

But through it all, the kindest stranger—and the most important to our growth—was a guy named Jay Regan. I had met him at a memorial service of a friend a few years back. Jay had earned a fortune on Wall Street in the 1980s by doing something no one had done before. He was fascinated by a mathematics professor at UC Irvine named Ed Thorp who had used computers to develop a theory for beating blackjack—the now widely known concept of card counting. Jay wondered if Thorp's pioneering work in probability theory could help him beat the stock market the way Thorp had beaten the casinos.

It could, and it did. The firm they created, Princeton Newport Partners, was the first of what came to be known as quantitative hedge funds. It garnered them millions.

It also gained them the notice of the feds. On the morning of December 17, 1987, fifty armed U.S. marshals in bulletproof vests bounded up the stairs to the third floor of PNP's offices in downtown Princeton, terrifying the employees and carting off three hundred boxes of PNP's files. Soon Jay found himself facing federal charges and, if convicted, real prison time.

"We were facing racketeering charges," Jay told me later. "And I mean racketeering is serious shit. I mean, you think about racketeering, you think, well, you must have been killing people and shooting people and all this stuff. But we were selling bonds and buying them back the next day. I mean, give me a break, right?"

The aggressive U.S. attorney in the case was none other than Rudy Giuliani, and it quickly became clear that Giuliani's target wasn't really Regan, or PNP, but the notorious junk-bond trader Michael Milken, with whom PNP had done business. Jay says his lawyers came to him and told him Giuliani was offering a deal: Testify against Milken and you won't go to jail.

Regan says he instructed his lawyer thusly: "Tell them they can go fuck themselves."

Jay and his partners were convicted of illegal stock manipulation, but before he served any time, the U.S. Court of Appeals in New York vacated the convictions, saying they were based on bad evidence. Jay was exonerated. He was also shaken to his very core. He had been absolved of all wrongdoing, but he knew that he'd been a hairsbreadth from prison.

He emerged from the experience a changed man. Out of the blue, one afternoon in 1992, I got a call from Jay, who came to visit me at Centurion. I started showing him pictures of the people we had freed from prison, and the innocent ones still behind bars, and I could tell it was having an effect on him.

"This could have been me," he said. "I was wrongly convicted, but I didn't spend one day in jail. Because I had the best attorneys in the world, and I could mount my defense and not worry about the cost. I had everything going for me, Jim. These guys have nothing going for them. What do they have going for them?" He went quiet for a second. "All they have is you, Jim," he said. "These guys have no hope of ever being free unless you guys are able to get them out."

I was never great at asking people for money, and I didn't know how to bring it up with Jay. But I didn't have to.

"Look, I know better than anybody what it costs to defend yourself when you're innocent," he said. "I'm gonna do everything I can to help you out."

From that day forward, Centurion was a changed institution. Not only did Jay donate generously, but he opened up his Rolodex to us and began introducing me to power players on Wall Street who could help our convicted innocents be freed.

"I got a lot of skepticism from these guys at first," Jay said. "You know, people would say, if these guys were convicted, they probably did it. But I would just sit down with them and say, look, I went through this crap. We got charged with something we didn't do. And I would tell the story of a specific case, and they would begin to see it. I could see the lights going on in their heads. And then, as each case came up and got resolved, they became big believers."

And there was a lot to believe in, in those heady days after I left the retreat. We freed another six prisoners in the three years after I'd shaken off my dismay and gotten back in the race. We weren't alone by then. The world had shifted in the decade since I'd started this work. Dozens of innocent men and women were being exonerated and freed each year, thanks in no small part to the growth of Barry Scheck and Peter Neufeld's Innocence Project and the exponential increase in the sophistication of DNA testing. Where I'd felt like a lone voice in the wilderness for so long, now it felt like the nation was finally waking up to the realization that false imprisonment was no rare occurrence or strange aberration but an endemic problem in the system. It helped, as we moved forward, to not have to start from scratch with every case, convincing everyone that it's entirely possible that our client was railroaded. The pendulum was finally starting to swing our way, and Centurion was riding high.

But there was some unfinished business I had to attend to. As thrilling as the rise of Centurion was in this moment, I couldn't rest until I finished a job I'd left undone.

□

The last time I had seen Kerry Max Cook, after his reconviction, he told me to get on the elevator and never look back, just to let him go. And of course, I ignored him.

I went back to see him whenever I could, but I could tell something had changed. The spark, the life, the torrent of words and arguments and ideas, the hurricane that was Kerry Max Cook, had abated. He seemed defeated, lost at sea.

"Kerry, I'm worried about you. Are you letting go?" I asked him.

"No, Jim, I'm not letting go," he said.

I wasn't so sure. But I will say this: Kerry was full of surprises. He was turning to Jesus, and the Bible, to help him through, as so many men and women in prison do. One day, when I came to visit him, he seemed more buoyed up in spirits than I'd seen him in a while. I asked him about it, and he told me he'd found a Bible passage that meant a lot to him.

"Can I read it to you?" he asked, and I said of course, but when I heard what the passage was, I almost fainted dead away.

He fumbled through a well-worn Bible for a few minutes. "Here it is," he said. He read, "Then Jesus told His disciples, 'If anyone wants to come after Me, he must deny himself and take up his cross and follow Me. For whoever wants to save his life will lose it; but whoever loses his life for My sake will find it.'"

He looked up at me. "Jim," he said, "you've got a weird look on your face."

"That's exactly the passage that got me into this work," I told him. "I read that one night and it literally changed my life."

"Mine too," Kerry said with a smile. "I guess God works in mysterious ways."

"Heard that once or twice as well," I told him.

But what I didn't say was this: I wasn't so sure I could count on God's help anymore. I was still determined to see to it that Kerry walked out of that cell a free man. But if I couldn't turn to God for help, I did know just where I should turn.

□

Paul Nugent had, quite heroically, represented Kerry pro bono through his second and third trials. But he told me he just couldn't go on working on the case for free anymore. Fortunately, he didn't have to. Another angel stepped up to the plate: One of the billionaire philanthropists whom Jay Regan introduced me to asked me how much I needed. I wrote a "back of the envelope" budget to the tune of $365,000, and the next thing I knew he'd wired it to our account.

Thanks to that beneficence, I was able to retain not only Paul but two other lawyers as well, Rocket Rosen and Cheryl Wattley, and pay for up to eight forensic experts. We agreed on a fee of $25,000 for Paul to write an appeals brief to the Texas Court of Criminal Appeals.

Best $25,000 I ever spent. Paul wrote an astounding 213-page brief, describing fifty-five points of error committed by the trial judge and the prosecutor during Kerry's last trial. And it worked! On November 6, 1996, in a 5–3 decision, the CCA reversed the conviction and ordered a new trial. The court ruled that the Smith County prosecutor's office "allowed itself to gain a conviction based on fraud and ignored its own duty to seek the truth" and that "the illicit manipulation on the part of the State permeated the entire investigation of the murder."

The DA appealed the decision, of course, but the CCA denied their request to reconsider. That day, Kerry remembers screaming so loud that the guards came rushing from the other end of the building, mistaking his screams for a riot.

I was ecstatic, too. It took a while, but Kerry was transferred off death row and up to the Smith County Jail again to await a new trial. On the morning of November 13, 1997, the hostile judge Robert Jones set bail at $100,000 cash—thinking we could never come up with that kind of money—but Jay Regan waved his magic wand and wired that amount to the court.

An hour later, Paul and I were in the sheriff's office, watching them take the handcuffs off Kerry Max Cook.

"Are you ready for this?" I asked him.

Kerry beamed at me. "I've been ready for twenty years," he said.

Later, in his brutally honest memoir, *Chasing Justice*, Kerry describes that first night of freedom—sitting in a chair on his mother's front porch until the sun came up: "Birds began to chirp and my mama's next-door neighbor's dogs barked. I was so mesmerized by the sights and sounds of my first morning as a free man that I could have been stark naked in the center of Alaska and felt no chill."

He wrote that his mother asked him if he'd slept at all. "No, Mama, I didn't," he said. "I want to savor every second of this because what if it doesn't last—what if they come back and get me? They always find a way to win."

Not this time, though. Inexplicably, as the fourth trial approached, the prosecutors finally submitted the panties of the victim, Linda Jo Edwards, for testing to see if they contained any semen and, if so, to test that semen for DNA. We were still waiting for the results of those tests when, just before the trial was to start, on February 26, 1999, the prosecutors offered Kerry a plea deal. If you plead no contest, they told him, you can go home a free man, your sentence reduced to the time you have already served.

Kerry was furious. He wanted nothing less than total exoneration. It was a horrible choice, and the judge had given us all of one hour for Kerry to make a decision. Kerry and I, along with his lawyers, retreated to the home I'd rented nearby for the month.

"Look, Kerry," I said. "It's your life. If you want to accept this, I can perfectly support you and understand why. After all you've gone through these last twenty-some-odd years. So if you decide to accept it, hey, man, I'm with you. If you want to go to trial, I'm with you. It's your life. You have to make the decision."

And so he excused himself from the room and went into the bathroom. And five minutes later, he came back out and said, "I want to go home. I want to go home today. Let's do it."

So we did.

Months later, the results of the DNA test came back—and yes, it turned out that there was semen on Linda Jo's panties. And guess what. The semen belonged not to Kerry Max Cook but to her lover, James Mayfield. Part of me wished that we'd waited so we could use that at the trial—but part of me wasn't sure it would have been enough to set Kerry free. So, in the end, I was resigned to the idea that we'd gotten the best deal possible, given all the circumstances at the time.

In the twenty years since he entered his plea—without an admission of guilt—and became a free man, Kerry has been determined to do everything possible to clear his name and achieve true exoneration. In 2016, Dallas attorney Gary Udashen, along with Nina Morrison of the New York Innocence Project, convinced the revamped Smith County DA's office to join with them and recommend to the CCA that it toss out Kerry's murder conviction. This was primarily based on a recent admission under oath by James Mayfield that he had lied at each of Kerry's prior trials regarding his sexual relationship with Linda Jo Edwards. Mayfield also admitted for the first time that he was indeed very familiar with the book titled *The Sexual Criminal,* which contained lurid photos of mutilated female victims whose wounds closely resembled those of Linda Jo.

Even though the recommendation could vacate the conviction, Kerry was upset that the agreement with the DA precluded holding Skeen and Dobbs accountable for their egregious misconduct at Kerry's prior trials. As of this writing, three years later, Kerry still awaits the CCA's decision, hoping against hope that the court will not only agree to vacate the conviction but find him to be actually innocent. That remains the only chance of final exoneration: James Mayfield died on July 12, 2019, and any hope of a deathbed confession died with him.

□

Through all this, Kerry has gone on with his life. He married a wonderful woman, Sandra, and they had a son named Kerry Justice; he named him that, he told me, because "that's the only justice I ever got from the state of Texas." KJ, as they call him, just graduated from high school; before college, he's going to take a year to do an internship. I am proud as hell to tell you that Kate and I are his godparents.

Kerry travels the world these days, speaking to groups of adults and children alike, on the importance of family, the importance of perseverance, and the importance of never losing hope. Because if the man who has suffered such indignity can keep hope alive, they can too.

This is a story about never giving up, he tells them. "I talk to them about how I learned that. I tell them what I overcame, how I overcame it, why I overcame it, and how you can overcome it, too. I wasn't born with superhuman strength. I'm you. And you're me. We can do this together if we just start believing in ourselves."

And while Kerry was going on with his life, I was going on with mine. Which of course meant Centurion, mostly. By now I was a confirmed lifelong bachelor; I spent lots of time with friends, but I was married to the work. And as the turn of the millennium approached, I was finding a new case to obsess over.

It was one of the clearest cases of wrongful imprisonment I had ever come across. It became a textbook example of how racial and socioeconomic differences can taint a case. It also illustrated how proving your own innocence might not be enough to get you out of prison. When we started, I had no idea how long I would find myself fighting to free this innocent man. Or how terribly, terribly agonizing our journey together would become.

☐

Benjamine Spencer isn't proud of the way this story starts, but he's honest about it. Not proud, because it starts with him as a newly married twenty-two-year-old making out with a high school girl in a park late at night, in his wife's red Thunderbird.

They'd been predicting thunderstorms that Sunday night in Dallas, in the early spring of 1987, but the rain had held off. There was plenty of turbulence in Benjamine's home, though. His wife, Debra, who was pregnant, had gotten upset with him earlier that day—he can't even remember why, now—but they were still carping at each other by dinnertime. So Benjamine decided to get out of the house and let them both cool down for a bit.

"Being that we were both young and expecting a child, we had our ups and downs," Benjamine would tell me later. "She would just get upset with me from time to time."

Benjamine drove around for a while, and someone told him that a high school girl he knew named Christi was asking after him. Benjamine stopped by Christi's house, and one thing led to another.

"We found a lot of things to talk about," Benjamine said. "Maybe our conversation was leading to something else, but we never had sex or anything. Maybe a few kisses, but nothing more."

About 10:00 p.m., one of Christi's brothers came in the front door of their home and planted himself in the living room. Christi kept asking him to leave, but he persisted, as little brothers are wont to do, so Ben took Christi to a park, and they sat in that red Thunderbird for a while, talking a bit, necking a bit, until Ben noticed it was midnight and figured he'd better take this girl home.

The next day Ben went about his business. Things between him and his wife had simmered down; he drove her to work, then headed off to the city pound to try to buy a car at auction for his mom. It didn't work out, so he planned to take his wife out to lunch, but before he got there, he was stopped by a friend, Robert Mitchell, who told him something shocking. "Hey, did you hear?" Robert said. "They found some white guy lying out in the street up on Puget on Sunday night." Ben didn't think much of it until a few days later, when a friend who goes by the name J-Mack stopped him on the street and said, "I heard you and Robert had something to do with the white man that was found dead up on Puget Street."

Ben was stunned. "It isn't fair for nobody to be spreading rumors like that," he said. "That could get someone in real trouble."

He didn't know the half of it.

Ben was coming down with a bad cold, so he spent most of the next few days in bed. That Thursday, he heard banging on the door. When he opened it, he saw a couple of police cars at the curb and an officer asking him for his ID. Before he knew it, he was told to turn around and put his hands on the wall. The officer told him he was under arrest for the murder of Jeffrey Young. The cops started searching the house, looking for what they were calling a "jam box"—what I know as a "boom box"—but found nothing.

Ben was sure this was a mistake, and it would soon be cleared up.

That was more than thirty years ago.

□

At Centurion's offices, Ben Spencer's case was the one that stood out to everyone who had looked at it. And it wasn't like we had just given it a quick glance: Ben had first written to us ten years earlier, in 1990, but because I was tied up on other cases, I was never able to give it the attention it deserved. Our volunteers had built up a good file for it over the years, though, and when I flipped it open, the first thing I saw was Ben's original letter. In his tiny, neat cursive, he laid out his whereabouts on the night of the crime, and everything that happened afterward, in minute detail. It was an unemotional letter, just the facts, but behind the facts was a desperate plea.

Get me out of here.

By then I was quite familiar with the crime. On a Sunday night, March 22, 1987, a thirty-three-year-old executive of a clothing importer drove to his office in a warehouse area in Dallas. He arrived at 8:21 p.m. At some point in the next ninety minutes, as he left the building, someone—or more than one person—violently attacked him. They smashed his head with a blunt object, cracking his skull in five places. They robbed him of his Seiko watch and wedding ring, went into the office and stole a silver jam box and TV, and then carried him to his BMW, parked outside the office. Sometime after 10:00 p.m., Jeffrey Young was pushed out of the car in a rough neighborhood in West Dallas. The killer then drove the BMW a couple of blocks away, ditched it in an alley, and ran away.

The crime immediately garnered huge attention. Young's father was a close associate of Ross Perot, the billionaire business magnate who later ran for president. The dad was in Alaska on business when Jeffrey was murdered; Perot sent a private plane to pick him up and immediately posted a $25,000 reward in the case, on top of the $10,000 offered by Young's company.

So you can imagine the enormous pressure on the police to solve the case—a young, up-and-coming business executive with high-profile connections, murdered and dumped in a poor, all-black neighborhood. That pressure fell on a young detective named Jessie Briseno who had never been the lead investigator in a homicide case before.

At first, no one in the neighborhood would talk to Detective Briseno, but after the rewards became public, witnesses started crawling out of the woodwork. One of them, forty-two-year-old Gladys Oliver, said at first that she'd seen nothing but a few days later told the cops she looked out of her bedroom window and saw two black men get out of the car and run away. One was a man named Robert Mitchell who lived around the corner. The other, she said, was Benjamine Spencer. Gladys led the police to two other young men in the neighborhood who corroborated her story.

So that's what convicted Benjamine Spencer. (That and, as you would expect by now, another "jailhouse confession" that was later found to be bogus.) The police never found a murder weapon; none of the stolen property ever turned up, and it certainly wasn't in Ben's house when they searched it. Police reports indicate that four fingerprints were lifted from items in Young's ransacked office and eight prints were obtained from Young's 1982 BMW, including a palm print found on the car's trunk lid. Ben and Robert's palm prints and fingerprints were compared with all those prints, but none matched.

Christi, the young woman Ben was with on the night of the murder—now a freshman at Prairie View A&M University on a track scholarship—testified to his whereabouts at trial. The jury discounted her. This highlights yet another reason so many innocent people are put behind bars: It's a sad truth that juries often tend not to believe alibi witnesses, because they're close to defendants and could be motivated to protect them. Think about it: Imagine a murder happened in your neighborhood yesterday. Where were you?

Most likely you were with friends and family. If juries tend not to believe friends and family, you're screwed, aren't you?

So Ben was screwed.

The more I read through Ben's file that late summer of 2000, the more the doubts about my faith that had crept into my life during the Kerry Max Cook case—the questions that I had to face during my retreat—receded into the distance. There was only one thing for me to do. It was time to go visit Benjamine Spencer.

□

I didn't go alone. Paul Henderson came with me. Paul was a journalist for *The Seattle Times* who always fought for the downtrodden and the misbegotten. At the same time that I was working on freeing Chiefie de los Santos, my first case, Paul was winning a Pulitzer Prize for a series of articles proving that a man convicted of sexual assault couldn't have committed the crime. So we were kindred spirits from the start, and Paul began working for us as an investigator on a case-by-case basis in 1988; in 1996, thanks to the money that had started to come in as a result of Jay Regan's largesse and connections, we were able to hire him full-time.

Paul was a guy with a heart of gold and the guts of a burglar. He'd go into the worst neighborhoods without blinking an eye. He was also the most disorganized person I ever met. We were working on a case in Santa Monica and staying at this classic noir 1930s hotel, and it was like rooming with a teenager; you could follow a trail of clothes, cigarette butts, and spilled coffee from one end of the room to the next. And driving with Paul was an adventure in itself; he'd have a cup of coffee in one hand, a cigarette in the other, and drive with his knees, his left turn signal perpetually on.

Paul didn't have a religious bone in his body, but one Sunday in Santa Monica I was headed for church and Paul said, "Oh, shit, I'll go with you." So there we were, sitting in a nearby Methodist church, waiting for the service to start, when the minister came walking up the aisle. Paul said, in his deep, gravelly voice, loud enough for all to hear, "Who the fuck is the guy in the black robe?" I burst out laughing, and we got the hell out of there before the service even started.

That's Paul. But as much of a mess as he was in his personal life, he was devoted with a laser-like focus to the cases he was working on. And I couldn't have had a better partner to walk into the Tennessee Colony with me.

The Tennessee Colony was a big complex of prison buildings located in a rural region a hundred miles southeast of Dallas. We found Ben in a visitors' area, his manner as courteous and reserved as his letters indicated it might be. He told us almost matter-of-factly that he was innocent.

"I know you guys must be very busy," he said. "There must be so many people asking for your assistance. But I need you. Nobody else is responding to me. Can you please give serious consideration to my case?"

I looked at him through the glass that divided us. Here was a man alone: It had become too painful for his mother to come visit, so she rarely came anymore. He had no one else. And yet he showed no bitterness, no anger. Just a patient plea for help.

And so we began.

□

Things didn't start off so well. Paul and I began by canvassing the West Dallas neighborhood where the body had been dumped. We pulled up in front of a house on a sunny, windy day—a decent house, but badly run-down. Five or six young men were congregating across the street, and we weren't feeling all that comfortable. They weren't threatening us but staring in a kind of "what are you two white guys doing in our neighborhood?" kind of way.

Paul put a manila folder on top of the car and went back in to look for something, and of course the wind picked up the file and blew the papers all over the street. We started running around, picking up the papers, and the young men were laughing their asses off at us.

But after that unpromising start, we began collecting useful evidence and were soon able to unravel the state's case point by point. We found another witness—a fourteen-year-old named Sandra Brackens—who lived much closer to the alley where the killer ditched the car than any of the state's supposed eyewitnesses. She said she saw a black male that night, running around the corner from where the car was abandoned, right by her house. He couldn't have been more than twenty feet away from her, and he was carrying—guess what?—a silver jam box on his shoulder. She knew Ben Spencer and Robert Mitchell and was sure it wasn't them. Incredibly, she was never called to testify at Ben's trial.

She also told us that one of the state's three witnesses, Charles Stewart, admitted to her that they had made up their story as a "come up"—a way to get the reward money. I also hired a forensic visual scientist, Dr. Paul Michel, to go back to the crime scene with me and see if it was at all possible for those three state witnesses to see what they said they saw.

Long story short: It wasn't.

Gladys was 123 feet away from where the car was abandoned; Charles Stewart was nearly 300 feet away; and Jimmie Cotton, the other supposed eyewitness, nearly 100 feet. Dr. Michel went back in March 2003, nearly the same date as the crime, and the same visual conditions: a moonless night, the light from the street the same, the interior kitchen lights and windows where eighteen-year-old Jimmie had been inside cooking dinner, all the same. He concluded that you'd have to have been within 20 feet of the car to make any kind of visual identification. You couldn't identify your own mother from where the state's witnesses were, given the darkness and the distance.

But Sandra was close enough. She said it wasn't Ben Spencer or Robert Mitchell, both of whom she knew from the neighborhood.

What more did I need? The real killer? Turns out, I think I found him, too.

□

Robert Mitchell, the man convicted in a separate trial for the same crime as Ben, was overwhelmed by prison life, especially since he was in for a crime he didn't commit. One night he tried to hang himself and survived only because his cellmate came by in time to cut him down.

His cellmate was another man from the neighborhood, a criminal named Kelvin Johnson. But he was a criminal with a conscience: Racked with guilt over Robert's attempted suicide, he told Robert something he hadn't told anyone before. He knew who killed that white man on Puget Street. He had his attorney contact the police and gave them the name of the real killer: He said it was Michael Hubbard, a violent twenty-two-year-old crack addict from the neighborhood.

Just a few days after Jeffrey Young's murder, according to Kelvin Johnson, Hubbard told Kelvin and another friend that he had killed "the white dude found on the street." He said Hubbard told them all sorts of details about the crime: for example, that he had taken a Seiko watch and a wedding ring, along with the jam box and the TV. And that the phone was ringing incessantly during the crime (in fact, Jeffrey Young's computer service provider had tried to call him repeatedly that Sunday night, right around the time the crime was taking place).

Kelvin couldn't have been aware of it—but these were all details only the police and the killer could have known. According to Kelvin, Hubbard also told them he was afraid that he'd been seen by one of the neighbors. That, to me, coincided with exactly what Sandra Brackens said happened, too.

For whatever reasons, Ben's defense team never spoke to Kelvin Johnson, the man who'd said he heard a confession from the real killer and who identified that killer as Michael Hubbard. But I did. I talked to Michael Hubbard, too.

It seems that a few years after Jeffrey Young was murdered, there was a string of terribly violent crimes that were strikingly similar to Jeffrey's case, and Michael Hubbard, a parolee recently released from prison, was the main suspect. During off-hours, at night or on holidays, police said, he would cruise office buildings in out-of-the-way industrial or warehouse areas, look for an upscale parked car, then wait for the car's owner to come out of the office building. When the owner did, Michael would ambush him from behind and bash him multiple times over the head with a baseball bat or another blunt instrument. They came to be known as the "Batman" crimes. Hubbard was arrested for them. He was convicted once, but the conviction was reversed; at his second trial, it took the jury all of one minute to convict him again.

I wrote a letter to Hubbard in 2002 asking for a visit, introducing myself, and explaining that his name had come up in my investigation of the Jeffrey Young murder in ways that I would like to discuss with him. Much to my surprise, he authorized my visit.

In my interview with Hubbard, he, of course, denied any involvement, but he did say something that I felt was quite telling. Toward the end of our one-hour conversation, he asked me straight out if I thought he killed Jeffrey Young. I responded, "The thought has certainly crossed my mind." He then asked why. I said, point-blank, "Because your m.o. in the Batman crimes was a virtual match to the Young homicide." I ticked off the similarities and waited for his reaction.

He thought in silence for what seemed like an eternity and then replied, "Well, I'm not the Batman."

Well, of course he was. There was no doubt about that. There was no doubt about what his non-denial denial meant, either. I just hoped a judge would see it the same way.

□

The smartest thing I did in this case was retain Cheryl Wattley, who I had previously hired as one of Kerry Max Cook's lawyers. She was a sharp, experienced attorney, one who had told *D* magazine a few years back, when she started a teaching stint at the SMU School of Law, that she had "become somewhat disenchanted with the judicial system and this opportunity provides me a better way to try and improve the system's conscience."

She put together a terrific writ asking for a reconsideration of Ben's case. As a result, in July 2007, an evidentiary hearing was held before Dallas County district judge Rick Magnis, and while he kept a judge's demeanor, I could tell he was flabbergasted by what he was hearing. All of our witnesses testified. So did Jimmie Cotton, one of the state's original eyewitnesses, who recanted his false testimony against Ben. (One of the other witnesses, Charles Stewart, had been murdered in a drug deal gone bad.) The "jailhouse witness" admitted he never really heard Ben confess. The judge even went so far as to visit the scene himself where the BMW had been abandoned.

Gladys Oliver did not recant her testimony, so the judge ordered the state to hire their own visual forensic specialist, who determined the same thing ours had: Gladys could not have possibly made that identification on that dark night, from a distance of more than 120 feet.

Based on all we had presented, the judge found, among other things, that the jailhouse confession was not credible; that none of the eyewitness testimony held any water; that Kelvin Johnson's testimony about Michael Hubbard included information that no one but the killer could have known at the time; and that, most important, and praise the Lord, Benjamine Spencer should be freed on the grounds of actual innocence.

Actual innocence.

That was his recommendation to the Texas Court of Criminal Appeals.

We were elated. Justice had prevailed. Or so we thought. For a maddening *three years*, the Court of Criminal Appeals sat on the ruling. Ben waited, and waited, and waited, and hoped, and prayed, and appeared to remain strong and hopeful. And yet, I knew, he was dying inside. A man alone, proven innocent, spending year after year behind bars. It was heartbreaking.

On March 28, 2011, *The Dallas Morning News* wrote an editorial proclaiming that the delay was "outrageous"—that a court had ruled him innocent and yet the CCA wouldn't budge. Well, that did it all right. Just three weeks later, the CCA issued their unanimous decision.

Rejecting the recommendation that Ben be set free.

I won't go through all the glaring errors of omission and commission that were found in that CCA opinion. I thoroughly believe that they were just pissed off at the *Morning News* for calling them out and that they wrote their recommendation out of spite.

I will tell you this. At the hearing, the courtroom was as racially divided as any I've ever seen. All of the victim's friends and relatives, who were white, sat on one side; all of Ben's supporters sat on the other. Much to my surprise, Alan Ledbetter, the foreman of the original jury that convicted Ben, came to every day of the hearing. He originally sat on the victim's side. But one day, after some of the testimony that clearly showed Ben's innocence, I looked up to see him sitting on the other side. Even he knew.

"We were very wrong," he told us later. "There's an element of guilt, and grief, that I carry for whatever role I may have played in robbing so much of his life from him."

I don't feel guilty. I know I did all that I could to free Ben Spencer. But I feel grief, because to this day Ben remains behind bars. We have not given up hope. A new DA was elected in 2018 who has agreed to reopen the case. We've added a new attorney to Ben's defense, the renowned Dallas lawyer Gary Udashen, who got the DA to agree to a new trial for Kerry Max Cook. We're continuing to push and we're continuing to pray.

As for Ben, he took solace in the chapel for a while, but he's abandoned that now. He still calls me most Saturday mornings, as he has for years. He still doesn't show his feelings; to me it seems that his hope has flickered but has never been extinguished. I promise him, when we talk, that I will never give up.

And I never will.

Eighteen

I had never given up on exonerating Roger Coleman either. It had been fourteen years since I sat on that cement floor and split a pizza with him on the night he was executed, but I don't think a week went by that I didn't think of him. I believed in my bones that he had not murdered Wanda McCoy that night in a rural corner of Virginia, the night he supposedly waded through a creek to surprise her in her home, the night that strange family in the house on the hill supposedly tucked themselves into bed while the murder took place.

With the help of a great D.C. attorney named Paul Enzinna (working pro bono, thank you very much), I'd made a number of attempts to get the courts to submit the semen that was found in Wanda's vagina for new DNA testing. All these years later, DNA testing had become so much more sophisticated I was sure it was at the point where it could prove Roger's innocence.

We were unsuccessful at every turn. But finally, in 2005, we started a last-ditch effort to get the governor, Mark Warner, to intercede. It took a while, but in December of that year he authorized the testing. A month later I was sitting by the phone in a Richmond hotel room, waiting for the results. Paul was with me. Finally, the phone rang.

It was the director of the Centre of Forensic Sciences in Toronto, the lab that was doing the testing.

"Jim, we have the results," he said.

He told me that conclusively, beyond doubt, some of the semen found on Wanda McCoy's vaginal swab belonged to Roger Coleman.

I hung up and turned to Paul in disbelief. "He's guilty," was all I could say.

I had prepared two statements for the press, one if Roger was found innocent and one if he was found guilty. I never thought I'd have to read the second one.

"Those of us who seek the truth in criminal justice cases must never be afraid of finding it," I said. "We must live or die by the sword of DNA." I made it clear, without equivocation—no matter how much we'd advocated on his behalf across the years—that Roger Coleman was indeed the killer of Wanda McCoy.

But I had my doubts. And all these years later, I have to say, I still do. It is indisputable that Roger's semen was found in Wanda. The question is how and when it got there. Over the years, I have wondered if Roger and Wanda were having a secret affair. As far as I know, there was never even a whisper to that effect; I have no evidence to suggest they were romantically involved.

So I continue to grapple with the question of his guilt. This I do know: He did not appear to have had the motivation, the means, or, most important, the opportunity to kill and rape her in the brutal manner in which it was done. It's important to keep in mind that Wanda had been vaginally raped and sodomized, that sperm was collected from both cavities, and that the 1990 and 2006 DNA testing both confirmed that the semen from the vaginal swab was a mixed sample, which means it came from two different men.

It is indisputable that from the time he left the coal mine at about 10:00 p.m., Roger was traveling alone until he arrived home at 11:05 p.m. So where could that second sample come from? It had been more than forty-eight hours since Brad had vaginal intercourse with his wife, and she had started to menstruate the day before her murder. It is highly unlikely that his sperm would have survived prior to her death. All of these forensic facts indicate that two men were involved in her sexual assault and murder.

This is the first time that I've ever publicly expressed my reservations. When the 2006 DNA results were announced, I believed that DNA trumped my reasons for believing in Roger's innocence. I said what needed to be said. But I must confess that now I don't know what to believe. It won't make anyone, on either side of the dispute, happy to hear me say so. In fact, I'm sure it will upset a lot of people. But I can only be honest, and knowing all that I know, I can't swear to God that Roger did it. In my mind there is an abundance of evidence that points to his innocence.

That said, the DNA certainly cannot be waved aside. Unless he was having an affair with Wanda, his semen had no business inside her and therefore can lead only to the conclusion that he is guilty.

I readily admit that those two ideas contradict each other. There is only one thing I'm certain of, and that is this: The question of his guilt or innocence will stay with me until the day I die.

□

I guess you can't keep doing this forever, and after the whole Roger thing was over, I was starting to think that I'd have to hand over the reins of Centurion to Kate and the others at some point. But with Benjamine Spencer still behind bars, and the punch-in-the-stomach end of the Roger Coleman case, I wasn't ready to hang up my spurs just yet. There was one more case kicking around our office that, the more I heard about, the more I knew was going to be my next—and maybe my final—battle.

It had started with letters from an inmate named Dominic Lucci. Dominic, we'd learn later, was a little bulldog of a guy, as funny as he was stubborn. Dominic first wrote to us in 2000, and he never gave up. In 2003, he wrote, "It's been a couple of years and this time I'm not taking 'no' for an answer. If McCloskey is retired, send somebody else down here to help us out."

He got our attention. We turned the case over to Jock McFarlane, one of our most trusted and meticulous volunteers. Jock, a quiet, sandy-haired guy in his sixties, did what had become standard procedure at Centurion: He started gathering every shred of paper related to the case. This is not an easy process; sometimes it can take a very long time to develop the case file, and in fact this time it took nearly six years. But when he was done, Jock, in his quiet, fastidious way, had amassed boxes and boxes of material related to the case, and once I started poring over those files, it was a no-brainer. I knew what my final battle was going to be. We were going to free the Savannah Three.

□

It all started on a Friday night in January 1992, when a twenty-year-old army private named Mark Jones was partying at his wedding rehearsal dinner with some friends in Hinesville, about an hour from downtown Savannah. The wedding was to be at the Fort Stewart base chapel in Hinesville at 2:00 p.m. the next day. They were expecting upwards of 150 people; the parents of the bride and groom had arrived from Florida, Texas, and Tennessee.

As the dinner ended, Mark was ready to call it a night, but two of his buddies, fellow soldiers Dominic Lucci and Kenneth Gardiner—with the smiling agreement of Mark's fiancée—persuaded him to go out on the town for one last night with the boys.

That night a thirty-five-year-old crack addict named Stanley Jackson was gunned down in a drive-by shooting by a barrage of bullets from an AK-47 in a neighborhood overrun with crime and drugs, the part of Savannah known to locals as Hazard County. A man named James White was about to enter his home when he heard loud gunfire coming from nearby. He turned and saw "fire coming from guns" being shot by two men leaning out of the passenger-side window of a car that had stopped in the middle of the intersection. A few seconds later, the car sped away, its tires screeching as it vanished into the night.

By terrible coincidence, about half an hour later, Mark Jones and his two buddies—lost in Savannah, trying to find a topless joint called Club Asia—stopped to ask a uniformed police officer for directions. She happened to be standing with James White, the witness to the crime, whom she was escorting to the nearby police station to make a statement. As they drove away, White happened to say to the cop that the three young men's car "looked like" the car used by the shooters.

And for that, the lives of the three young men would be destroyed. They were arrested that night in the absence of confessions. No guns or bullets or physical evidence linked them to this crime, or any other crime for that matter. They had no history of arrests and no connection to the victim, and there were no holes in their story about where they'd been that evening. But there was one thing: an ominous racial undercurrent.

Violent crime and homicides had skyrocketed in Savannah the previous year, and it appeared that the city's all-white law enforcement establishment had been pouring resources into the few cases in which the victims were white and not being nearly as vigilant in those with African American victims. Outrage in the black community had been growing, and it burst like a rain cloud on what should have been Mark Jones's wedding day, letting forth a torrent of anger that, sadly, washed away any chance of a fair trial in this case.

When the three young white men were charged with the murder of a black man, the entire city turned its attention to the case. A vigil was held for Stanley Jackson, with more than two hundred in attendance; the next day the mayor allowed a spokesperson for those mourners to address the city council. The speaker admonished the city for treating the cases of black victims differently than those of their white counterparts and then prayed for "equal treatment in Savannah."

I need to say at this juncture that this case was very different from the cases we usually take. The majority of those we've freed at Centurion are African American, and in case after case, as you've seen throughout this book, the inherent racial prejudice that is endemic to the American criminal justice system has been one more huge boulder we had to try to overturn in getting those innocent men and women freed. So often, when the suspect is black and the victim is white, it's "guilty until proven innocent."

But in this case, it was the white defendants who were guilty until proven innocent. And there was a great deal of pressure on the district attorney to deliver a swift conviction. He wasn't about to disappoint.

The prosecutor had James White's testimony, which by now had gone beyond just saying he thought their car looked like the shooters' car; at a preliminary hearing he had also identified Jones and one of his companions, Kenneth Gardiner, as the shooters leaning out the car window with AK-47s.

The prosecutor also had a bizarre theory, which he presented to the jury: The three young men spent a lot of time on the base playing Dungeons & Dragons, a role-playing game. He theorized that they had tried to live out their fantasy game by going out and killing an "evil" person.

Based on that narrative, the three young soldiers were convicted and sent to prison, sentenced to life.

□

As I read through the case file, it became more and more evident that these guys were innocent. I spent day after day poring over the voluminous files that Jock McFarlane had gathered. Some of the first things that drew my attention were James White's police statement and pretrial and trial testimony. They appeared at best to be unreliable—he couldn't have identified the men from so far away, in just a few seconds, at night, while already traumatized by the gunfire—and at worst intentionally false, a fabrication, once again, brought about by intense police pressure.

But beyond that, as I read the case file, it became enormously obvious that the three young men could not have committed the crime. The facts made it impossible.

Here's why. The wedding rehearsal dinner went from 8:15 p.m. to about 9:30. That was easy to establish. Mark and his friends left the restaurant in Hinesville at about 9:30, and it was a fifty-minute drive to Savannah. They stopped first at a bar called the Tops Lounge, at about 10:15 at the earliest, where they were turned away because Jones was three months shy of his twenty-first birthday. Another customer had told them to try Club Asia. Looking for it and getting lost, they asked the police officer—standing with James White—for directions at 10:35.

The murder itself took place at 10:05 p.m.

So to believe they're guilty, you'd have to believe that after a ridiculously high-speed drive from Hinesville to the Tops Lounge, they first detoured to a dangerous part of town, gunned down Stanley Jackson with two AK-47s, stashed the weapons somewhere, proceeded to the Tops Lounge (where they appeared, to all who saw them, as just three happy-go-lucky young men "looking for a titty bar," as one witness said), then, turned away from the bar and having committed a brutal murder, stopped to ask a cop for directions.

Unbelievable. Literally. So how could we prove it?

Once again, the inimitable Paul Henderson was working with me. His slovenly ways had become as endearing to me as his incredible investigative skills were invaluable. Paul was convinced of the young men's innocence and so was I. We set out on the road.

We started with the three soldiers themselves. My certainty about their innocence was absolutely reinforced when we walked into that prison. I could tell from the get-go that they were as clean as a hound's tooth. First off, all three were nerds to the first degree. Two of them, Mark Jones and Dominic Lucci, didn't even drink, which I thought was fairly unusual for young army guys barely into their twenties. Dominic—"Dino," they called him, the one who'd written to us—was the more forceful of the two; brash and funny and outspoken, he was full of piss and vinegar and still very angry at his fate. Mark was the more thoughtful one, kind of chubby and sloppy and, I could tell, a bit of a screwup. But I mean that in a sweet way; he really was the kind of guy who, you could just sense, didn't want to harm a fly if he could avoid it. Far from the racist crazies that he and his friends were portrayed as, Mark was an affable, articulate, and intelligent young man.

Kenneth Gardiner was probably the smartest of the three, and the quietest. He would open up a little more as time went by, but on this first visit he didn't have much to say. They all said, in their manner as much as their words, what I needed to hear.

We are innocent. Help us. And so Paul and I set out to do just that.

□

The first thing I did, that late summer of 2009, was try to hunt down James White, the supposed witness who identified Jones and Gardiner as the shooters. James considered himself a minister, saying he was ordained by a local Baptist church; he preferred to be referred to as Reverend White. I hoped that his religious leanings would work in my favor.

It took until December, but I managed to get ahold of some relatives of his in Atlanta and gave them my card. Much to my surprise Reverend White called me and told me to get in touch after the holidays.

I don't like to talk to prospective witnesses over the phone. It's easy to say no and hang up on a phone call, but if I can present myself at their door, 90 percent of the time they invite me in. So after the holidays I flew down to Atlanta and showed up at the door of one of the relatives I'd found. She told me the Whites were now homeless, and she didn't know where they were living. But a few phone calls later we had their location: They'd checked into a Super Motel about forty miles south of Atlanta.

When I pulled up thirty minutes later, James and his wife, Suzette, were unloading groceries from an old beat-up Oldsmobile with tape where the rear passenger window used to be. I introduced myself to James while his wife hung back, wary of this strange white guy in the parking lot. They told me to give them an hour and then come back. When I finally entered their room, James—close to three hundred pounds and lying on the bed dressed in only his underwear, T-shirt, and black socks—was polite to me; his wife was still wary, though, busying herself by pretending to clean up the messy room.

As always, I started by chatting, trying to establish some rapport, respect, and trust, telling them about Chiefie, and how I'd started Centurion Ministries, and about John Sessum's recantation in the Clarence Brandley case. Eventually I worked the conversation around to the soldiers. James told me something that would have been startling if I hadn't come to expect it by now. He said he had been under intense pressure to make an identification, both by the police and by black church leaders. If he didn't testify, they told him, the three men would be found innocent of killing a black man, and "there would be race riots in the streets."

His wife, Suzette, chimed in that before the trial they had gotten a lot of phone calls urging James to "do the right thing"—to testify against the three soldiers—including several from the prominent pastor of the leading black church. The pressure, she said, was "overwhelming."

The room got quiet. I asked if this was the first time they'd told anyone about all the pressure they'd been under. They said it was. I took a gamble and told them everything I knew—why I thought it was obvious that the three men were innocent. James and Suzette told me that the cops had told them the three had been on a "rampage," killing black people throughout Savannah, in order to gain his cooperation. I told them flat out that it was a deliberate and bald-faced lie. I told him how the three soldiers couldn't possibly have gotten to the scene of the crime. I didn't accuse James of lying, but a question hung in the air.

James sat up in bed. "How are them boys holding up?" he asked me.

"They're doing better than their mothers and fathers," I said, staring right back.

At that point, James started to cry. I'd broken through.

"Please tell their parents I am so sorry for what has happened. I—I just—" He couldn't go on. He was sobbing now, and instinctively I walked over and hugged him, and we sat at the edge of his bed, frozen, his sobs muffled in my shoulder. Each of us knew, in his heart, what had to happen next.

It wasn't until a few months later, over lunch at an Olive Garden, that James told me the whole story: how in the dark on the night of the shooting, and in fear for his life, he couldn't possibly identify the shooters; how he'd lied about the identification because of community pressure; how he told the prosecutor right before the trial that he couldn't make an identification and was threatened with jail and perjury charges, since he had already made an identification at the preliminary hearing earlier in the year.

That was it. I had what I needed to reopen the case. Until I didn't.

By this time I had retained Steven Sparger of Savannah and the great Peter Camiel of Seattle to represent the soldiers. This was Peter's fourth Centurion case. Peter prepared affidavits for James to sign, but when Peter and I tried to find him, he had disappeared. He wouldn't answer my phone calls. I had one last chance—an address for one of his sons, Donte, a musician in LaGrange, about an hour south of Atlanta. As usual, I knocked on his door unannounced. If this didn't work, I was sunk. He gave me an address of one of his brothers, and the next day, Sunday morning, at 9:00 sharp, Peter and I knocked on the door.

I heard Suzette's unmistakable voice: "Who is it?" And when I responded, I heard her yell to James, "It's Jim. I told you he would find us."

They welcomed us in like long-lost friends, and we talked for a while. Finally I put the affidavit in front of James. He read it, and I asked him if it was accurate, and he said yes.

He put it down and stared at Suzette for the longest time. A long, heavy silence hung in the air. Finally, Suzette sighed.

"James," she said, "be a man. Sign the fucking thing."

And that was that.

□

I made sixteen trips to the South over the course of four years. Paul Henderson and I interviewed 130 witnesses in seventeen different states. Even for me, that was a lot, and if it sounds kind of obsessive, I will say right now, "Guilty as charged." I was absolutely obsessed with this case, bound and determined to get these guys out. Their innocence was so obvious, the miscarriage of justice so blatant. The original defense lawyers in the case, although they had done their best and been blindsided by the prosecutors, were eaten alive by their guilt. "When I shave every day, I think of these guys," Bill Cox, one of the lawyers, told me.

We spent hundreds of thousands of dollars on this case, which we were able to do thanks to a benefactor from New York City who was outraged by this perversion of justice. The mounting evidence fueled my obsession, and the lawyer Peter Camiel was just as fixated.

But of all those trips, of all those interviews, for all the hundreds of thousands of dollars we spent, who knew it would all come down to one piece of paper—a paper that, if it were not for that very same obsession, might have been lost forever.

□

Peter and I had filed a public records request with the Savannah PD. They sent six hundred pages to my Princeton office, and I looked at every page. And then one jumped out at me.

It was just half a page, handwritten, dated February 1, 1992—the day after the crime. It was about an incident in Yamacraw, a mainly black neighborhood in Savannah. A resident of the Yamacraw public housing projects reported to the beat patrol officer that at 1:00 a.m. two vehicles occupied by several white males with military-style haircuts, and armed with semiautomatic weapons, were threatening to shoot blacks who hung out on street corners.

Let me point out to you that Mark Jones, Dominic Lucci, and Kenneth Gardiner were in custody at the moment that this event took place; that what the men were threatening was exactly what had happened to Stanley Jackson three hours earlier; that evidence of this event would certainly open up the possibility that there were other suspects in this crime; that our three soldiers never had access to this evidence at their trial; and that not giving them access to the Yamacraw report would almost certainly be considered suppression of evidence that was material to the crime and conviction.

And let me say that when I read that report, I jumped up and started screaming at the top of my lungs.

☐

Largely on the strength of the suppressed evidence, as well as James White's recantation, we were able to get a new evidentiary hearing for the Savannah Three. We had twenty-three witnesses, ranging from fellow soldiers testifying to the character of the three defendants—all saying they didn't have a racist bone in their bodies—to a professional twenty-year veteran taxicab driver who testified that it's impossible to drive from Hinesville to Savannah, a drive he's made thousands of times, in less than fifty minutes, making it impossible for the three young men to have committed this crime. These witnesses, collectively, dismantled every element of the state's case at trial.

But our star witness was the remorseful James White, and his words rang out in the courtroom.

"I want to correct something I did twenty-one years ago," he said, "and that's false witness against the prisoners. The police kept pointing and pushing me towards the defendants. I wanted to make sure it was done the way they wanted it and that's one of the most horrible things I ever did in my life. 'Cause being a minister of the Gospel I know it say in the book of Exodus you can't be a false witness. Thou shall not kill, steal, or be a false witness against people. And I did that. And that hurt me so bad and it's been torturing me for years and I'm so sorry. I lied on these three gentlemen here."

It was a triumphant moment. But I've learned to temper my joy with the reality of the justice system, and sure enough—believe it or not—the judge refused to give the Savannah Three a new trial, for the most unbelievable of reasons: She said that the defendants should have brought up the suppressed evidence—the Yamacraw report—at their original trial or under direct appeal, even though the evidence hadn't been revealed until eighteen years later!

We were incredulous, but we were not done. Far from it. We appealed to the Georgia Supreme Court. We prayed that that foolish, ridiculous, nonsensical ruling would not stand the scrutiny of an objective court.

It didn't.

At the end of 2017, the court, by a unanimous 9–0 vote, vacated the conviction of the three soldiers—citing the fact that the police withheld exculpatory evidence and saying that if the defense had had it, the outcome of the trial would most likely have been different.

Ordering a new trial, the court said, "The Yamacraw report was evidence that others similar in appearance were threatening a racial attack similar to that suffered by Jackson . . . and that other persons, not the defendants, were in the area that same night, apparently ready to engage in racially motivated violence." It went on to say that "the outcome of the trial might well have been different" if the jury knew about the Yamacraw incident.

As fantastic and incredible as this was, it wasn't enough to free the Savannah Three. Not yet, anyway. When your conviction is tossed out, you are still considered charged with the crime; in essence, you go back to square one, after you were arrested but before your trial. What that meant was the DA's office could keep them in prison awaiting another trial, if they wanted to.

We were almost certain that the DA would relent; she had to know now that the Yamacraw report had surfaced and White had recanted. She'd have no chance of getting a conviction at the second trial, but again, I had learned enough in my thirty-seven years in this work to know that anything can go south for any reason. At least, I hoped, we could get them out on bail before Christmas, while we waited for that decision to be made.

And so on December 20, 2017, as we walked from our hotel to the Chatham County Courthouse, hoping to get the Savannah Three released, the guy who was supposed to be Mark's best man at his wedding—a towering, six-foot-eight figure affectionately called Tiny—said to me, "So, this is going to be a slam dunk, right, Jim?"

"Tiny," I told him, "nothing in this business is a slam dunk."

We entered a courtroom that, except for some modern-looking computer terminals, looked exactly like the courtroom in which the Savannah Three had been convicted decades earlier. All of their family members were there; we filed into five rows of benches that looked exactly like church pews, which seemed appropriate to me since all the family members were silently praying.

The three men—young men no longer, aged by the years and the torment of false imprisonment—filed in quietly, heads down. I was holding my breath, until I heard the DA tell the judge, "The state leaves the issue of bail entirely at the discretion of the court." And at that, the judge set the bail, and we knew it was only a matter of a few hours of paperwork before the Savannah Three would be freed.

The three respectfully kept their heads down, but just before they went back to the local jail for what we all hoped would be their last few hours behind bars, Mark Jones, looking like an old John Lennon in round spectacles and with a serene look on his face, found

257

his family in the back row and allowed himself a little smile, then got up to leave.

The same New York benefactor who'd kept the case alive to this point immediately wired $100,000 to the sheriff's office to cover the bail. Hours later, we all stood in the lobby of the jailhouse, Mark Jones's mom rocking back and forth, saying to the universe, "Come on, give me my son back." And then, at 3:32 p.m., the three men walked out into a sea of hollers and whoops and cheers, hugging their families with all their might, then heading toward the door.

Mark Jones's mother had to be persuaded to let go of him so he could make it out of the building. "Except for his birth," she said, "this is the greatest day of my life."

Back at the hotel, an impromptu party broke out in the lobby—a subdued gathering, until Tiny pulled a little prank. One of the family members got a call on his cell phone, listened for a minute, and then hung up. "Tiny just called," he announced. "He's outside, setting up for a game of Dungeons & Dragons."

□

Mark Jones   Kenneth Gardiner   Dominic Lucci

Top row: The night of the soldiers' arrest on January 31, 1992. Bottom row: The day of their freedom, nearly twenty-six years later, on December 20, 2017. *Diane Bladecki*

We threw a small dinner for the three men and their families that night, at the home of John Watts Jr., Mark Jones's trial attorney, and afterward Mark had a moment to reflect on what he had been through. He seemed inordinately tranquil, and someone asked him, was he really feeling that calm?

"Remember at the time I was only twenty-one, twenty-two years old," he said by way of response, "and I'd had something happen to me that should never happen to anybody. And the whole world thought I'm this racist killer for a crime that I had absolutely nothing to do with. And I didn't have the experience and wisdom to be able to deal with that at the time. That took me years to learn how to deal with it, to learn how to deal with those emotions, how to shunt negative emotions away.

"The problem for me is not experiencing the emotions; it's showing them. Because of the environment I've been in, you can't show those type of emotions unless you're amongst people that you absolutely trust. And trust in that environment is very rare. So, I learned how to bury those emotions so I wouldn't show them, and basically put forth a very calm facade. It took me a lotta years, but it's gonna take me even longer to remove it, and I don't know how I'm gonna do that."

I heard him, and I looked around the room, at all the mothers and friends and fathers who had not only gathered for this day but had also kept the faith, fighting to keep hope alive for nearly twenty-six years, and I thought, these are the most heroic people in the world. The families of the innocent. The ones who held these three young men in their hearts when the rest of the world had forgotten.

I looked back at Mark, and I looked over at his mother, Debbie, sitting by his side, and in my mind I said to him, I've seen many an exoneree walk this path alone. Not all of them have thrived back out here in the real world. But you have your incredibly devoted mother beside you, a mother who has stood by you through your entire incarceration and who will walk this path with you. Step by step—I believe, with all my heart—you will find your way.

Nineteen

WHERE ARE THEY NOW?

I'm almost at the end of this book, but in truth I've only told you half the story. Because for the most part, I've focused on telling you how the cruelty and indifference of our criminal justice system puts innocent people in prison, and how a bald Irish minister from New Jersey put together an organization that freed as many of them as we could.

But getting out of prison, for an innocent man or woman, is not the end of this saga. In many ways, it's just the beginning. There is a "future shock" that so many of our exonerees have told us about: When they went into prison, people had beepers; now everyone has a cell phone. If they're looking for a job, employers ask if they're familiar with Excel and Photoshop, and many of them have never touched a computer. Or used an ATM. Or owned a credit card. Or taken an Uber. Or ordered from Amazon.

Or made a friend they could trust.

Some of the exonerees need help with the simplest things: Buying toothpaste can be overwhelming—to walk into a drugstore and see all the choices, when you have never been asked to make a choice in your adult life, when everything you do is what you're told to do, everything you own is given to you by the state. I remember one exoneree telling me about running out of the drugstore shaking in fear because he couldn't handle that much selection. Another told me about his first fight with his wife, after he was freed from prison: Whenever she asked him what he wanted to do each evening, he'd say, "I don't know," and she thought it was because he just didn't care. It took her a while to realize that no one had given him the power to make a choice for more than twenty years; he hadn't learned how to adapt to being asked that kind of question.

Some of the stories of our exonerees' lives after prison are nothing short of heartbreaking. That includes the man who got me started on this calling, Jorge "Chiefie" de los Santos. The exuberance of getting my first innocent man out of prison faded quickly. Because a year or two later, Chiefie was convicted of a drug-related robbery. He got out again in the early 1990s, I learned, although not from him; he was too ashamed to talk to me about it. I lost touch with him completely at some point, and when I did finally find out what happened to him, it was about the saddest news I could imagine. Chiefie had been found murdered in a vacant lot in Brooklyn, killed, apparently, over a bad drug deal.

I tell people all the time that if it were not for this Puerto Rican drug addict from Newark, Centurion Ministries would never have existed, and another sixty-two men and women would more than likely still be languishing in prison. I would still be wandering through the wilderness, searching for my purpose in life. I thank God for Jorge de los Santos. May he rest in peace.

And so early on, I knew that freeing the innocent from prison, as exhilarating as it was, was not the end of our work and that our success came with great responsibility. So from that day forward, all of us at Centurion made sure to stay in touch with our exonerees as best we could, visiting them whenever we were in their cities and trying to help them make the enormous adjustment back to the real world. One came to live with Kate and then with me for a while; others became part of our extended family.

Nate Walker, another of our early exonerees, nearly met the same fate as Chiefie: When he got out, he started using cocaine for the first time in his life. It was his own way of trying to cope, I guess. But the great news is that he beat it, and got straight for the rest of his life. He settled a civil suit against the state—Paul Casteleiro was his lawyer for that—and got $300,000, a pittance when you think of the years of his life that were stolen from him, but still one of the first-ever suits of its kind. And I'm proud to say he donated $25,000 of that to Centurion—a godsend in those early days. Once Nate straightened his life out, he became quite influential in advocating against New Jersey's death penalty, which was abolished in 2007.

Nate died of a stroke in 2010. He was sixty-eight. Overall, sixteen of our exonerees have died, and it's part of our heartache at Centurion that so many of them died after having just a short taste of freedom, or else died at a relatively young age. Among those were Joyce Ann Brown, Damaso Vega, and Clarence Brandley; none of the three made it through their sixties.

□

I also want to make sure I don't leave you with too rosy a picture of our work. Yes, we've freed sixty-three innocent men and women in twenty-one states and Canada—who, collectively, have spent 1,330 years falsely imprisoned.

But I have to take a moment to note that there were fifteen other cases where we did not free our client, for a variety of reasons. I've mentioned some of those—Jimmy Wingo and Roger Coleman—but there were others.

Two died in prison during our work on their behalf; we dropped six because we discovered we were wrong and that they were, in fact, guilty. We had to leave five others behind because we were just never able to develop enough new evidence or present a new legal argument to warrant a judicial review. So there were a number of failures, as can only be expected, both in trying to get them free and in trying to help them find their way in the world once they had been freed.

Some of our exonerees did incredibly well after they left prison; others had a really hard time. It's never clear why one person will find a path out of the darkness and another will never find their way, but sometimes—often—I believe it was the family members who stood by them that made the difference.

That was certainly the case with a young man—young at the beginning of this story, anyway—named Mark Schand. Mark, a wiry, balding man with boundless energy and a great enthusiasm for exercise and healthy living, has a tattoo on his left arm recording the time he spent in prison for a crime he did not commit: "26 years, 11 months, 20 hours, 26 minutes, 8 seconds, 4 nothing."

On October 26, 1986, Mark, then just twenty-one years old, was stopped on the street in Hartford, Connecticut, and hauled to the police station, where he learned he was a suspect in a murder in Springfield, Massachusetts. Year after year, he languished in Walpole prison. Year after year, he endured assaults and witnessed murders and stabbings. He was stabbed himself once, while he was talking on the phone.

And year after year, month after month, week after week—almost every single week for twenty-seven impossibly long years—his wife, Mia, came to visit.

"It meant everything to me," Mark told me. "It keeps you grounded. It sustains you. It lets you think, okay, I have a reason to get out of here. I have someone to come home to. If I didn't have Mia, I think I might have started acting like a convict, and fell into every little convict cliché, and I think I'd still be in there. But Mia coming to visit, it made me feel . . ."

Mark paused as he told me the story, searching for the right word.

"It made me feel human."

Mia was pregnant with their first child when Mark first went to jail. Mia brought little Quinton on her weekly visits; Mark had two sons from previous relationships, living with their mothers, and Mia would bring them as well, whenever she could. It was a two-hour commute from Hartford, but except for when severe snowstorms made the highway impassable, she faithfully trekked back and forth.

"I did it for us," she told me, "to keep the strength in our family. My family is very close; that's how I grew up, and that's how I wanted the boys to grow up."

And so the years went by, Mark playing board games with his sons when they were little, and chess when they got older, and helping with homework during the school year and sitting down for big lobster-and-corn picnics in the summer when Mia got permission to bring food in. How they all kept from losing faith I will never know, but Mia and Mark always told the boys that one day their father would get out. They truly believed it.

"I always pictured Mark walking through that front door, and when he finally did, it was absolutely a blessing," Mia said. "It's been six years that Mark's been home, and every day is better for us."

Working alongside Mark's long-term attorneys John and Linda Thompson, Centurion's investigator Richard Hepburn and I were able to exonerate Mark in 2013. Mark got a $450,000 settlement from Massachusetts for his wrongful conviction and used it to open a smoothie shop in Hartford, and it's doing pretty well.

Mark also filed a wrongful-imprisonment civil lawsuit and in September 2019 achieved a landmark victory: A federal district

With Mark Schand and his wife, Mia, moments after his release on October 4, 2013. *Diane Bladecki*

court jury awarded him $27 million, $1 million for every year of his imprisonment. It was the largest civil judgment ever awarded against city police. Of course, the city has appealed the verdict.

"It feels good," Mark told me after the verdict came in. "It feels really good. Not because of the monetary damages. Because first of all, I don't have it. Second of all, there's a 90 percent chance I don't get most of it. What feels good is the fact that the judge actually apologized to me. And that someone finally acknowledged that there were people responsible for what happened to me. That's more important to me than anything else."

In the meantime, Mark is happily working away at the smoothie shop and says he won't give it up, even if the money does come through. His specialty is coming up with new and surprising combinations of flavors. One day he was doodling around with some ideas and came up with a combination of banana, pineapple, raspberry, almond milk, and honey. I was stunned when I walked into his shop and found out he'd named it the Centurion Freedom. I asked him why.

"It tasted so great and brightened up my day, and sincerely, you all brightened up my freaking life, so I thought it was the perfect fit," he said.

Centurion's been given a number of honors over the years, but I have to say I don't think any one of them meant more to me than that.

□

As I said earlier, one of the most astounding things I experience when I talk to our exonerees is how many of them have managed to get rid of the deep, all-consuming anger that possessed them when they were wrongly convicted. And how many of them say the same thing: that the anger is another prison, binding them to those who conspired against them; that to be truly free meant more than walking beyond the prison walls, that it also required walking beyond the walls of that rage.

Harry Granger remains one of those who has managed to let go of his anger, to find a place of contentment—joy, even—in the simple fact of being free, even though his was one of the most outrageous cases we ever handled. He and a friend, David Alexander, were convicted of a 1976 murder in Iberia Parish, Louisiana. What happened later is something I never saw before, never saw again, and still can't quite believe. The actual killers confessed, and even led the sheriff to the buried murder weapon, but the sheriff convinced them to retract their confessions because he'd already indicted six people, including Alexander and Granger, and didn't want their confessions to conflict with his indictments.

So Harry and David wound up spending an unbelievable *thirty years* behind bars, most of it at the infamous Louisiana State Penitentiary in Angola, until attorney Peggy Woodward and I convinced the parole board to finally release them. Harry walked free in the summer of 2006, and David a few months later.

The gravel road Harry grew up on was paved when he came home. The mother who stood by him through his decades of false imprisonment was now diabetic, and so there was little time to relish his newfound freedom; he had a mom to take care of. "She couldn't walk, so I had to pick her up and put her in bed," Harry told me. "And put her in a recliner. And give her her medication, and she liked that cup of coffee in the morning. So that's what I do. You do what you have to do."

He got by on Social Security and some odd jobs, until he found regular work offshore, doing galley work on commercial ships—working with the cook, making beds, that sort of thing. And against all odds, he has kept his happy-go-lucky attitude.

I asked him how he kept up such a positive demeanor, given all that had been taken from him.

"Hatred will destroy you, you know?" he said. "You can't feel sorry for yourself. You have to move on. You can't live in the past. You have to live for the day."

□

Not all of our exonerees are able to shed their fury. Dominic Lucci, one of the Savannah Three, the one who wrote to me and convinced us to take the case, roils with anger at the injustice that was done to him and the injustices he has to face every day.

"I'm still excited as hell to be out," he told me the last time we talked, "but I didn't know it was going to be this hard to get work. And it's not fair."

The nightmare of the Savannah Three officially ended on July 18, 2018, when the DA decided not to retry them and all charges were finally dismissed.

Mark and his mother, Debbie, have found work cleaning houses and are making decent money; they recently invited Kenny Gardiner to come down to their part of Texas and work with them. Kenny and Mark are living in trailers side by side.

But for Dominic, living up near Cleveland, a new nightmare was beginning to surface. Exonerees, he said, face problems that even those who are paroled, or who serve their time, don't have. "When you get paroled," he said, the anger barely contained in his voice, "there's all these programs to help you get a job, to help you get housing. They help you get an apartment, to get career skills, whatever you need. But when you're exonerated, they just open the gates and say, 'Good luck.'"

Dominic has faced the prejudice that so many ex-convicts face. "People believe that if you go to prison, you're an animal and you deserve to be treated like an animal," he said. There was the humiliation of going on job interviews and thinking he had the job—until he didn't. "One job I interviewed for, after the interview, the guy over at HR called me and told me, 'Hey, lookit, the vice president of operations gave me your application and told me to hire you,' and

I said, 'Excellent!' and he said, 'Basically you have the job, but we have to go over the basics so I can fill in the blanks.'"

And all goes well, until they get to a certain twenty-six-year gap.

"And he says, 'Well, where were you?' And I say, 'I was in prison, and I worked as a team leader on two projects.' 'You were in prison!' and I say, 'Well, do you have my résumé?' And he says, 'Well, I have it right here in front of me.' And I say, 'Well, it's right there at the top. I was in prison for twenty-six years,' and he says, 'Well, it was really nice talking to you, sir. Have a nice day.'"

That's happened to Dominic more than once, and it's left him bitter and disillusioned. He lives at home with his father and has finally landed a job, answering phones for the local VA office. He doesn't date, he says. "What's the point? Women don't need some fat, bald fifty-year-old former prisoner talking to them."

I suppose the fact that the Savannah Three have received no compensation for their time is one of the reasons that Dominic retains so much anger, and it's not uncommon: Compensation laws are wildly inconsistent from state to state. They can seem as capricious and arbitrary as the criminal justice system they're meant to compensate for. There are fifteen states that offer no compensation at all. Of those that do, the amounts—and the limitations on eligibility—vary greatly. As you've seen, getting a conviction vacated doesn't necessarily prove innocence; it just awards the accused the right to a new trial, and a DA can take months to decide whether to pursue that trial. If the DA decides to appeal the decision itself, that process can add years. In Jimmy Landano's case in Hudson County, New Jersey—one of our early exonerations—it took nine years. Nevertheless, some states require a finding of "actual innocence" before compensation is awarded. So for some exonerees, the years they've lost can be followed by years in limbo, fighting for the simple compensation they deserve.

Like Mark Schand, Michael Austin was one of the "lucky" ones—and I use the term extremely loosely—in that he was awarded $1.4 million for the twenty-seven years he was in prison, wrongly convicted of a Baltimore murder in 1975. Working with Baltimore attorneys Larry Nathans and Booth Ripke, and our own investigator Steve Delaney, we freed him just after Christmas in 2001.

Michael and I were at a ballgame together in Baltimore to celebrate my seventy-seventh birthday a while back, and it happened to be the day that a Michigan man who spent forty-five years behind bars had been awarded about that same payout—$1.5 million. I thought that was a pittance for the time he served—and I think it's a pittance for what Michael went through too—and I asked him what he thought.

"Absolutely, man," he said. "What is the price of a day of life? How did you calculate and come to the conclusion that this is enough money? I didn't ever look at it as okay that this here was sufficient as to what I did. There's not enough money to do that."

Michael, like anyone coming out of prison, was thoroughly unprepared to handle that amount of money, anyway. He blew through a lot, he gave a lot away, and he realizes now that what he was going through was nothing short of post-traumatic stress disorder.

"I was released out of my cell straight into society," Michael said to me a while back. "I didn't have a chance to acclimate back into the community through the normal process that they send you to a halfway house, let you actually get out and go into the community. When I was released, I just came straight home and the future shock and all that was presented to me, it was really something that my mind wasn't ready to get a grip on. I was bombarded with things I have never experienced. I felt like an alien who came from another planet."

The process of recovery, Michael said, was a matter of reinventing himself: realizing he was not the same person he was in prison, and having to introduce himself to the new Michael Austin. Fortunately, he had an ally: music.

Michael has told me he nearly went crazy in his years in prison, so consumed was he by anger. But through the grace of God he crossed paths with a convict who had a BA in music, and Michael and some others convinced him to start a music theory class. The convict became Michael's cellmate and mentor, setting him on a path of education and self-improvement, teaching him the fundamentals of music. Michael took up the trumpet—to the consternation and annoyance of some of the convicts in the nearby cells—but he stuck with it. Now he's a practicing musician in Baltimore; you should go look up his albums. He's a fabulous singer, too, and performs in clubs around the city.

Michael talks to students wherever he can—at schools, libraries, churches—to share his message that the anger inside you, and the world around you, doesn't have to shape the path you walk. You get to do that yourself.

"I try to share how to live life through your experiences," he says, "but don't let the negative aspect of your experiences be the controlling factor of who you are. Do those things by conditioning yourself to keep a cooler state of mind, and just keep moving, man."

Just keep moving. In the end, sometimes, that's all you can do.

□

It's not just the wrongly convicted themselves who suffer so much during their years in prison. I've stayed in touch with many of their family members, both during their loved ones' incarceration and through this period of transition that follows. It can be terribly hard on them, too.

Thelma Lloyd thought her young son was joking when he called one day to say he'd been arrested for murder. "He was such a trickster," she remembers now. She soon realized her son, Richard Miles, was dead serious, and in the fourteen years between his conviction and the time Centurion got involved in his case, she realized how many horrors she would have to endure.

"It's hard because so many things is happening," she said. "You're losing friends; family members are turning against you. My sister, she never visited with Richard; they never asked about how he was doing. We pastored a small church, and some walked away from the church. They didn't say they were leaving for that, but it was hard for them to see a pastor pastoring and their child going to jail for murder. That was heartbreaking.

"And so to have your child suffer through something like this, and then you're having the pressures because of what he's going through—you have no support. No one to understand and go through this with you. You are so alone."

The visits with her son were just as heartbreaking. "When we first visited, we couldn't touch him. And it took some months before he was able to have that contact. And then having to walk away and leave him. And you see all of this. It was just, it just ripped my heart out. Every time. But I didn't want him to see my tears." She saved her tears for later; when she was with Richard, she always tried to keep his hope alive. "When you look out the window," she would tell him, "don't look at the bars. Look at the sky."

It is this ability to keep hope alive that has always humbled me so deeply, when I experience it in the lives of our clients and their families. Saint Paul, in his letter to the Romans, said, "Suffering produces endurance; endurance produces character; and character produces hope." Thelma and her son and so many of our exonerees have taught me this very same lesson, again and again.

I was there with Thelma in Dallas the day in October 2009 when her son Richard walked free. Cheryl Wattley, the lawyer who was instrumental in helping me gain his freedom, was there too, and she asked Richard what he wanted to do first.

"And I didn't know," he recalls. "And she asked me, 'Well, what do you want to go eat?' And I didn't know. I had no direction, walking out of prison. And basically what I did was I followed after the suggestions of Cheryl, even when it got to the point of me picking something to eat." We all went to a barbecue restaurant in South Dallas. Richard says, "I remember walking right behind Cheryl Wattley, and everything she ordered, I ordered it."

Richard Miles and his mom, Thelma Lloyd, in 2016. For his work after his release, Richard was named one of CNN's 2019 Heroes. *Diane Bladecki*

That feeling of not knowing how to function as a grown man outside a prison—Richard was just nineteen when he went in—persisted. His mother remembers sitting at the table with Richard and him always asking for permission to go to the bathroom. But over time, and with the loving help of his family, Richard adapted. He met a woman named Latoya and got married, and in 2012, when he was finally fully exonerated and received a compensation package of $1.2 million, he found his direction as well. He and a friend he'd made in prison founded an organization to help others like him. It's called Miles of Freedom.

"Miles" for Richard Miles, of course, but "MILES," as well, to represent the pillars that he teaches others coming out of prison: to become Motivated, Inspired, Law-Abiding, Enthusiastic, Successful citizens. The organization helps former prisoners find jobs and housing, gives them a three-month employment-readiness workshop, teaches them personal finance and relationship skills, and helps them find work. Miles of Freedom also runs a lawn service and—in what is perhaps closest to Richard's heart—a shuttle service to allow families to visit their loved ones in prison. Because Richard knows that those visits from his mom—when she never wanted to let him see her cry—were as important as life itself.

And still today, Richard says, his family has to remind him, in his sister's words, to "take a minute to live." "I have not begun to live yet," he says, "because I haven't really found out who Richard is. I've been out just really trying to either fight or build the organization, Miles of Freedom. I would say I'm experiencing life as I grow. Am I living? I don't know yet, you know? I'm just experiencing life. I think once God allows me to mentally settle down, then that's when I'll be able to truly experience and appreciate everything that he's blessed me with."

But the one who is teaching him how to live, Richard says, is his five-year-old daughter, Raelyn. "Raelyn loves for me to play in her room," Richard told me. "She will give me multiple cartoon characters so I have to be Peppa Pig, and I have to be the PAW Patrol, and we do these tea parties.

"I missed so much of my life," Richard told me. "But what I do with Raelyn, I get to be an adult, and I get to be a child again."

And in the end, that may be what coming out of prison as an innocent man is: a chance to be born again, to start life anew.

□

I am proud to say that I am godfather to Raelyn, who just got a little sister; Aubreigh Joy Miles was born in December of 2019. But I never did have a family of my own. My on-and-off relationship with Crystal Star, the sister of Chiefie's wife, went on for a while—nearly twenty years, in fact—but faded away quite some time ago.

I do still think of Yoshiko from time to time. It turned out that boy I met, that day in Yokohama, was not my child; once I learned of his birthday and compared it with the last time I'd seen Yoshiko,

I knew it couldn't be. As for Yoshiko, after she and her husband retired from the navy, they settled again in Utah, where her husband was from. I hope that she found contentment and lived a happy life. After fifty-two years of marriage, they died within ten days of each other, as those in long marriages sometimes do.

I do have family that I'm very close to: The love of my sister, Lois, and my brother, Rich, has always sustained me, and I cherish the time I get to spend with them and my nieces and nephews.

But the exonerees, and the people of Centurion, have always been my family as well, and I love them as deeply as if they were my own. We have a "family gathering" from time to time, when as many of the exonerees as can make the trip get together, along with their families and all of our supporters, and share their experiences. It's always a powerful bonding time, but never as powerful as the one we held in the spring of 2019.

All the exonerees, nearly twenty of them, got up on stage, and just as they were about to leave, Willie Green stepped up to speak. Willie, who spent twenty-four years in prison for a murder he did not commit, had run a life-lessons program for other inmates in San Quentin prison in which he would help them get their GEDs and learn other important skills. One of the hardest lessons he taught was public speaking.

"That's the scariest thing you can get a person to do, is stand in front of his peers and speak," Willie told me once. "So, the first thing that jumps in his mind, he's fixing to be judged. Or people looking at it as a sign of weakness when you start telling people stuff about yourself. So, you have to get him to get up there and you make him comfortable by talking to him, letting him know, you need to get this stuff out."

Now, at the family gathering, it was Willie's turn to speak. And he couldn't.

"I just want to say—" Willie started, but then was overcome with emotion.

The room waited silently. Other exonerees gently put their hands on his shoulders, to let him know he was not alone. Finally, Willie gathered the ability to speak.

"When I was in prison, I had a dream," he said. "I had seen Mr. McCloskey on *60 Minutes*. And when I saw him, I said, 'That's the man that's going to get me out of prison.' And then I had that dream. You don't dream in color, but in my dream I saw Mr. McCloskey, he had on some beige khakis, he had on a blue shirt, he had on a gray jacket, and he came to get me, and he said, 'Come on, Willie, they can't hurt you no more. You're free to go. Let's go.' And the day I was released from prison, he had on those same clothes that I saw him in, in my dream, and he was holding me on my back and I knew that meant he cared about me.

"So I had to say something to you all, to let you know how I feel. I don't have no family outside of Jim, except for my wife, my high school sweetheart. I married her a few years ago. I met her in 1958, when we were in first grade. I pulled her hair and I ran away. And then a few years ago I went to the class reunion and met up with her. And we got married. And I'm as happy as happy can be."

Everyone in the room was overcome with the joy of that moment, but when Willie walked off the stage, Mark Jones, one of the Savannah Three, came up to him. They'd met the day before, at a session where the exonerees all shared their tales with each other. Now Mark walked up to Willie, looked him in the eye, and said, "There's one thing you said wrong up there."

Willie looked up at him, puzzled.

"Jim and your wife are not your only family," he said. "We are your family. I just met you yesterday, but you are my brother for life."

And the two men embraced, and in that embrace I knew all I needed to know: about family, about freedom, and about the grace that can heal us. Because, yes, sometimes God works in mysterious ways. But sometimes those ways aren't mysterious at all. God works through each of us. And, if we're very lucky—as I have been, so very, very lucky—God allows us to heal each other. And, by doing so, heal ourselves.

When I "retired" in 2015 (I use the term loosely), twenty of our exonerees came from all over the country to wish me well. *Diane Bladecki*

☐

As for Centurion, the work continues. In May 2015, I retired from active management of the organization and turned the reins over to my incredibly capable and enormously dedicated partner of the last thirty-two years, Kate Germond. She's been involved in every aspect of the organization since she joined me—conducting a lot of Centurion investigations herself—and I consider her nothing short of God's gift to me and to those whom we serve.

Paul Casteleiro—the lawyer who helped me on my very first case and worked closely by our side for years—closed his own private practice and has taken over as the full-time legal director of Centurion. To date he's exonerated seventeen innocent individuals—a record unmatched by any other single practitioner in America.

As of this writing Centurion has a caseload of twenty and remains the only group nationwide that works to free the innocent investigating non-DNA cases. We have a dedicated staff of fourteen employees and a cadre of twenty volunteers. We still get more than a thousand requests from inmates every year, and we still answer each and every one.

As for me, even though I retired from the day-to-day operation, I did stay on the board and kept working the cases of seven men. Five of them have been freed; I have two to go.

The organization's budget is consistently in the low seven figures these days. There's never been a year when we haven't worried about our ability to receive the financial support required to do our work, but somehow the windows of heaven have opened and provided for our needs. These days we depend on anywhere from a thousand to twelve hundred donors a year—mostly individuals, but a healthy handful of family foundations and churches keep us afloat as well.

God bless them all.

□

I do want to take a moment to add one last personal note. Many ask me, after all I've seen, what the state of my faith is today. As I tried to convey in this book, my faith was quite clear when I started this journey. There was no doubt in my mind that Christ led me into this work. I believed that God's hand would continually guide me.

Now my faith fluctuates. It is less certain. I still believe that Christ led me to this. But there have been stretches of time when I have felt the absence of God and when I questioned God's very existence. I'm still wrestling with essential beliefs of the Christian faith. But my faith remains; perhaps in a more skeptical form, but I'd like to think a more mature one as well. Despite the ups and downs of my faith, I retain a deep gratitude to God for sustaining me and Centurion Ministries from the very beginning.

In the Gospel of Mark, the father of an epileptic son pleads with Jesus to heal the boy. Jesus tells him, "All things are possible to one who believes," to which the father responds, "I believe; help my unbelief." Which is what I find myself saying, quite often.

But when I don't find myself quoting the Gospel According to Mark, I do find myself returning, over and over, to the Gospel According to Satchel Paige, the great baseball pitcher of yesteryear: "Never let the odds keep you from pursuing what you know in your heart you were meant to do."

Amen, Satchel. Amen.

Epilogue

Thirty years ago, I wrote an article in the John Jay College of Criminal Justice journal *Criminal Justice Ethics* about wrongful convictions in which I said, "An innocent person in prison, in my view, is about as rare as a pigeon in the park." Very few were aware then how widespread the phenomenon of the "convicted innocent" was in the United States. As we've seen throughout this book, a lot has changed in the thirty years since. But a lot hasn't, too.

As I've noted, back then I felt like a lone voice crying in the wilderness. Centurion Ministries, when we started up as a ragtag operation in Mrs. Yeatman's home, was the only organization in the country—in the world, for that matter—fighting to free those who were innocent and living their lives away behind bars. The positive changes I've seen since those days are everywhere. They make my heart soar, as they do for anyone who believes in justice for all.

So what I'd like to do, in summing up what my colleagues and I have learned, is to talk about three things. I want to convey how things have changed for the better; I want to summarize what we know about why these wrongful convictions persist; and I want to talk about what needs to be done to make sure that, to whatever degree possible, no innocent man or woman ever hears those prison bars close behind them again.

That's my impossible dream. This is why I dare to dream it.

WHAT'S GONE RIGHT

Let's start with the positive.

The advent of genetic evidence in criminal exonerations has been transformative for the wrongly convicted. Since the first DNA exoneration in 1989, DNA evidence has—as of this writing—vindicated 367 falsely imprisoned people nationwide, 21 of whom had served time on death row. That and other forensic developments, as well as initiatives such as sociological research into the study of memory and perception, have dramatically changed the landscape of the criminal justice system. They awakened a sleepy and self-confident legal community to the realization that our system wasn't nearly as foolproof as they had thought.

When Centurion started out, it was commonly assumed by both the public and those who came together in a criminal court of law—defense attorneys, prosecutors, judges, juries, the media—that the verdicts rendered in those courts were, by and large, correct and true. If by chance an innocent person slipped through the cracks and got convicted, that was an isolated instance of justice gone awry. It was often coupled with a sense that, well, he probably committed another crime anyway or he wouldn't be here. So justice got done one way or the other.

At about the same time as the advent of DNA evidence—and largely as a result of it—there arose a widespread innocence movement in the United States. Collectively, its participants have not only freed countless innocent people but also helped to educate the public and successfully pushed for much-needed reforms. In the last twenty-five years, dozens of organizations, operating as legal clinics on a pro bono basis, have sprung up to free the wrongly convicted. At last count, fifty-five of them are based in the United States and twelve are located internationally. As I mentioned earlier, Barry Scheck and Peter Neufeld's Innocence Project has become the most visible of these, and it has done an incredible job shedding light on a phenomenon that only a few decades ago was buried in the shadows of the justice system.

The innocence movement has begun to take root within the criminal justice system itself. As of the end of 2019, fifty-nine prosecutor's offices across the country had established Conviction Integrity Units to review possible cases of wrongful convictions. Some, I'll say, do so with more authenticity and vigor than others, but the fact that this movement has started to grow within the system itself is an enormously positive sign.

Beyond that, several states have established independent "innocence commissions" to review possible wrongful convictions. The first, in North Carolina, was established in 2007 and so far has exonerated twelve innocent people. I'm proud to say that the attorney general of my home state of New Jersey just started a conviction review unit—triggered by the exoneration of two men represented by Centurion and the Innocence Project together.

In 2012 the National Registry of Exonerations was established by several prestigious law schools to keep track of the exonerations that have taken place since 1989. By their count, more than 2,500 men and women have had their convictions reversed. Of those, 123 had been sentenced to death.

Think of that. If not for the innocence movement, states would have killed 123 innocent people in thirty years. Four times, every year, for three decades, we, the people of the United States, would have killed an innocent person. To me, this simple fact is the greatest argument against the death penalty. Because think, for a moment, about all the innocents behind bars who did not get to meet someone from Centurion Ministries, or the Innocence Project, or one of those other groups. Think, for a moment, of all the innocents who have died. It has to give any civilized society pause.

I know many of those reading this book are proponents of the death penalty. I know there are arguments on both sides. As someone who has lived with the reality of it as a constant presence, I believe it to be ineffectual, inefficient, and arbitrary in its application; far too expensive; racially biased and disproportionately used against African Americans; and just plain wrong. States—and now, once again, the federal government—should not be in the killing business.

As we've seen, for those who do escape the gallows, or a life in the hell of prison, the transition home can be a prison of its own. Compensating those poor innocents for the time they've lost can help ease that transition, and the number of states passing laws to compensate victims of the system is growing each year. As of this writing, thirty-five have enacted statutes to compensate the wrongly convicted for the years they've lost, although the amounts vary and, in my opinion, are never enough. Some of our exonerees have won larger amounts in federal lawsuits against their respective states, for civil rights violations—in amounts, as you've seen, ranging up to $27 million—but winning such a lawsuit is far from a sure thing. Three of the men you met in this book—Clarence Brandley, Willie Green, and Darryl Burton—lost, and they got nothing.

There are more reasons for hope, though: More than a dozen states have tried to reform police practices that—as we've seen throughout the book—can be ground zero for what develops into a wrongful conviction.

So all in all, there's great momentum in the world of the wrongfully imprisoned. I'm buoyed by how the cause is spreading and the ways in which more and more people are rallying to their side.

But we still have a long, long way to go.

WHAT'S STILL WRONG

We've learned a lot of lessons, in our battles to free the innocent, about why so many of them wind up in prison. Certainly, some are there because of honest mistakes, but as we've seen throughout the book, the vast majority—in my experience—are there as a result of lying witnesses, dishonest law enforcement officials, pro-prosecution judicial bias, and juries that remained uninformed about the ways in which prosecutors can manipulate their perceptions, and hide evidence, to bring them to the wrong conclusions. So before we can talk about what needs to be done, it's crucial that we summarize the main causes of this ongoing epidemic.

THE SYSTEM DOESN'T WANT TO CHANGE. America's criminal justice system is a cruel machine responsible for an untold number of wrongful convictions. No one knows how many, but I believe they total in the tens of thousands.

Once some poor innocent soul is singled out, and law enforcement is convinced of his guilt, the train has left the station; there is no turning back. Truth has been left behind.

Then, once that train has pulled up to the prison and deposited its human cargo, there will be hell to pay, and many fruitless years of fighting for his freedom and redemption. Even in the face of new and compelling evidence of innocence or wrongdoing at his trial, the stubborn and stiff-necked system will not let go of his conviction without a no-holds-barred fight to the bitter end.

PERVASIVE PERJURY. In the late 1980s, former Philadelphia district attorney Ed Rendell said, "In almost any factual hearing or trial, someone is committing perjury; and if we investigate all of those things, we would be doing nothing but prosecuting perjury charges." I'm hard-pressed to think of a single Centurion case in which a primary witness for the prosecution did not lie in a material way. If you'll remember, it happened in every case you've read about in this book. Such is the rule, not the exception. As you've seen, it's not just inveterate criminals making up lies to save their own skin— either on their own or goaded (or forced) into doing so by police and prosecutors trying to nail down a conviction. Everyday citizens lie as well, for any number of reasons: for a reward, for revenge, or even just to gain attention for themselves.

It is frightening how easily people can be influenced or pressured to say the wrong thing. Our insecurities and fears, as well as our desire to please those in authority, allow us to be far more malleable than we like to think. Few of us have the inner strength to resist such overreach by the law. Those who are new to the criminal justice world tend to trust the people in charge, naively believing they know what they're doing and have the best of intentions. Those who live on the margins of society are particularly susceptible to police pressure, because they feel powerless to resist. So again and again, we find truth in what one of our Louisiana clients told Ed Bradley on *60 Minutes:* "Those that lied went home and those who told the truth went to prison."

POLICE PERJURY. I'll never forget the words of a police lieutenant, a twenty-five-year veteran of the Newark police force back in 1981, when I was a rookie investigating Chiefie's case. Talking about his perception of how defense teams work, he said, "Look, Jim, they lie, so we lie. I don't know one of my fellow officers who hasn't lied on the stand." It's an open secret in the criminal court community: It's not unusual for police officers to lie under oath. Judges and prosecutors know it, but they turn a blind eye to it.

Let me be clear: I believe that most police officers are good people who have one of the most difficult and dangerous jobs on the planet. But we have to be honest and realize that it's not just "a few bad apples" we're talking about. It's a pervasive culture that needs to be changed from the bottom to the top.

A retiring inspector in a big East Coast city once admitted to me that his homicide unit sometimes planted a suspect's fingerprints at a crime scene. Aghast, I asked him why. "We knew he did it, but we couldn't prove it," was his cynical reply.

That is one of the reasons for police perjury: a culture in which the ends justify the means, that if you get a "bad guy" off the streets, then you've done your job, even if you had to bend the truth—or obliterate it—to do so. The planting of fingerprints, by the way, is more common than you'd think: In the years 1984–1992, for example, five members of the New York State police identification unit were convicted of planting fingerprints at crime scenes in at least forty felony cases.

FLAWED FORENSIC TESTIMONY. This is an intractable and insidious problem. Juries take forensic testimony as gospel: Blood and hair samples, bite marks, gunshot residue, fingerprints, autopsies, and fiber analysis sound incontrovertible in the quiet air of the courtroom. But in the real world, those so-called sciences are often as flawed as the testimony they're used to support. The analysts are often poorly trained and reckless, or they're from labs that work closely with a police force on a daily basis and come to see their job as supporting the police narrative, not searching for truth.

There have been major scandals at many labs across the country, but the most scandalous of all was at the FBI. In a 2015 report, the FBI did an internal review of five hundred trials that occurred before 2000 and that relied on evidence from the FBI's microscopic hair analysis unit. After 2000, DNA technology was available to replace that hair analysis. Looking at the DNA and other factors, it was clearly demonstrated that the hair analysis was often wrong. Not just in some cases. Not even in most cases.

It was clearly demonstrated that the analysis was wrong, or exaggerated, 96 percent of the time!

Among those five hundred cases were thirty-five death row inmates. Nine of whom had already been executed. Five others died on death row. I can only pray that their deaths not be in vain—that they be a constant reminder of the work we have to do, to give truth a seat in the courtroom.

RECANTATIONS. As you've seen throughout this book, a lot of our cases involved witnesses who recanted their false testimony. And as you've seen, that should have been enough to get an innocent person out of prison, but it wasn't. So the question is simple: Why?

The causes rest with the judiciary. Judges tend to discount recantations because of a sense of false equivalence: *Well, if you say you lied at the trial, who is to say you're not lying now?* It's also their long-held custom: Recantation testimony is treated as unreliable simply because it always has been. Judges are generally reluctant to defy a precedent. They're also hesitant to concede that such egregious perjury took place in their courtroom years before, resulting in the false conviction.

It's my experience that the vast majority of recantations are reliable and should be seriously considered by the courts, not dismissed out of hand. It's important for you to remember that those who have recanted in our cases didn't come forward on their own. We found them, we approached them, we appealed to their conscience, we tried to help them fight off their fears. Without exception, I truly believe that they recanted not because of what I said but because of the guilt borne by their own conscience.

In almost all of our cases, the recanter had no relationship to the person in prison. No reason to admit the shameful, painful fact that their lies destroyed the life of another. I can think of no earthly reason why anyone would divulge such a humiliating secret if it weren't true. Their reason for recanting, I have concluded after all these years, is nothing short of a spiritual one. The confession is a balm to a tortured soul.

Whenever I talk about this, my mind goes back to John Shafer, who was all of nineteen years old when the Pennsylvania State Police coerced him into falsely incriminating a man for the brutal murder of a mother and her two children. John's recantation helped us free that man, Milton Scarborough, in 2013. What John told *The Philadelphia Inquirer* stands for what so many of our recanters felt in their hearts: "I'd been thinking about it for years and years. What I did was wrong. It was wrong, wrong, wrong. . . . I don't want to be dying with this on my head."

INDIGENCE. It is extremely rare for a person who is falsely accused of a violent crime to have the financial means to defend himself. Every one of our clients is indigent. They are at the mercy of the state to provide them with an attorney. Often, that lawyer is court appointed, with little murder or sexual assault case experience, the crimes most likely to land someone a life or a death sentence. The lawyer is paid a pittance in fees, and hardly any funds are allocated for an investigator or relevant forensic experts.

Meanwhile the prosecutor has whatever resources he needs to investigate, develop, and present the case at trial—including the use of crime lab criminalists who, as we've seen in this book, are often not nearly as competent or impartial as the jury is led to believe, or else who rely on faulty evidence. The defense just doesn't have the means to challenge them.

The scales of justice are out of balance from the get-go.

UNRELIABLE EYEWITNESSES. So often, the cause of a wrongful conviction comes down to a witness who didn't see what he thought he saw. Remember my first day on a prison block—when I "remembered" that the inmate who cursed at me was a black man? Juries put way too much weight on eyewitness testimony. Memory, as we've seen, is a tricky thing. I suspect a lot of those witnesses who help convict innocent people aren't lying per se, but your own false memories can, very quickly, seem as true as reality.

MISTRUSTED ALIBIS. As you saw in several of our cases, including those of Nate Walker, Ben Spencer, Joyce Ann Brown, and the Savannah Three, judges and juries often dismiss alibis as unreliable. As I mentioned in those cases, a person's alibi often involves a friend, relative, or co-worker—unsurprisingly, since those are the people you spend the most time with. It makes me crazy how quickly juries dismiss such alibi evidence because they think those people are lying to save a friend's skin.

Has it happened? Yes, of course. But among the sixty-three people we have freed, a significant number have presented credible alibi evidence, including timecards from work, only to be dismissed or ignored by police, belittled by prosecutors, and disregarded by juries. This mind-set alone has resulted in many an innocent person going to prison, often for decades.

Mark Schand—the guy who finally won the $27 million civil suit for his wrongful conviction—is a notable example of this. When the Springfield, Massachusetts, murder for which he was convicted took place, he was thirty miles south in Hartford, Connecticut. At closing time, Mark was at his wife's hair salon to pick her up and drive her home.

Six witnesses, including customers and the owner, testified on his behalf to that fact. They recalled that he was in a great deal of pain from a root canal procedure he had had earlier that day, which the dentist confirmed in his testimony as well. It doesn't get much better than that for an alibi. Nevertheless, the jury chose to disregard all of that in favor of some very problematic eyewitness testimony.

That cost Mark twenty-seven years of his life.

RACIAL DISPARITY. There is a reason that the majority of Centurion Ministries' clients are black. Disproportionately, the wrongly convicted in this country are black.

If you are African American, the chance of being wrongly convicted is far greater than it is for whites. Of the sixty-three innocent inmates Centurion has freed, thirty-nine are black, and only twenty are white (four are Hispanic). As of late 2016, the black population of the United States stood at 13 percent, but according to the National Registry of Exonerations, of the nineteen hundred exonerees recorded at that time, nearly 50 percent were black.

The causes for this should come as no surprise. Throughout my career, I've seen it time and time again: an ingrained bias, either conscious or subconscious, on the part of those in law enforcement, to see black people—particularly black men—as inherently more likely to be guilty. This spreads to juries as well and, in my experience, to white jurors more than black jurors.

I don't think it's insignificant that according to a report published a few years back, which looked at the race of twenty-four hundred elected prosecutors, 95 percent of the country's elected prosecutors were white.

PHONY JAILHOUSE "CONFESSION" TESTIMONY. As you've seen throughout this book, it's all too common for habitual criminals to fabricate phony confessions supposedly made by their poor unwitting cellmates who are awaiting trial. In exchange for these bogus confessions, these witnesses—who will say anything to avoid incarceration—are paid by prosecutors, often in secret, with a "get out of jail free" card for their own felony crimes. We have seen it far too often, not only in Centurion cases but in countless instances across the country. Such testimony is a perversion of justice, perpetrated by desperate prosecutors, and should be banned in all courts of law.

FALSE CONFESSIONS. In addition to the phony "jailhouse confession" testimony from dishonest snitches you've seen throughout this book, police frequently draw false confessions out of the wrongly accused themselves. The process by which police obtain those false confessions—and how those confessions become an enormous obstacle that the accused can almost never overcome—is perhaps the most pervasive, and most insidious, reason for innocent people being convicted. It has happened in countless cases—including, famously, the Central Park Five, whose wrongful convictions outraged the nation.

I know it's hard for you to imagine why someone would confess to a crime they didn't commit—which is why these confessions carry so much weight with juries—but I'm here to tell you I've talked to so many who have endured the relentless, overwhelming questioning by detectives, hour after nightmarish hour, that frankly I don't think I could withstand it myself. I'd venture to say you couldn't either.

Just imagine sitting in a windowless room, no food, no water, three detectives screaming at you, spewing lies, saying that they have your fingerprints or your DNA at the murder scene, and your friends say you committed the crime, and you're confused and exhausted after going over your story again and again, and then they tell you that if you don't sign this paper, they're going to make sure you go to the electric chair, but if you sign it, we'll call your mom and you can go home and we'll sort it all out in the morning.

Are you sure you wouldn't sign?

And if you want to imagine just how pervasive this is, consider this. Remember those 367 people who were previously convicted of serious crimes in the United States and who had been exonerated by DNA testing? Proven to be unmistakably innocent of the crimes they were convicted of?

One in four of them had signed a confession to the crime.

One in four.

So the fact that such false confessions are much more common than you'd imagine is one thing. But the fact that confessions are given such enormous weight in the courtroom, whereas recantations are not, is one of the most difficult prejudices we need to overcome, if we indeed want to find justice for all.

PROSECUTORIAL MISCONDUCT. When I started out, trying to free one innocent man forty years ago, I believed in my heart that prosecutors want to make sure they're convicting the right person. But the overwhelming amount of evidence to the contrary—the number of times we've seen prosecutors intentionally falsify information, hide evidence, manipulate witnesses, and just plain lie—makes me wonder how true that might be.

What boggles my mind is that prosecutors are rarely seriously admonished by the courts for their illegal and unethical behavior. I've seen the occasional prosecutor get disbarred, but rarely does he get criminally charged for such conduct. I'm aware of only two cases in which a prosecutor was criminally convicted of illegal conduct that resulted in an innocent person's conviction, and both times the prosecutor spent only a day or two behind bars. The innocent people they helped convict were incarcerated for decades.

And I was stunned to learn that prosecutors are immune from civil suits, that they can't be sued for anything they do illegally at trial. You can sue the police but not the prosecutor. It's this total lack of accountability that allows these pervasive illegal activities to persist.

The cases in which there is evidence that the accused is innocent but the DA ignores it and bulldozes on are just too common to be ignored. Suffice it to say that in the course of our work freeing sixty-three innocent men and women at Centurion, we encountered clear evidence of prosecutorial misconduct in forty of those cases.

That has to change.

So much has to change.

WHAT TO DO

So how *do* we change all this? I believe that it begins with faith, and it begins with hope.

Faith, as ministers much smarter than I am have said for more than a hundred years, and as Martin Luther King reminded us, that the arc of the moral universe is long, but it bends toward justice.

And hope that as more and more people learn of the reasons for wrongful convictions, we can, working together, be the agents of change to help that come to pass.

Here are just a few of the ways I think we can help make that happen:

• One of the great saving graces of our broken justice system is that most district attorneys and state attorneys general are elected. It is imperative for the electorate to ensure that those candidates seeking such high office recognize the importance of conviction review units and that they staff these units with people who are genuinely interested in rooting out prior bad convictions. They should work hand in hand with the defense attorneys who represent inmates with what appear to be legitimate claims of innocence.

There is nothing sweeter than when Centurion or any other innocence group is able to partner up with a prosecutor's office in seeking justice for an innocent inmate. We've done this on twelve occasions. It is a beautiful relationship that has saved those inmates many years of further suffering, and, I might add, saved the county a lot of money. I'm always amazed how the Red Sea parts, how fast the innocent can pass through to the other side of imprisonment, when a district attorney joins the defense and asks a judge to vacate a conviction.

• An area where the U.S. system of justice falls far short is in not conducting official postmortems on proven wrongful convictions. We should take our cue from the Canadians in this regard. Once a false conviction has been established by the Canadian courts, the provincial government has, on occasion, initiated a public inquiry—usually headed by a respected retired judge—to discover what went wrong, determine who was responsible for the misfiring of justice, and recommend changes to prevent similar mistakes from happening again.

This commission of inquiry has full discovery subpoena power for all relevant files and can compel witnesses to testify under oath. This has occurred in seven different cases that I'm aware of, including the two Centurion cases from Canada, David Milgaard and James Driskell.

With the twenty-five hundred or more exonerations that have been documented in the United States since 1989, not once has such a commission of inquiry taken place in this country. That needs to change.

• I believe states should pass what is called an "open file" law. This requires prosecutors to share, with some minor exceptions, their entire case file with the defense. Right now, a handful of states have such a law, and a few progressive district attorneys practice this as a matter of course. It seems to me that true justice seekers—which is what DAs profess to be, and ought to be—should not be afraid of complete transparency. This one step alone would significantly reduce the chance of convicting innocent people and greatly enhance the opportunity to exonerate the wrongly convicted.

- Judges need to learn that recantations count. Recantations should be an integral part of the appeals process, not dismissed as they so often are now. I believe with all my heart and soul that the thirty-five recantations we've developed in our post-conviction work are as solid as any DNA evidence.

I'd swear to it in a court of law.

- Similarly, each and every city, town, county, and state should, by this moment in the history of the innocence movement, make sure that their police, sheriffs, and prosecutor's offices revamp and reform their procedures when it comes to handling and preserving evidence, interrogating suspects, and conducting eyewitness photo and live lineups. This includes videotaping interrogations, preserving in perpetuity the biological evidence taken at crime scenes, and employing the double-blind lineup method, in which neither the administrator nor the witness knows who the suspect is.

- It also seems to me that if a case for innocence appears to have a semblance of merit and credibility, it deserves to be moved to the front of the line on both the prosecutor's and the judge's calendars. An expeditious evaluation by all parties could save an imprisoned person from many more years of unjust suffering. Even in cases where we prevailed and got an innocent person out of prison, the extra years of that person's life that this took, just because the wheels of justice grind so slowly in such cases, is absolutely heartbreaking. Consider the fact that on average our exonerees spent over twenty-one years behind prison walls. One of them, Lou Thomas, spent forty-five years; another, Walter Lomax, thirty-nine years, for crimes they didn't commit. We have to do better.

- I think people unfamiliar with the workings of the criminal justice system would be shocked, as I was, to learn that federal law and U.S. Supreme Court rulings forbid a prisoner to appeal his conviction to a federal court based solely on new evidence of his innocence, no matter how compelling. Among the justices, Antonin Scalia was the strongest proponent of this view, writing in a 1993 opinion in the case *Herrera v. Collins*, an opinion that still stands: "There is no basis in text, tradition, or even in contemporary practice ... for finding in the Constitution a right to demand judicial consideration of newly discovered evidence of innocence brought forward after conviction."

Currently most states have procedural bars in place that make it extremely difficult for the post-conviction petitions of innocent inmates to qualify for judicial review. A common hurdle demands that newly discovered evidence be submitted to the courts within one to five years of the direct appeal's denial. Stacking the deck in this manner is unfairly restrictive and, in my view, should be eliminated altogether so that evidence of innocence can be presented regardless of how long it took to surface.

The good news is that a handful of states are way ahead of the Supreme Court on the matter of presenting new evidence. In response to the vast number of wrongful convictions that have been chronicled in the United States in the last two decades, these states have enacted statutes, and their state supreme courts have upheld them, demanding that inmates who have compelling claims of innocence based on new evidence be entitled to return to their original court of conviction at any time and present this evidence for judicial review, even if their conviction has no constitutional defects.

That's enormous, but it's not widespread.

Yet.

But it could be.

☐

And so, as I said at the beginning of this summary, it begins with faith, and with hope. I believe that we can help that arc of the moral universe bend toward justice. I believe it's what I was put on this earth to do, and what so many others have found as their calling as well. This book is, at least in part, my attempt to ask you to join us— to walk beside us, when you can, in whatever way you can.

Because the justice system is not just.

But it could be.

ACKNOWLEDGMENTS

I am so appreciative of those who, during the past forty years, gave so much of themselves to the work and the mission of Centurion Ministries, not to mention those whose love and friendship gave me the strength and sustenance to do this work. And how can I ever express enough thanks to those who made this book possible?

I am forever indebted to my literary agent, Deborah Grosvenor, who stuck with me through thick and thin and without whom this project never would have gotten off the ground. She deftly and patiently managed this five-year effort and led me to my co-writer, Phil Lerman, and finally to Doubleday. Phil is not only a highly talented writer whose prose brings this story to life; he is a mensch with whom it was a pleasure to work and collaborate.

I thank God for the entire Doubleday editorial team led by the very wise senior editor Yaniv Soha, whose thoroughness, insight, and skill added immeasurably to the narrative. I can't imagine having a more caring editor than Yaniv. He was ably supported by assistant editor Cara Reilly. Editorial Production Manager Bette Alexander and copy editor Ingrid Sterner superbly saved the manuscript from a number of unforced errors. A hearty thank-you goes to the creative jacket designer, Michael Windsor.

And a huge thank-you to John Grisham for volunteering to write the foreword. What a nice gift that was.

There would be no Centurion Ministries were it not for three people: the Reverend Richard Streeter, pastor of my home church, Paoli Presbyterian Church; the Reverend Joseph Ravenell, chaplain at

Trenton State Prison; and Jorge de los Santos, the first inmate I ever worked for. Dick was instrumental in guiding and encouraging me as I struggled with my decision to leave the business world and go into the ministry, and then he insisted that if I felt called to do this, I must go to Princeton Theological Seminary. Reverend Ravenell set up the student chaplaincy program between the seminary and the prison and assigned me to the Vroom Building. If not for that assignment, I never would have met Jorge. Jorge challenged the authenticity of my faith and insisted that God had led me to him so that I could help free him.

It is said that if you build it they will come. I shudder to think where Centurion would be without Kate Germond and Paul Casteleiro. Both were godsends. As partners working side by side during the last thirty-three years, Kate and I grew Centurion into what it is today. There is no one with more passion and compassion for the falsely imprisoned than Kate. She was born to serve these forgotten and forsaken souls. And there is not an attorney in the land more devoted, skilled, and experienced in exonerating the imprisoned innocent than Paul. He never gives up and leaves no stone unturned, regardless of the forces arrayed against him or how many years it takes to complete the mission.

There are many Centurion exonerees among the sixty-three we have freed who, regrettably, have not been mentioned in this book or whose stories have not been told in the detail that they deserve. Every one of them is just as important to me as those who are depicted in these pages. I can't tell you how excruciatingly difficult the decision was to leave those compelling stories for another day. But let me say this to the entire family of Centurion clients, both to those we have freed and to the twenty we are still trying to free, whether included here or not: Rest assured that I and my colleagues are in absolute awe of your courage, grace, and unending patience, which have enabled you to endure the unendurable. None of us can even dare to imagine the suffering that goes with decades of false imprisonment.

Serving all of you gave meaning and purpose to our lives and has been a privilege and an honor unattainable in any other field of work. Thank you for trusting us with your lives and allowing us to become a part of your families as all of you are a part of ours.

For the last forty years Centurion Ministries has been admirably served by a dedicated staff, hundreds of volunteers from all walks of life, thousands of benefactors across the nation, and a board of directors without which we could not have done our work or operated with any degree of effectiveness. Please accept my deep gratitude and immense appreciation. You are the real heroes because you receive no public acclaim but nevertheless lend your talents to those we serve, giving your all and expecting nothing in return except the satisfaction of knowing that what you do is essential to the accomplishments of Centurion.

I do want to thank and recognize a few board members individually because of their longstanding and critically important service and support: Charlie Crow and Ed Pisani, for twenty-seven years of service on our Board of Directors and especially for helping us navigate at times in very choppy waters; Jay Regan, for serving as chairman of our board for twenty-three years prior to his retirement and for his unflagging effort over the last twenty-eight years in taking us to an entirely new level of fundraising; Rob Mooney, for succeeding Jay as Centurion's board chairman; Bill Scheide (who has passed away) and Judy Scheide for significantly raising our profile in the Princeton community and for their extraordinary and most generous financial support over the last twenty-five years; and the Beinecke family of the Prospect Hill Foundation, for their thirty years of continuous generosity. Thank you from the bottom of my heart.

I also want to thank those many attorneys nationwide who worked with us over the years, some in multiple cases. It would have been impossible to free those that we did without your invaluable legal expertise and service. These lions of justice are far too numerous to list here, but they represent a virtual Who's Who of the criminal defense bar. A grateful tip of the cap also goes to the score of forensic experts who have assisted Centurion in getting to the truth of the matter in numerous cases. Thank you.

I want to extend a special appreciation to current staff members who make the Centurion engine run so smoothly and efficiently and without whom we and our clients would be at wit's end: Executive

Director Corey Waldron, Janet Baxendale, Kim Weston, Gene Truncellito, Jim Cousins, Alan Maimon, Diane Bladecki, Laila Wilson, Tyler Spikes, Lori Freedman, Priyanka Banerjee, Rosemary Kay, and Madison McCoy. I happily include my past assistants, Lisa Kurtz and Joan Jennings, each of whom for twenty years uncomplainingly put up with my many "eccentricities." And I will never forget and will always appreciate former Centurion investigators Steve Delaney, Richard Hepburn, Bill Raynor, and, of course, Paul Henderson (may he rest in peace). Thank you one and all.

I would be remiss if I didn't take a moment to honor the memory of the woman I've called "Yoshiko." I've changed her name and the name of her son to protect the family's privacy. She was the love of my life who will always have a special place in my heart.

I am blessed to have many friends from early life up to the present day with whom I have stayed in steady contact and from whom I've drawn sustenance. Friends, especially old friends, are treasures to be cherished. Among mine are those from grade school through high school; my Bucknell Phi Gamma Delta fraternity brothers; and friends from the navy, as well as those from Japan, Princeton Seminary, and the Nassau Presbyterian Church here in Princeton, pastored by the Reverend Dave Davis. I am particularly indebted to Dave and his family, with whom I am very close, for quick action when I suffered a heart attack in their home in 2012.

In closing I'd like to add that I am part of a loving family spread out across the country consisting of my brother, Rich, and his wife, Lynn; my sister, Lois; and my four nieces and two nephews and their families. Thank you to them and to the entire Centurion Ministries family for enriching my life and sustaining me in this work.

ABOUT THE AUTHORS

Jim McCloskey is the founder of Centurion Ministries. He served in the U.S. Navy, patrolling rivers in the Mekong Delta of Vietnam, and spent twelve years in international consulting. He has a master of divinity from Princeton Theological Seminary. Today McCloskey is retired from active oversight of Centurion, although he continues to pursue cases.

Philip Lerman has been the national editor of *USA Today*, co-producer of *America's Most Wanted*, and executive producer of PBS's *Made in Spain*. He is the author of *Dadditude* and the co-author of numerous nonfiction books. A native of the Bronx, New York, he lives in Washington, D.C.